AF470708

LOST NORFOLK LANDSCAPES

THE PAINTINGS OF HORACE TUCK

(1876–1951)

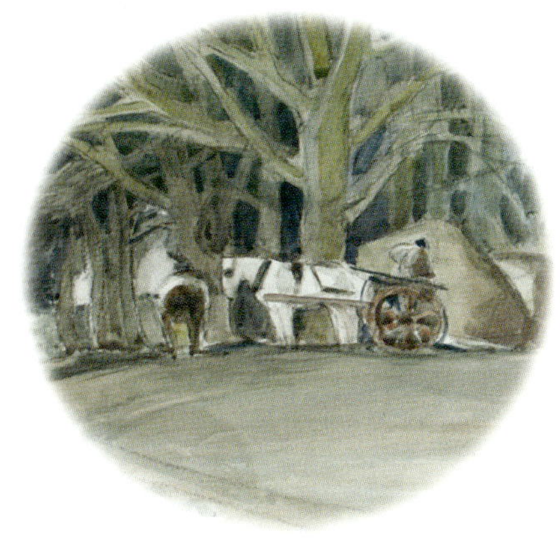

Simon Butler FRSA
IN ASSOCIATION WITH Cyril Nunn

WITH A PERSONAL MEMOIR
BY Jennifer Tuck

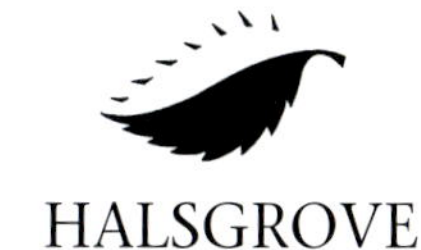

HALSGROVE

First published in Great Britain in 2006

DEDICATION
*This book is dedicated, with love, to my wife Renate,
for all her patience over many months.*
Cyril Nunn

British Library Cataloguing-in-Publication Data
A CIP record for this title is available from the British Library

ISBN 1 84114 521 1
ISBN 978 1 84114 521 1

HALSGROVE

Halsgrove House
Lower Moor Way
Tiverton, Devon EX16 6SS
Tel: 01884 243242
Fax: 01884 243325
email: sales@halsgrove.com
website: www.halsgrove.com

Printed and bound by D'Auria Industrie Grafiche Spa, Italy

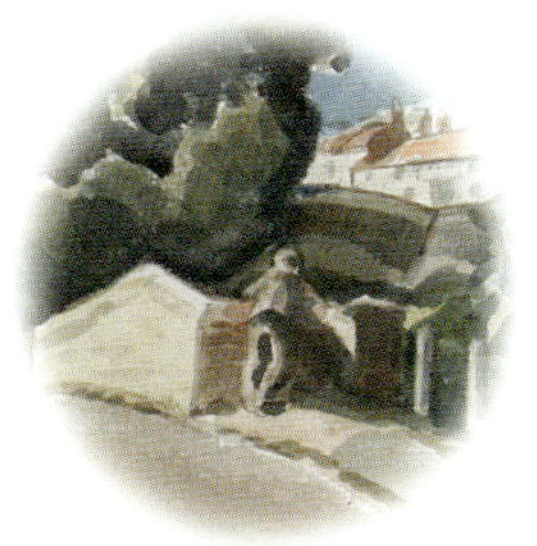

Contents

Acknowledgements

I thank all those who have contributed in any way to the compilation of this book. Principal among these are Cyril Nunn and his wife Renate, Jennifer Tuck and Brian Garrood, Liz Keevill and Mrs Lena Pye.

Seeking information from a variety of sources regarding Tuck's life there has inevitably been instances where the information proffered describing particular incidents and events has not always been in accord. I have not taken it upon myself to act as umpire in such instances, as what is on offer here is a quick sketch of the artist, drawn in order that we might gauge his work and character. Following Frank Lloyd Wright's tenet that the truth is more important than the facts, I leave it to future biographers to sift such evidence more finely.

Grateful thanks are also due to Sadie Butler, Alan Childs, Gavin and Nicky Dollard, Adrian and Michael Hill at the Picturecraft Gallery, Judy Hines, the Pallant House Gallery, Colin Self, Keith Skipper, Andy and Phil Thomas, and Maggie Willmore. Thanks also to my colleagues at Halsgrove.

Among a mountain of relevant literature the following books have been referred to in particular and I would recommend them to readers interested in background information on painting in Norfolk and Norwich: *Wide Skies - A Century of Painting and Painters in Norfolk*, by Adrienne May and Brian Watts, Halsgrove 2003, and *A Happy Eye*, by Marjorie Allthorpe-Guyton, Jarrold & Sons, 1982.

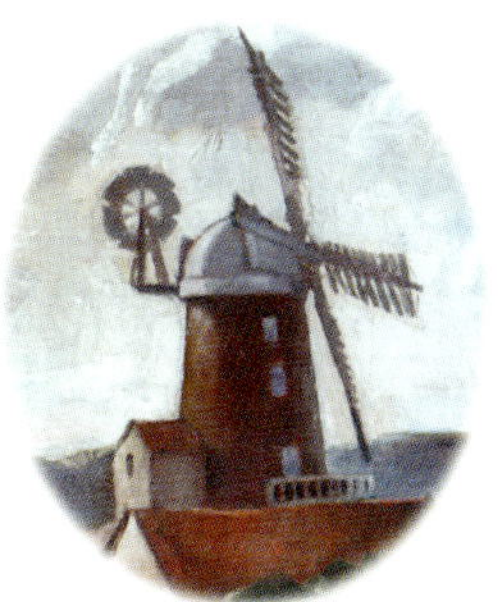

Foreword

I never met my great uncle, Horace Tuck. I would love to have done but, sadly, he died four years before I was born. Yet, I feel I've known him all my life. I grew up with his paintings displayed on the walls of every room in our house. And when we visited relatives on the Tuck side of my family, their homes were full of his paintings too. Intriguing tales were told of him at family gatherings and I was fascinated by the sound of his rather bohemian lifestyle.

After his wife Bessie died, when I was 9, we visited Far End (Tuck's last home, in Sheringham, Norfolk) before it was sold. Though still children, my brother and I were captivated by the sense of his presence: that it had been the home of an artist was palpable. We were astonished still to find his oil paints and brushes in his airy studio, and brought them home with us. My brother and I started experimenting with the paints on old pieces of cardboard. For the first time, I considered whether a career in art might be a possibility for me too.

So, 'Uncle Horry', as I have always known him, was not just a legend in my family but a source of great inspiration. Here was somebody who not only made a living doing something that he loved, but a very good living. And despite initial disapproval from his parents, Horry's example gave respectability within the family to the idea of pursuing an artistic career. My father – Horry's nephew – inherited the Tuck art gene and, encouraged by his uncle's example, went to the prestigious art school at Goldsmith's College, South London. I followed in my father's footsteps by going to Norwich Art School and Camberwell School of Art and Crafts, and I am now a university art history lecturer. So Uncle Horry's legacy lives on.

When Horry died, his nephew Stephen Tuck produced some bound sets of wood-block prints, which he printed himself from Horry's blocks and distributed to family members. Stephen's introductory text ended with the words, 'Horace Tuck died near his birthday in 1951. How much of his work will live on after him, only time will tell'. The beautiful book you are looking at now is evidence not only that my great uncle's work is living on but, over 50 years after his death, is finally being appreciated by the wider audience it deserves.

Liz Keevill, 2006

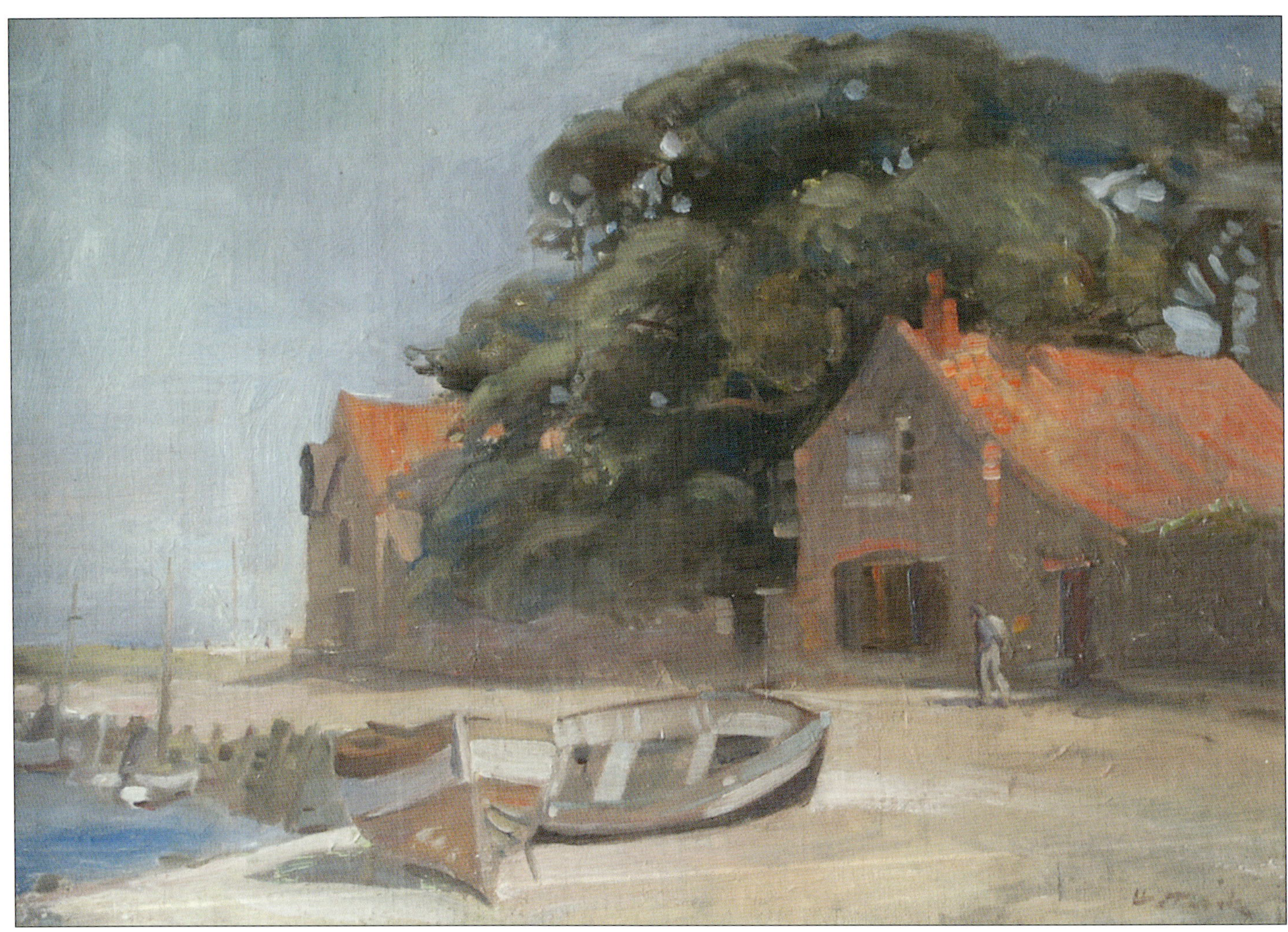

Blakeney Quay
oil on canvas
8x10 inches

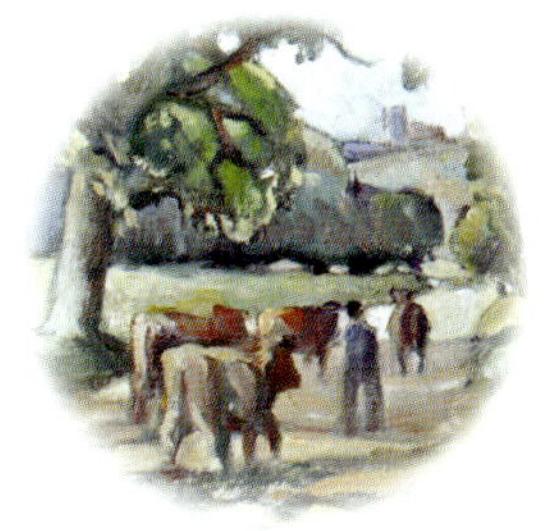

Introduction

I first came across a painting by Horace Tuck while working with the Norfolk and Norwich Art Circle on the publication of their history, *Wide Skies*, in 2002. Visiting the home of one of the contributors to that book, I noticed and commented on a seascape, one of many paintings by Norfolk artists that filled the walls of his house. It looked to me like an important painting, boldly executed and painterly. This was my first encounter with the work of Horace Tuck.

A year or so later, and in a different part of the county, I was visiting an author of a book based on the life of the photographer Olive Edis, whose wonderful portraits of fishermen from in and around the north Norfolk town of Sheringham, formed part of a book, *Face to Face*, on that celebrated society photographer's life. Again my eye was caught by a small painting that happened to be propped up on the floor against a wall. While its subject was insignificant, a doorway and window overlooking a snowy street, the use of colour in the painting immediately made one suspect it was the work of a considerable artist. This was to be my second encounter with Horace Tuck.

My visit on that occasion was to see retired photographer and art collector, Cyril Nunn, who noted my interest in the painting and made some offhand remark about owning more works by the same artist. Only later did it become clear that the house contained not a handful of Tuck paintings, but a veritable gallery of his work comprising over 150 oils and watercolours, along with linocuts, woodcuts and various other ephemera. As my friendship with Cyril grew, we agreed that such a large collection held in private hands of works by an artist with such a worthy pedigree merited a possible publication. The quality of the paintings and their local interest would make a wonderful book. Under the helpful eye of his wife Renate, Cyril and I spent many hours photographing and cataloguing the Tuck paintings with a view to including them in this book.

As it happened, Cyril had first met Horace Tuck as a schoolboy when Tuck visited Upper Sheringham School in the 1930s. At that time Tuck was acting as a peripatetic art teacher, travelling to schools throughout the county. Tuck's sister-in-law, a Mrs Garwood, was head teacher at the school (one of her daughters, now in her nineties, still lives in

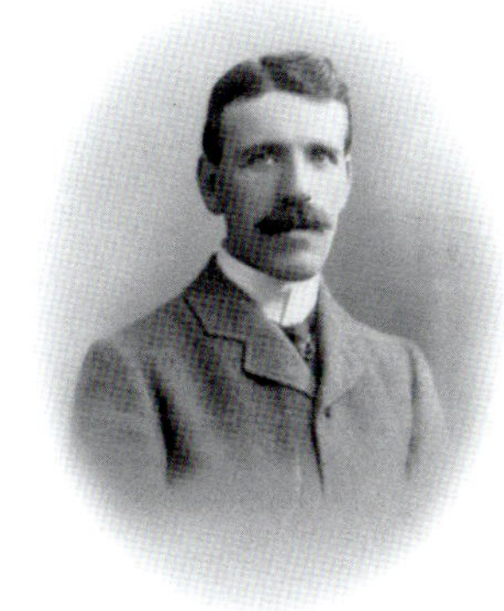

Portrait of the artist as a young man.
(Lena Pye)

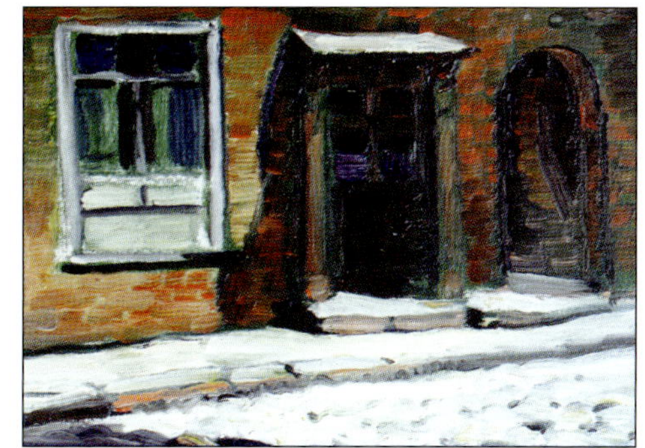

Doorway and window in the snow.
oil on canvas

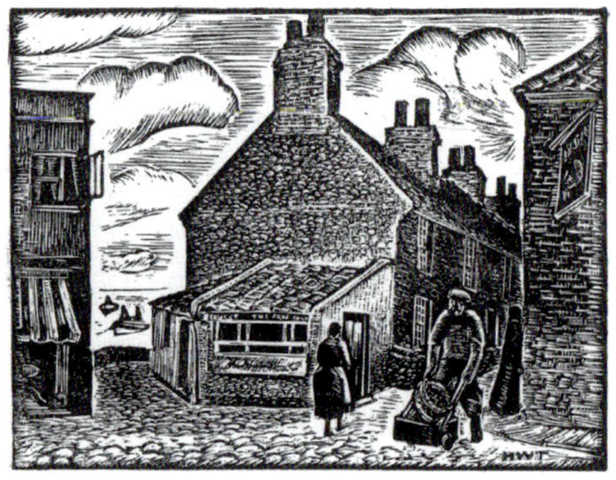

A favourite corner in Sheringham - woodcut. (Liz Keevill)

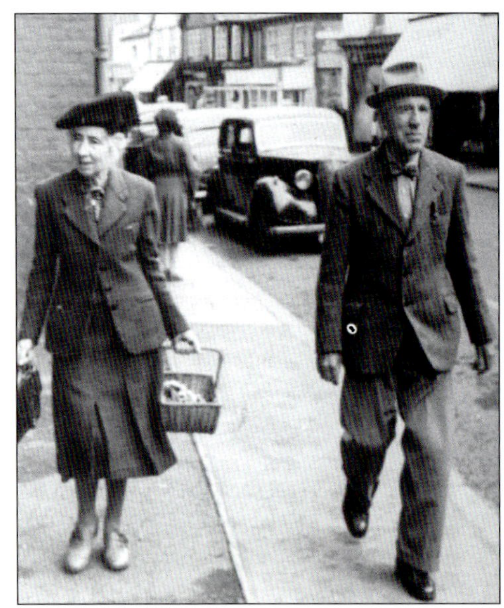

Horace and Bessie Tuck in Sheringham c.1940. (Lena Pye)

Sheringham), and Cyril remembers Horace, 'a very amiable and modest man,' turning up with items of fruit, props from which he and his fellow students would attempt to draw a still life. Another student recalled that those adjudged to have produced the best drawings were then awarded the pieces of fruit as prizes!

Later, in 1947, Cyril joined the West Runton Art Group. Several teachers, some from The Slade, a Mr Dodds who taught at Gresham College, and Horace Tuck were among the artists who came to instruct the group. Tuck would also spend time painting in Sheringham, and Cyril recalls a favourite location being at the corner where the Lobster Inn met Gun Street.

In 1939 Tuck and his wife Elizabeth Mary, 'Bessie' (1874–1965), moved from Branksome Road in Norwich to their new home 'Far End', a bungalow in Knowle Road, Sheringham. Returning from service in the RAF Cyril remade their acquaintance and, while running a shop associated with his photography business, Cyril began to sell Horace Tuck's paintings of the area: 'Commercial travellers were always keen to buy them, although the total number sold was not great.'

Cyril remembers Bessie as 'a real lady and a good friend'. Though they did not have children of their own, Cyril recalls that both she and Horace were fond of youngsters, and would often have children of relatives staying with them during the summer months. Horace's fondness for young people is evident from all those who have spoken or written about him and his kindly and patient nature undoubtedly added to his effectiveness as an art teacher.

After Horace died, in 1951, Cyril remained friends with his widow, buying paintings from her from time to time and eventually purchasing the entire contents of the studio when Bessie decided to leave Sheringham. This included a number of paintings by Bessie (some of which are included in this book). Bessie died in 1965.

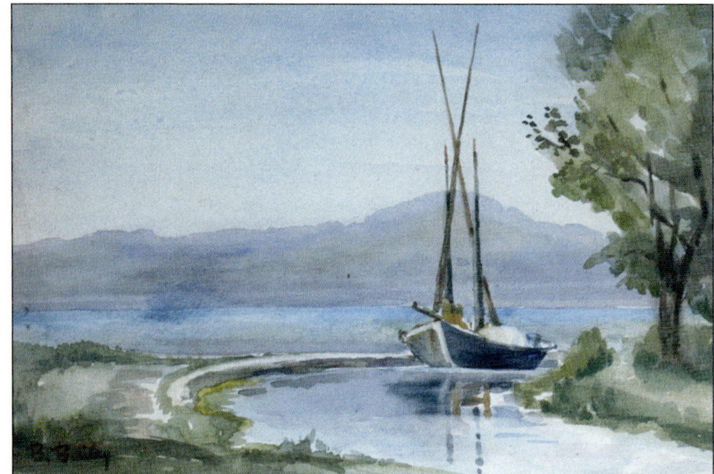

The Blue Boat, *a watercolour by Bessie Tuck.*

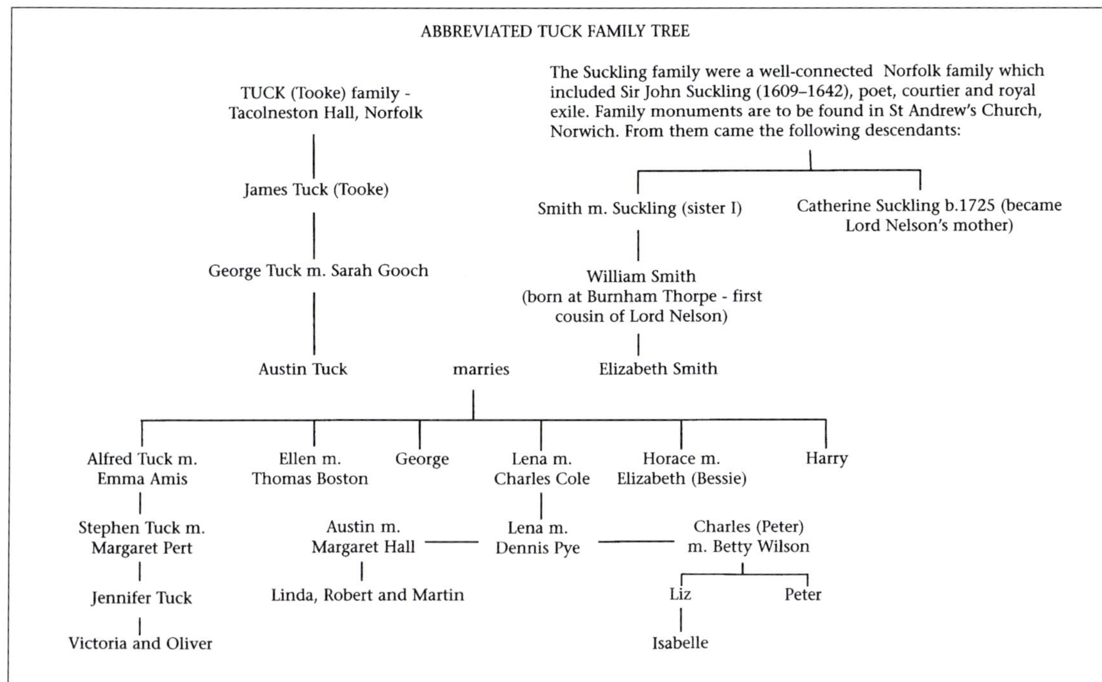

Abbreviated Tuck family tree. (compiled by Stephen Tuck)

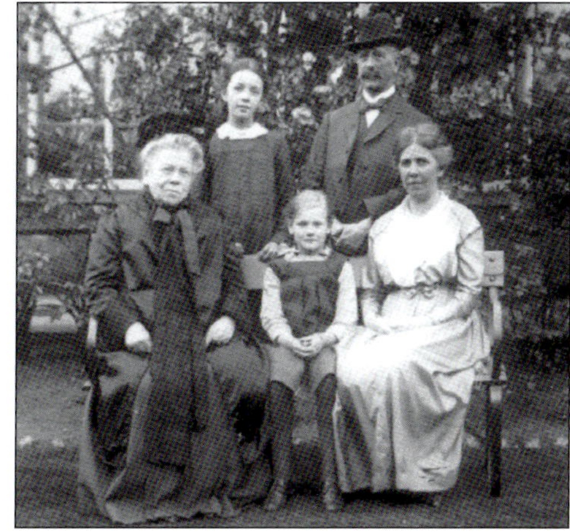

HWT's mother and (far right) one of her daughters Nellie, Horace's sister (she lived to be almost 100. The man behind her is Nellie's husband, Thomas Boston, a local and very successful businessman (Tuck's brother-in-law).

Along with our work cataloguing the collection, I began a search for further information concerning the artist and his life. Through Norfolk-based broadcaster and author Keith Skipper, a plea for information in his *Eastern Daily Press* newspaper column resulted in a dozen or so responses and, as I'd hoped, contact with Tuck's relatives. Among these was a letter from his niece, Lena Pye, and two great neices, Liz Keevill and Jennifer Tuck. Without their help and enthusiasm this short introduction to Tuck's life could not have been written, and the memoir included later in this book, by Jennifer Tuck, provides a perfect miniature portrait of Tuck.

In contrast to this personal memoir, this introductory essay attempts to provide a overview of Tuck the artist from which the reader might better appreciate his paintings within the context of the world of art and education during his lifetime. I soon came to recognise that my own ignorance of Horace Tuck could not be taken to imply that he was an unknown. On his home turf, during his lifetime, Tuck cut a well-known figure. Today his paintings and drawings form part of the important collection at the Castle Museum and Art Gallery in Norwich, residing there alongside the Cotmans, the Cromes and the Munnings. His paintings also appear from time to time at auction, are increasingly sought after, and continue to demand respectable prices.

*   *   *

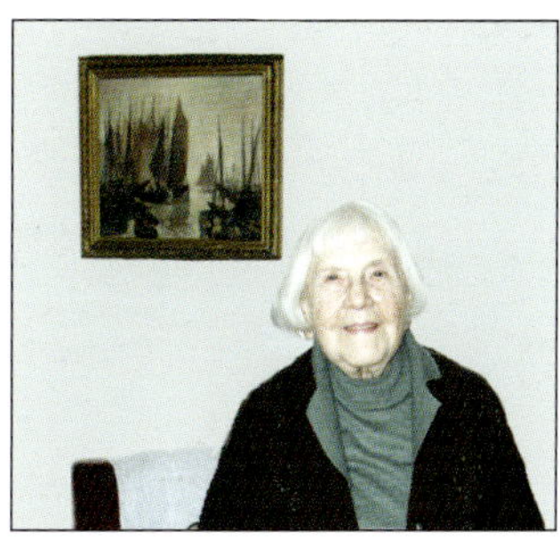

Lena Pye, Horace Tuck's niece, a photograph taken in 2004. Mrs Pye provided much of the background information for this book.

I owe the title of this book to my friend, the artist Colin Self, who on being shown a few of Tuck's paintings, admired them for the way in which they evoked the Norfolk of his childhood – a rural way of life even on the immediate outskirts of the city of Norwich. Yet it was a landscape that was rapidly disappearing as Tuck's life came towards its end. In the post-war decades the wholesale introduction of mechanisation into farming and the progress of the motor car was to accelerate the drawing to a close of a rural idyll that once characterised Norfolk. Indeed, during the 75 years of his life, Tuck possibly saw more changes to the character of the Norfolk landscape than had taken place in the previous five hundred years.

Not that Tuck set out to produce a body of work of a deliberately nostalgic nature. He was a professional artist painting the scenery of his native county in a way that provided some measure of financial support. His style, both in his watercolours and oils, is largely traditional, no doubt informed by the strong influences of the Norwich School led by John Crome (1768–1921) and John Sell Cotman (1782–1842). Such traditions have been somewhat sniffily described as having their origins in 'a form of modest self-expression by provincials; a record by simple men of their own happiness in their fields and villages', but Tuck wholeheartedly embraced such simplicity and his paintings are imbued with a passion and sense of joy in depicting a landscape he belonged to and which he loved.

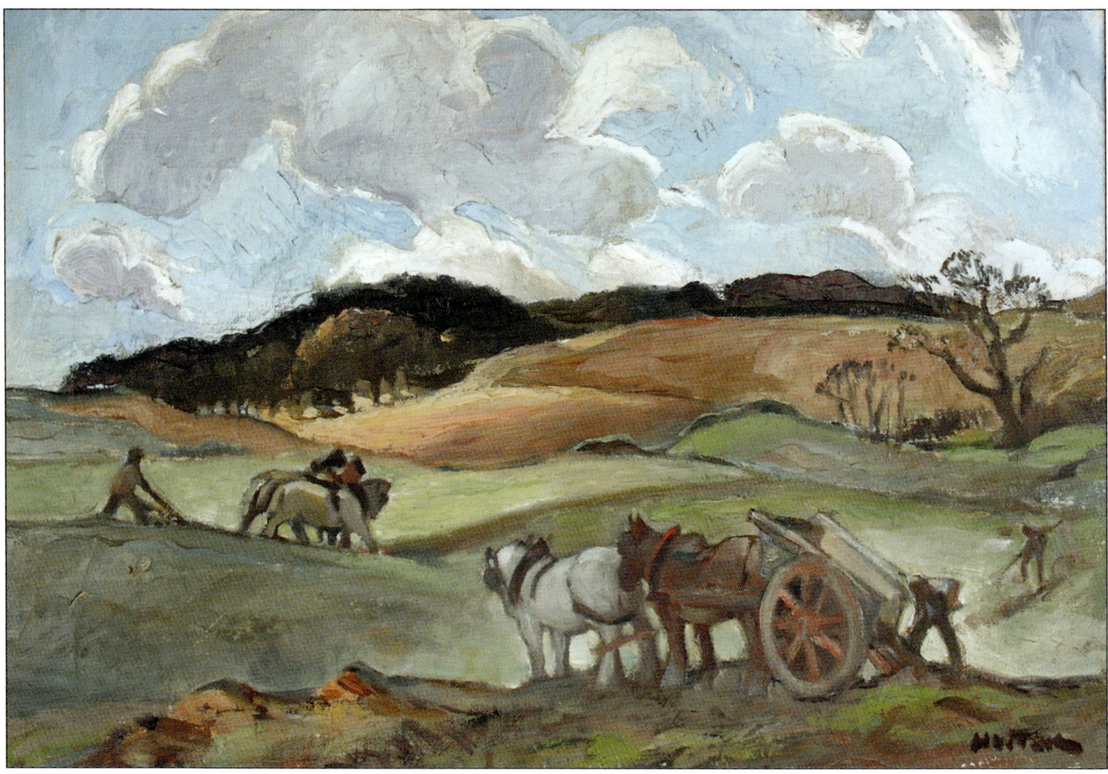

'Happiness in their fields and villages'. Tuck painted scenes that were soon to disappear, as in Spring Landscape.

Tuck's adherence to tradition would have been a deliberate choice on his part, for he would certainly have had a keen appreciation of the unquiet revolutions that ran like lightning bolts through the art world during his lifetime.

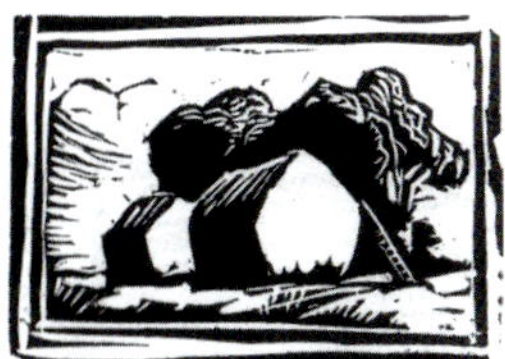

Horace Tuck was born in Norwich and chose to study art somewhat against his family's wishes, first at Norwich School of Art (as it became), one of the country's premier provincial art colleges, and later at Borough Road Training College in Isleworth, west London.

The Norwich Government School of Design opened its doors to pupils in 1846, its principal aim being to improve industrial design. Financed by the Board of Trade, provincial Schools of Design had been set up to train artisans to design for industry. In common with other provincial schools, Norwich never actually achieved this aim. The pupils that it later attracted were not the artisans, but essentially middle-class, many of them women, interested more in the fine arts than in design for commerce. The School did, however, become the training ground for many of the artists who later formed the Norwich Art Circle.

Wide Skies Adrienne May & Brian Watts, 2003.

Borough Road, now part of Brunel University, originated in 1798, moving to Isleworth in 1889. After completing his training in London Tuck returned to Norfolk and, prior to the First World War, he was employed by the Government School of Design as a peripatetic tutor for Board Schools (as locally administered schools were then known). A large area such as Norfolk, with its thinly spread population, meant Tuck travelled widely to a large number of small schools often in remote villages and towns. The railway served many of these rural communities and Tuck no doubt got to to know his home county well during these years.

In 1920 Tuck joined the permanent staff of Norwich School of Art, remaining there until 1939, and eventually acting as deputy to Charles Hobbis who had arrived as head of the college in 1919. During these teaching years, Tuck would have witnessed many of the major art movements both in Britain and on the Continent. From Impressionism, through Fauvism to the Dadaists and Modernists, Tuck and his students would certainly have debated the merits and demerits of such movements, and some no doubt took them up, though there are few signs that Tuck himself was ever moved to follow them. But that is not to say that Tuck ploughed a lonely furrow, or that over the years changes in the style of his work are not evident. On the contrary, many of his paintings evoke the work of esteemed contemporaries, now seen as leaders of the British School in the first half of the twentieth century.

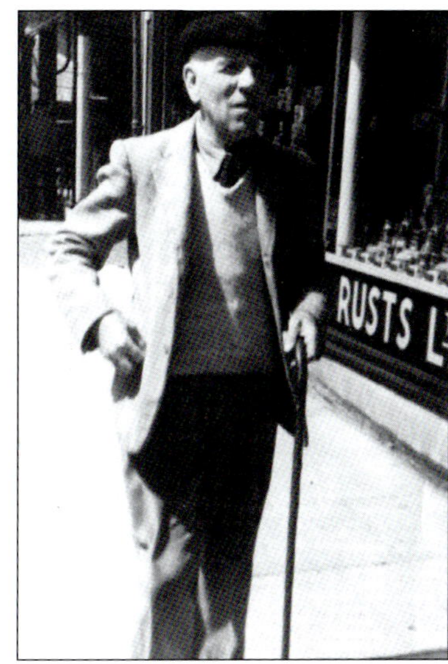

Man about town. Tuck c.1935.

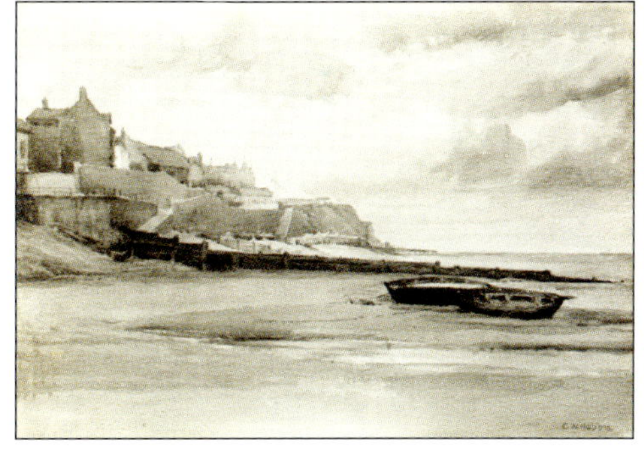

A view of Sheringham by C.W. Hobbis, Head of Norwich School of Art from 1919 until 1946. This was a Christmas card sent in 1926 by Hobbis to Horace and Bessie Tuck inscribed with the message 'With best wishes to you two from we three'.

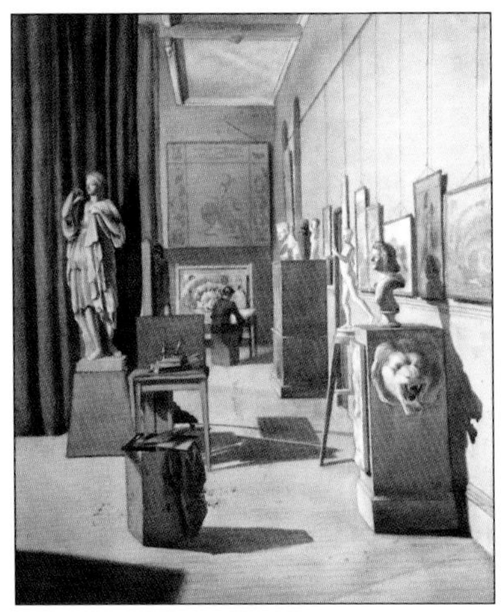

A wash study made by Horace Tuck of the drawing room at Norwich School of Art.

Staff and students at Norwich School of Art in the early 1920s. Horace Tuck fourth from left, middle row.

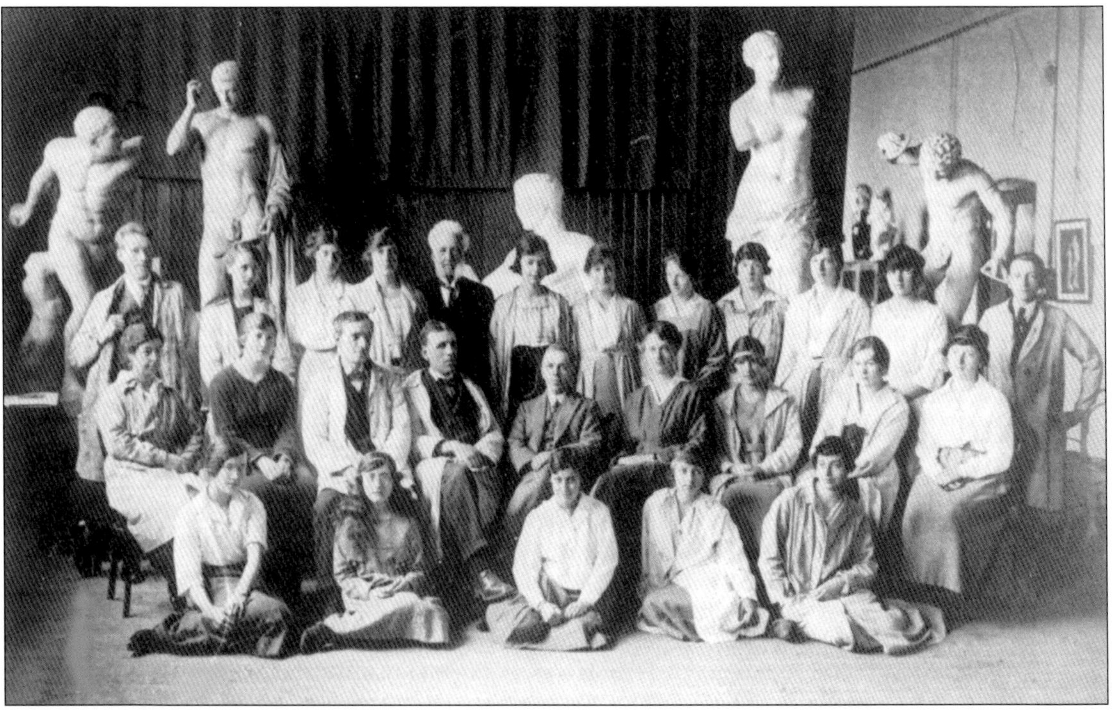

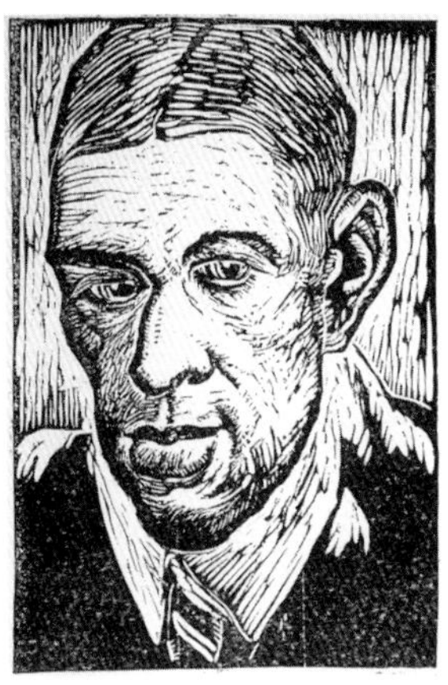

'That huge jaw...' a woodcut, believed to be a self-portrait of Tuck. (Liz Keevill)

As a teacher Tuck is remembered with great fondness and clearly made an impact on his students: 'he seemed about eight feet high with a huge jaw and a very pontifical manner... you couldn't help but have Tuck brush off on you.' At Norwich he was employed to teach painting in oil and watercolour, as well as sculpture, and his study of the drawing room at the School illustrates the conservative approach to the teaching of art during Tuck's tenure.

The Art School, the Woodpecker Art Club, and the Norfolk and Norwich Art Circle, each provided for artists in the region a variety of opportunities to paint and draw and exhibit their work in an atmosphere of mutual support and competition. The Woodpecker Art Club, founded in 1887, took its name from its founding group of wood engravers and their principal activity, 'pecking' at wood. The Woodpecker Art Club amalgamated with the Art Circle in 1925 which continued to hold annual exhbitions at the Castle Museum Gallery. Formed in 1885, the Norwich Art Circle over the years attracted many major figures, among them Frederick Cotman, Sir John Alfred Arnesby Brown, Sir Alfred Munnings and Edward Seago. Tuck, with his gregarious nature, thrived.

We know also that Munnings and Tuck were friends (see the memoir that follows) and that they went on excursions together into the Norfolk countryside – and a small number of Tuck's paintings do call to mind Munning's work, in style and certainly in choice of subject.

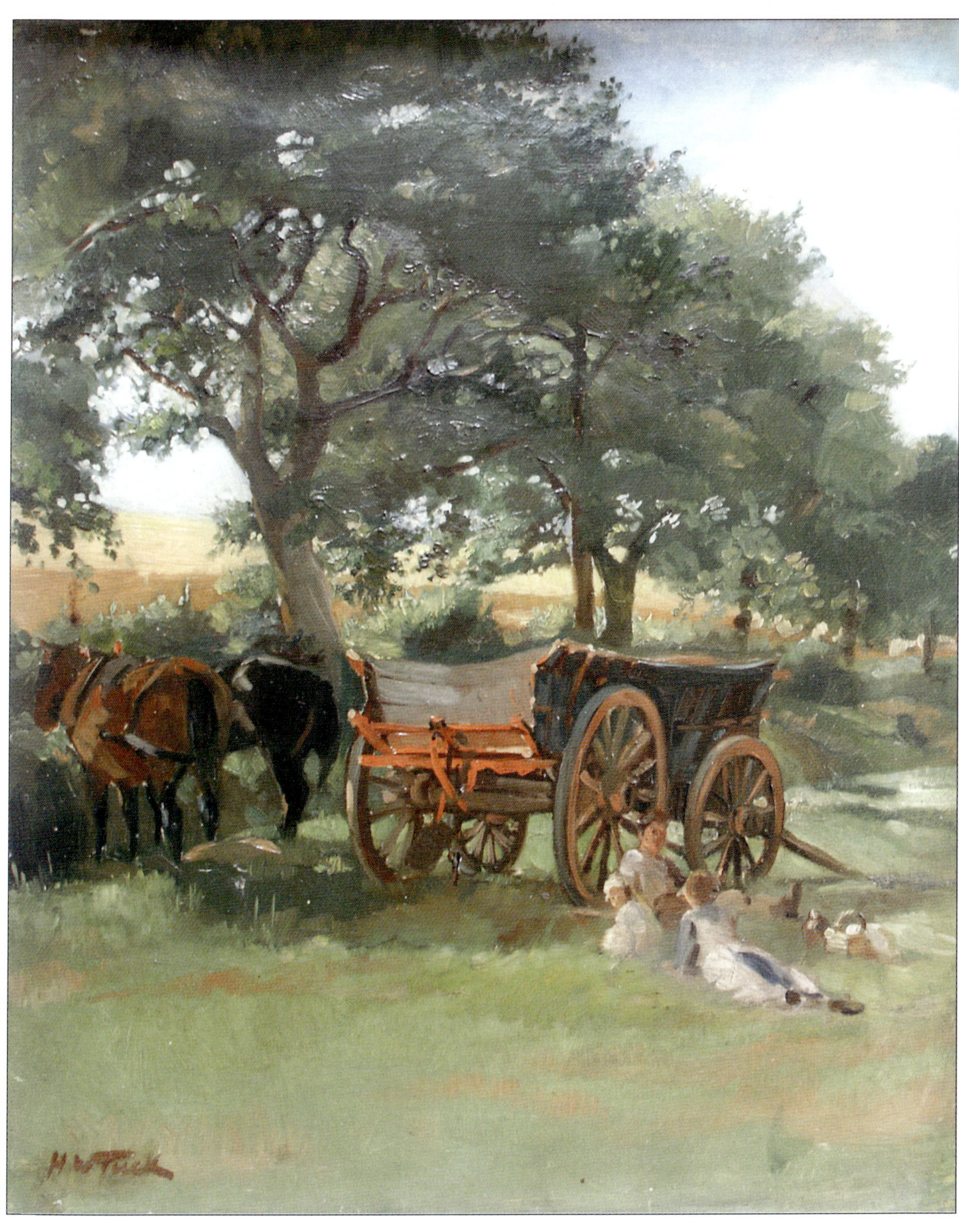

Munnings-like, at least in choice of subject, Tuck's figurework in this painting is far more 'Impressionist' than is typical in his other work.

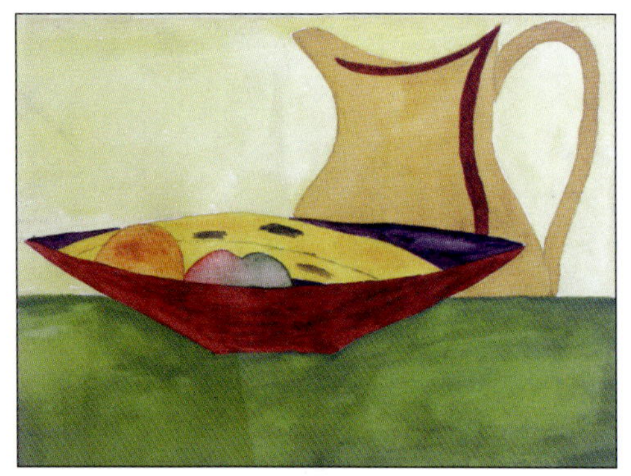

Found among the ephemera of Tuck's studio is this watercolour - a foray into abstraction perhaps?

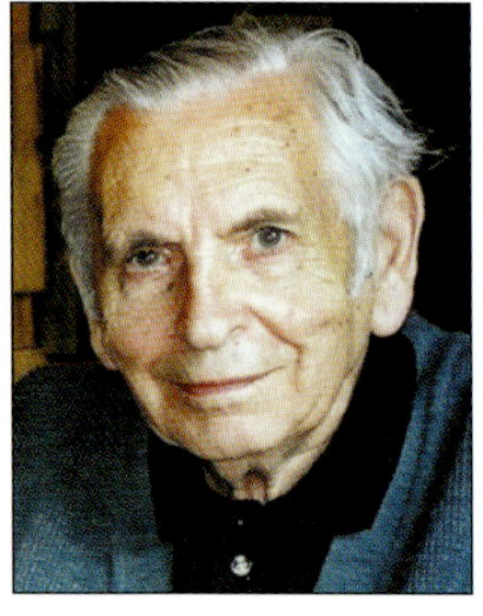

Charles Taylor Cole (Peter), Tuck's nephew and Liz Keevill's father.

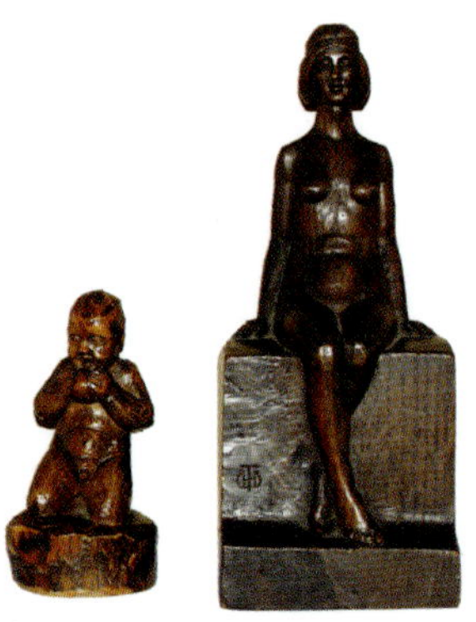

Tuck obviously felt at home among his Art Circle contemporaries for he remained a member for almost fifty years, from 1904 until his death. He also served variously as Vice Chairman, Vice President and eventually as a life member, each year providing work for their prestigious annual exhibition. Nor was the membership comprised only of traditionalists for in 1944 (two years before Tuck became an honorary life member) a small group formed the Norwich Twenty Group whose aim was to debate modern art and produce their own work in this area. But most of this group remained members of the Art Circle and so, no doubt, provided Tuck and his colleagues with every opportunity also to debate the merits of Modern Art. While Munnings' views and extreme disapprobrium of Modern Art are well documented (he was President of the RA at this time), we might suppose that Tuck's sunnier disposition allowed him a more open mind on the subject. There is even a small shard of evidence that he experimented in abstraction himself.

In his forties at the outbreak of the Great War in 1914, effects of a childhood illness prevented Tuck from active service, yet he would have seen many of his students going off to the fighting. There is no evidence in his surviving work of the tortured psyche that so many artists, poets and writers were to exhibit as a result of trauma the war brought to them both at home and abroad, and yet stories told by his family suggest he was not entirely untouched by the horrors of that conflict, nor of the World War that followed.

His great niece, Liz Keevill, recalls her father telling the tale of Horace visiting wounded servicemen in a local convalescent home in the county during the 1940s, and how Horace (having never served himself), felt under an obligation to help where he could. Presumably in the hope of providing some therapeutic and creative motivation for these soldiers, Tuck would take along wood and the necessary tools for 'chip' carving, as he called it, and demonstrate his own facility in making small wooden figures such as those illustrated here. In recollecting these times, Liz's father retold the story of the way in which the soldiers, hardened by life on the front line, would sometimes laugh behind Horace's back, the veterans considering such artistic pursuits altogether too soft.

In his late sixties by the time of Second World War began, Tuck again had to watch his fellow countrymen march away to war, again because of age unable to participate himself. But there survives from this time a fascinating watercolour painting that demonstrates not only how close this war came to the Home Front, but also reflects on the sensitivity of Tuck's nature. The painting (startling in similarity to a watercolour by Paul Nash entitled 'Raider on the Shore', 1940) shows the wing of a crashed German bomber lapped by the tide, and with a body floating nearby. There seems no doubt that this perturbing image is taken from an actual event at Sheringham in 1939, the year Horace and Bessie moved there. Newspaper reports of the time, and surviving photographs, provide a vivid reminder of the effect this tragedy, so early in the war, must have had upon the people of this remote Norfolk community. Tuck's painting of the scene is quite different from his usual landscapes, and is painted with a dreamlike quality, with the remains of the aircraft depicted almost in abstract, the rounded metal form echoed by the waves in the roiling sea.

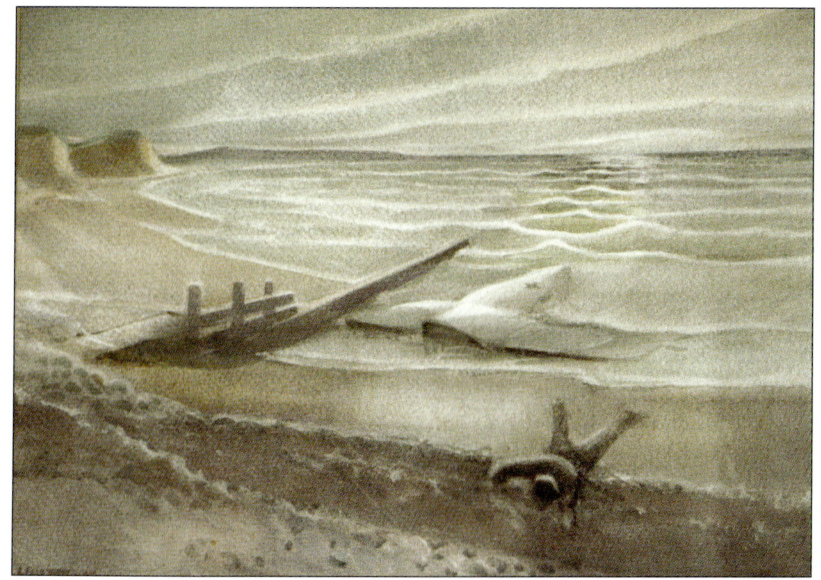

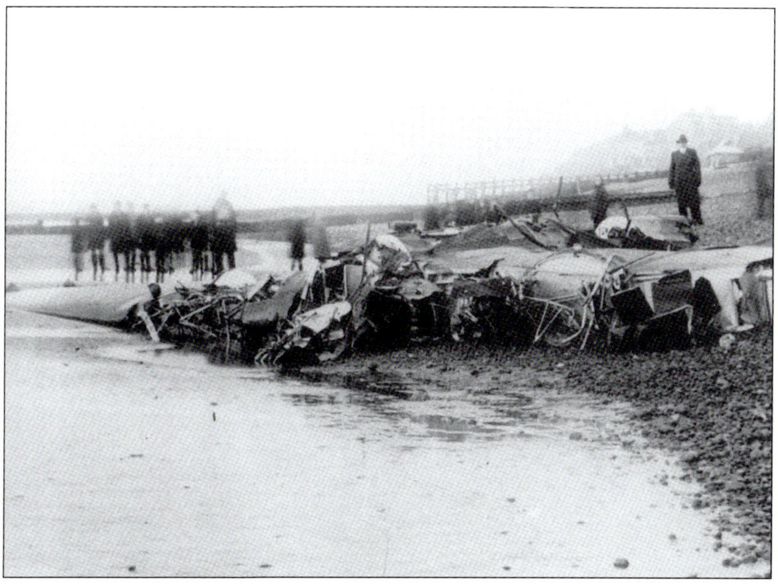

In the early hours of the morning on 6 December 1939 a Heinkel bomber came down in the sea off Sheringham, Norfolk. All three crew members were killed and the body of the observer Emil Rodel, aged 29, was washed ashore. He was later buried with full military honours at Great Bircham churchyard. Tuck's poignant painting of the scene shows the wreckage of the aircraft, identified with the German cross, with the body of the airman alongside.

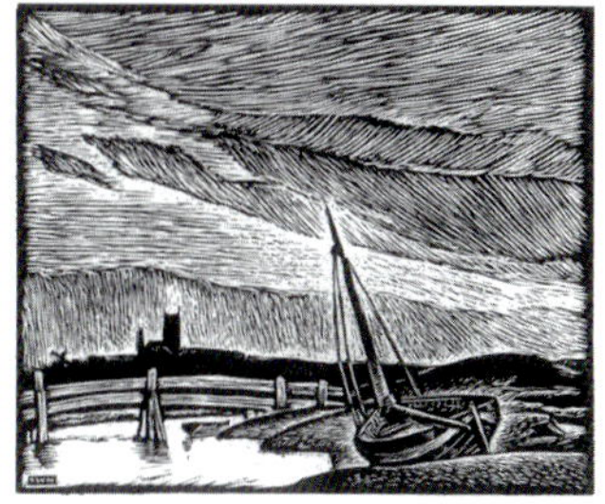

It is difficult, from the evidence to hand, to be certain of the motivation, the 'drive' behind Tuck's urge to paint. Lena Pye recalls his family, middle class people who frowned upon his insistence to attend art college. It is possible to infer from this that his desire to paint went far beyond having an 'artistic bent', and that his lifelong commitment to painting, and to teaching, implies a more complex and dedicated commitment than might first appear from 'amiable' first impressions.

And we can glean from the following extract, a newspaper article written by Horace Tuck under the title 'The Wheelwright's Yard', that his appreciation of the countryside, rural life, and his awareness of its fading from view, was acute, and though tinged with regret, was largely devoid of sentimentality. Interesting too, with his passion for including them in his paintings, that he should write about the craft of the wainright and wheelwright:

At Morston *(inset) - woodcut*

Cart in a Norfolk Lane *includes Tuck's favourite motif.*

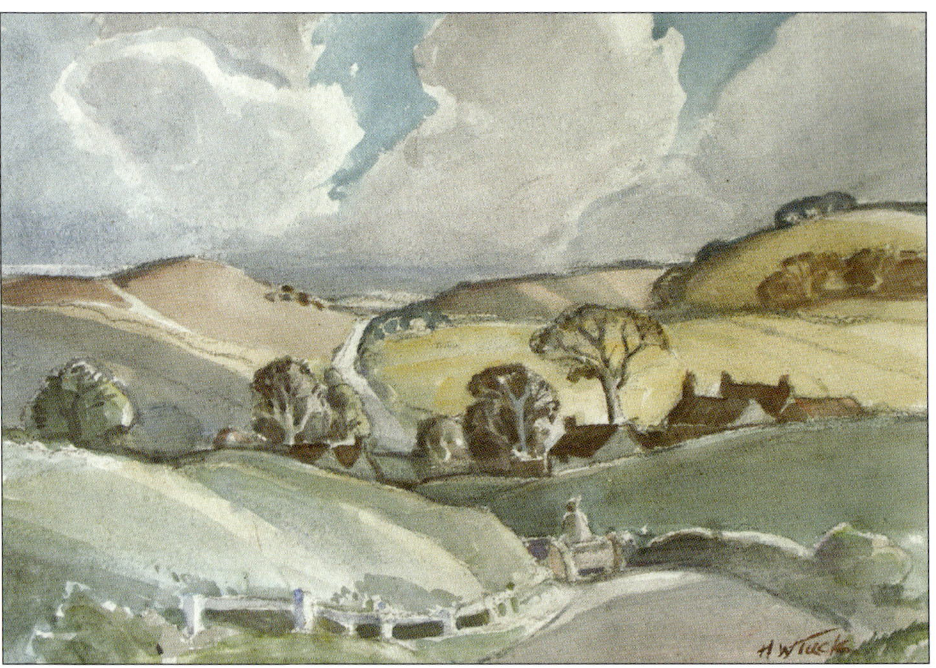

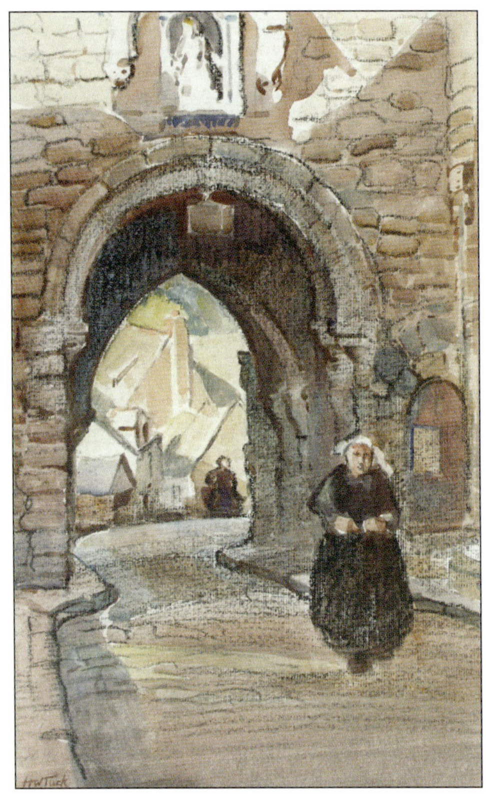

Gateway in a Breton Town. *Tuck painted a number of scenes in and around Dinan in Brittany.*

..at the foot of the black tower of this mill was a timber yard piled high with the severed limbs of great trees, and under its clacking sails, in yards and enclosures, were carried on the little one-man industries in crafts for local needs; a stonecutter's yard, a joiner's shop, shoemakers, even a dyer tented his clothes on frames in his back garden, and in a few cottages, on the last of the handlooms, horsehair stuff was woven, But the wheelwright's shop and the yard of one appropriately named Wright, was the attraction for a schoolboy allowed to hang around and sometimes with pride to lend a hand.

Yet his interests carried beyond the Norfolk landscape, as the final chapter of this book shows. Well travelled, at least in Britain and France, Tuck revelled in novel scenery, often changing his style, particularly in his depiction of French townscapes, as though in celebration and appreciation of that country's painting traditions.

Surviving newspaper clippings provide an insight into Tuck's ambitions to have his work recognised beyond East Anglia. Yet London is an unforgiving place for 'provincial' artists, or those who fail to fully embrace the market makers who peddle what's 'fashionable' in art. Tuck is certainly not the only Norfolk artist who might be said to have been ignored in London as a result of remaining true to his roots. Even so, the critics generally praised his exhibited works, including *The Times* correspondent in 1936:

Though they are not very sensitive in drawing, indeed they are a little wooden, the landscapes in watercolour by H. W. Tuck at the Brook Street Art Galleries win approval by the evident attempt in them to treat things constructively. The impression given is that Mr Tuck will gain flexibility when he has mastered the landscape 'architecture' which engages his attention at the moment. 'The Beech Wood' Sheringham Park', 'The Winding Road', and 'Spring, Sheringham' are among the most successful studies, the colour in them being nicely adapted to the constructive purpose.

Unsurprising perhaps, less reserved praise for the same exhibition came from his peers in the *Norwich School of Art Magazine* for 1936:

Mr. H. W. Tuck, one of our members who is on the Staff of the Norwich School of Art, has a collection of 30 watercolour landscape drawings on view in the Brook Street Galleries New Bond Street. They are comparatively small in size, averaging quarter-imperial, and cover a very wide range of subjects, suggesting the extensive variety of Mr. Tuck's sensibility to land-scape charm. They are handled with unusual freshness and skill. His method is in the best tradition of watercolour, for they are simple drawings with all the added fascination of colour. Every one of them seems to be a spontaneous outdoor study, swiftly and surely ren-dered with an eye to the subject as a whole in form, colour, lighting and atmosphere com-bined—a group of interrelated conditions that only a ripe skill and experience can grasp in unity. In addition there is an invariable sense of pictorial design, so that besides being a study each sketch is an attractive picture. His treatment of clouds as integral elements of the landscape is particularly happy. There is none of the rather familiar sensation of these being added afterwards (as some are) or painted first and then forgotten while the landscape is gradually built up. Much can be said in praise of Mr. Tuck's direct and telling style, his

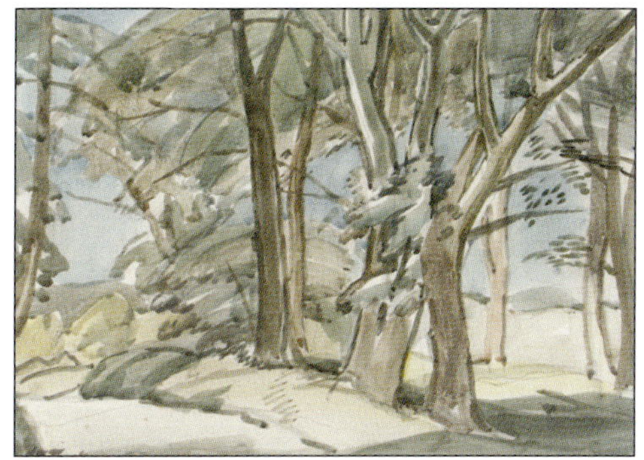

Parkland Glade. *Such watercolour sketches were often studies for more finished oils.*

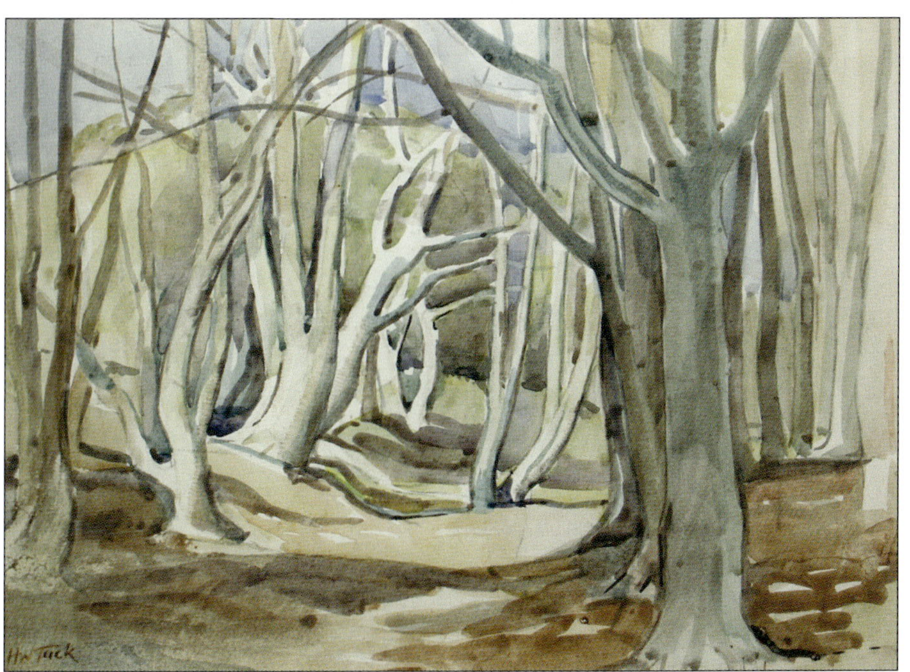

Winter Trees *typifies Tuck's adherence to a simple and spontaneous watercolour technique.*

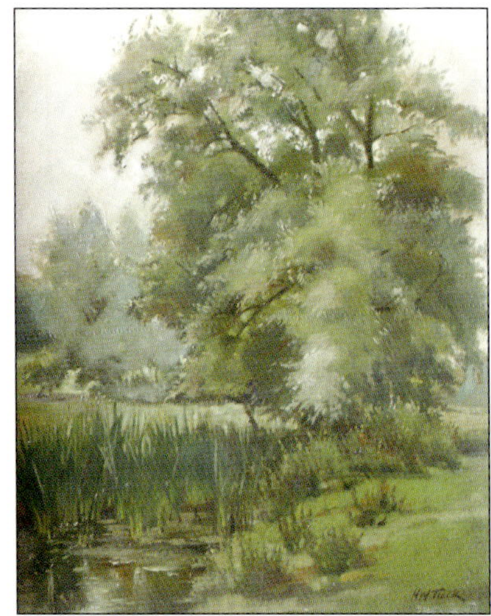

Willows - *Corotesque?*

bold use of broad washes and his instinct for the suppression of non-essential detail. It is a most agreeable and satisfying show, and it was interesting to note that a considerable number had sold.

In the year of his death, 1951, a painting by Tuck, one of his French scenes ironically, titled 'Dinan on the Rance' was chosen to be included in a travelling exhibition celebrating The Festival of Britain. A further exhibition of his watercolours, was held at the Flint House Gallery in Elm Hill, in Norwich shortly after his death:

The many people in Norfolk who remember Mr. H.W. Tuck with affection will be interested by a visit to an exhibition of his landscape paintings. Mr Tuck was for many years teacher of drawing and painting at the Norwich School of Art, and students who came under his guidance remember him for his geneality and tolerance. Nevertheless he had very definite views on the nature of art and his personal style in drawing and painting was well marked.

This style is evident in all the works exhibited; each one is what has come to be known in Norwich as a 'Tuck' and reminds one strongly of the man himself.

It is easier to detect the earlier works which though equally competent, do not have the freedom with which the artist noted down the essentials of the view in 'Earlham Meadows' or 'Sheringham Common'.

Some paintings, like 'Willows', have a Corotesque quality, but most of the works, especially the views of the North Norfolk coast, have a marked flavour of the Norwich School,

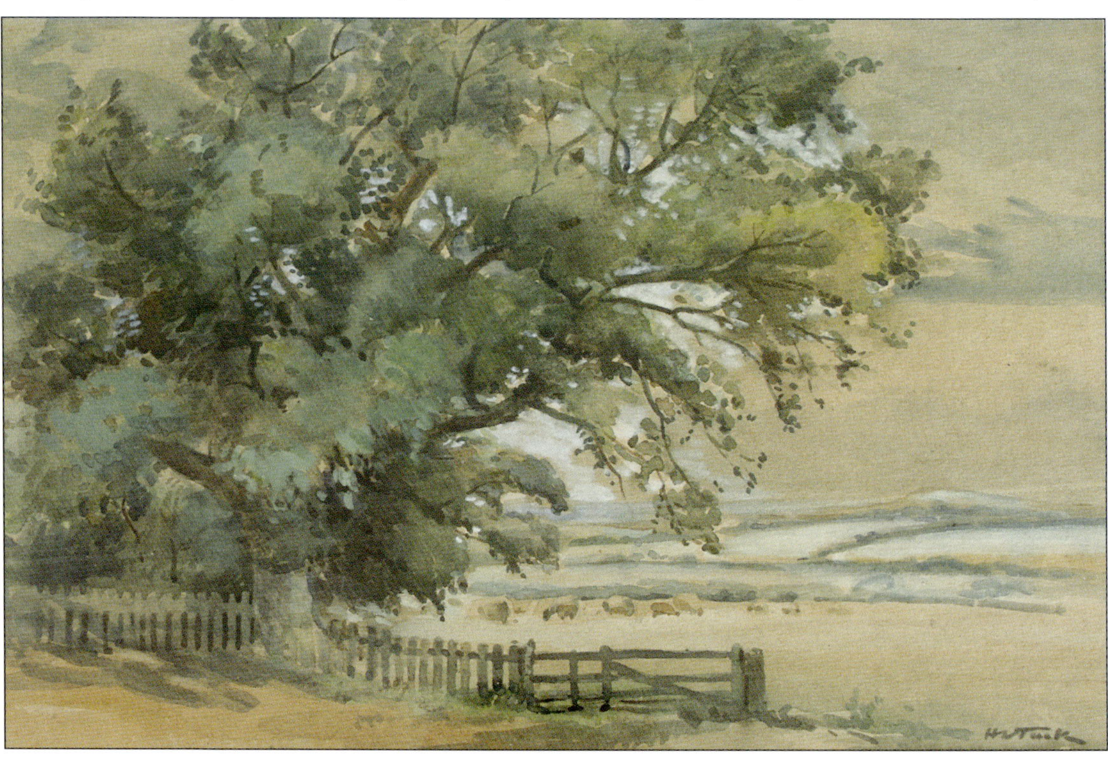

This early watercolour reveals far more of a traditional approach to landscape painting, lacking the freedom of Tuck's later studies.

and in particular of Cotman, but they are in no sense imitations. Rather they are a development of Cotman's capacity for simplifying and clarifying what he saw and subordinating details in the interest of the broad design.

It is somewhat to be regretted that the exhibition is limited to the artist's landscapes, since he is much remembered by his old students for his sure grasp of what he regarded as the essentials in drawing the human figure, as in painting a landscape, and his search for form in life-drawing contributed not a little to his discovery of it in landscape.

Interesting that the newspaper's critic should compare individual Tuck paintings to those of Corot and to Cotman and, whatever the veracity of such comparisons, Tuck's seeming ease at adopting a variety of styles leads inevitably to such observations. On seeing Tuck's oils for the first time, Colin Self referred to the burgeoning landscapes looking like 'baked bread' - the shape of the hills rising yeastily amid the wooded valleys.

Nor did Tuck only choose rural scenes for his paintings. Indeed some of his best work in watercolour is of urban scenes, particularly of Norwich, including several paintings of the building of the Roman Catholic Cathedral.

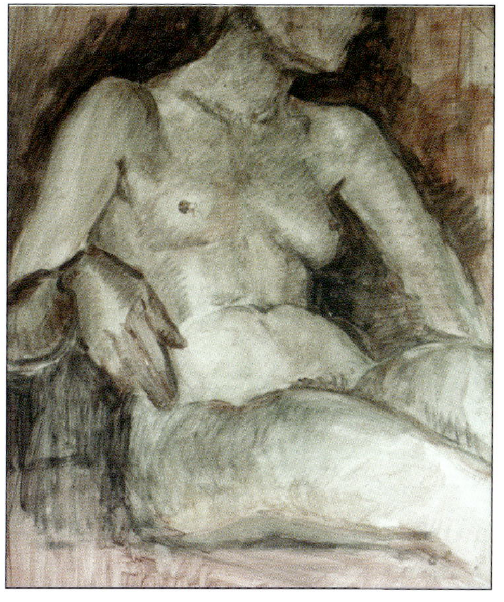

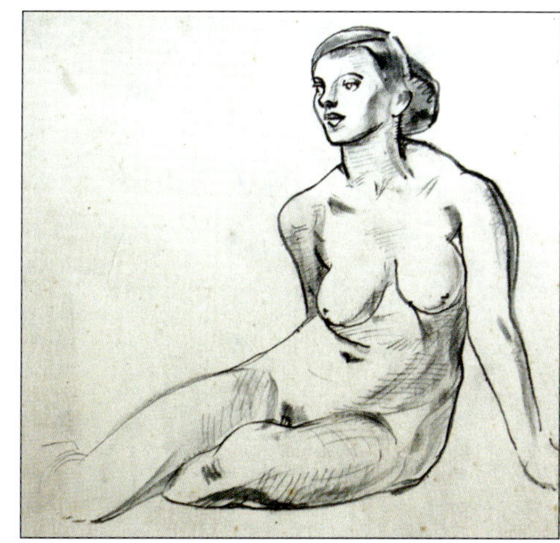

The few surviving life studies by Tuck reveal his fine sense of form and 'a sure grasp of the essentials in drawing the human figure'.

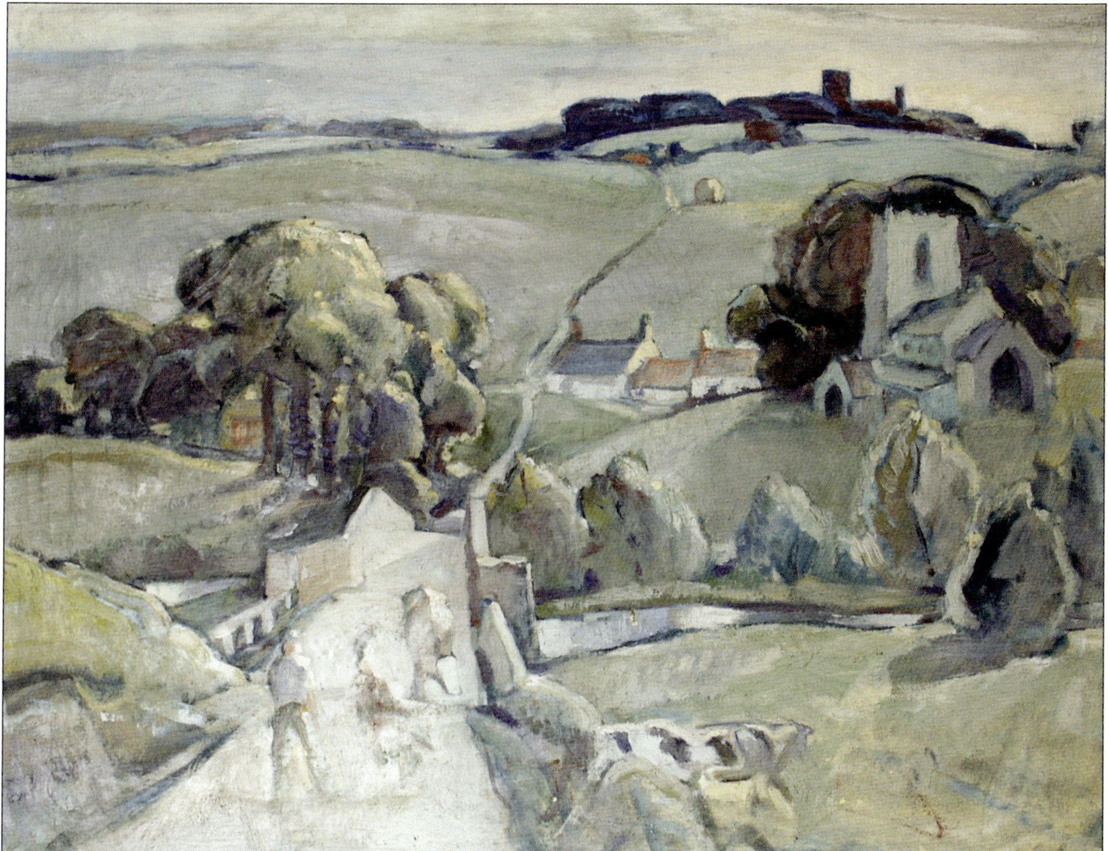

Rounded hills and trees rising 'like baked bread'.

Norwich Market - *woodcut..*

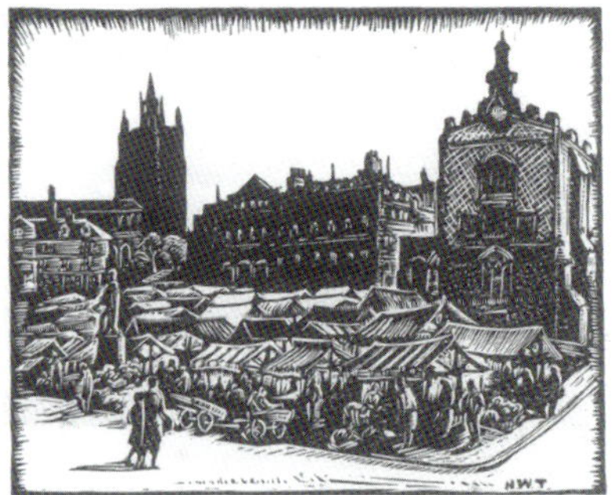

Comparisons between artists' works in a given period are invidious, yet inescapable if we are to attempt to place Tuck's work in some sort of historical context. Whether we are correct in divining direct influences on Tuck from particular of his contemporaries we can be assured that his work forms part of a collective movement in art during the first half of the twentieth century. Generally Tuck's paintings might be said to fall within what has become known as British Modern Art in which artists moved away from the nineteenth century traditions of art as practised by painters such as Whistler and Sickert. It was as though the tidal surges that changed the face of art in the twentieth century, swept clean the canvases of former times, and in receding left at the high watermark, on each successive tide, new concepts and ideas for artists to pick over.

Whittenham (1935) by Paul Nash, watercolour (courtesy Pallant House Gallery) and (right) Copse a watercolour by Horace Tuck.

The works of Paul Nash (1889-1946) and Ivon Hitchens (1893-1979), illustrated here are intended to indicate how Tuck's work, while continuing the traditions of the Norwich School, also paid homage to aspects of modern art. Perhaps had he been born 15 years later, Tuck too would have embraced abstraction as wholeheartedly as Hitchens later did.

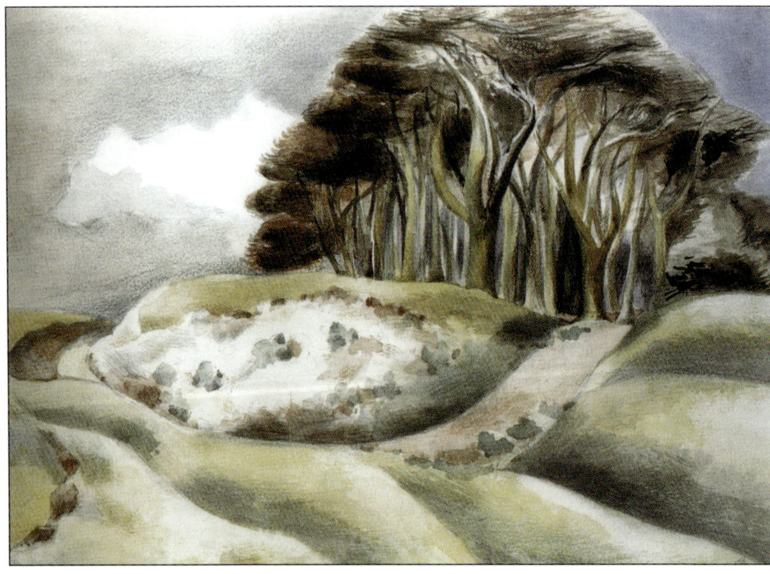

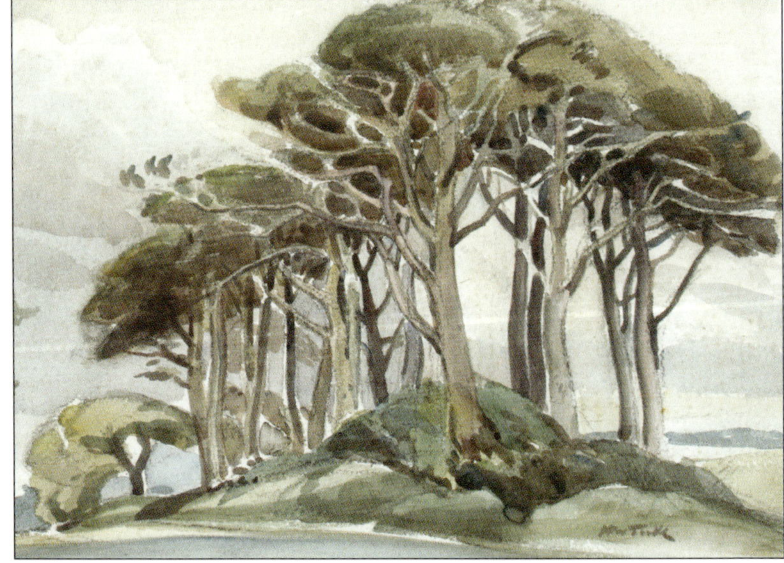

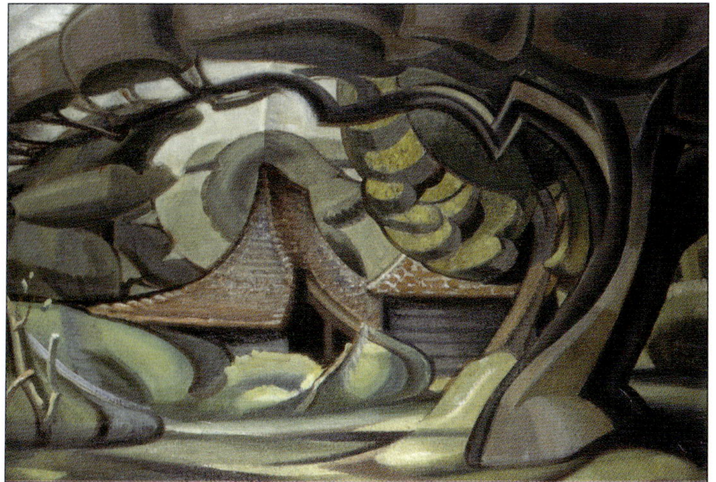

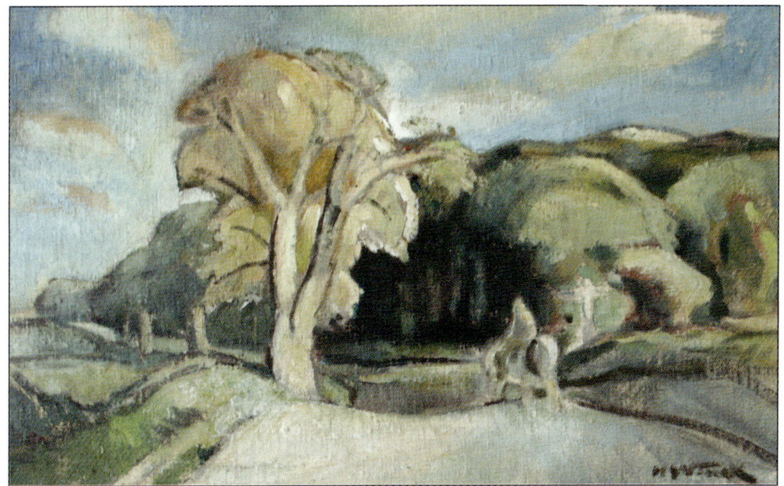

Reference has already been made to Nash's painting of a crashed warplane which is so similar to that of Tuck's watercolour, but Tuck's study of a clump of trees in his water-colour illustrated here is also worthy of comparison, especially in line and tone to Nash's 'Wittenham' on the Berkshire Downs. Similarly, Hitchen's swept lines in 'Curved Barn' have echoes in Tuck's painting alongside. One is reminded of Clive Bell's statement 'Who has not, at least once in his life, had a sudden vision of a landscape as pure form? For once instead of seeing fields and cottages he has felt it as lines and colours'.

Curved Barn (1922) by Ivon Hitchens, oil on canvas (courtesy Pallant House Gallery) and (right), Oakwood *an oil by Horace Tuck, painted on the coast road between Sheringham and Cromer.*

*   *   *

But Tuck, both by inclination and by background, was conservative. No doubt too, those who purchased his work preferred a traditional approach to interpretation of the land-scape. We should also remember that for most of his working life, Tuck's principal means of livelihood was teaching. This undoubtedly influenced his output and the range of media in which he worked. Many of his finished paintings have references in another medium - the same scene repeated in a linocut or woodcut. In teaching his students his facility for handling everything from oil to woodcuts to watercolour would have imposed a necessary orthodoxy.

It is in Tuck's later figurative work that we discover a willingness to move away from tra-dition and his paintings of people, which are rare among his work, have echoes in the painting of Stanley Spencer, Lowry, even Beryl Cook. The painting 'Card Players' shown opposite, and paintings of the Scottish fishergirls and the Salvation Army band included elsewhere in this book contrast with the nudes illustrated earlier.

Tuck was also in demand for illustrative work. A number of modest publications include Tuck's fine drawings and 'decorations': *Norwich - A Book of Drawings* and *A Ballad Upon a Wedding* by Sir John Suckling, the latter being interesting, for Suckling was a celebrated

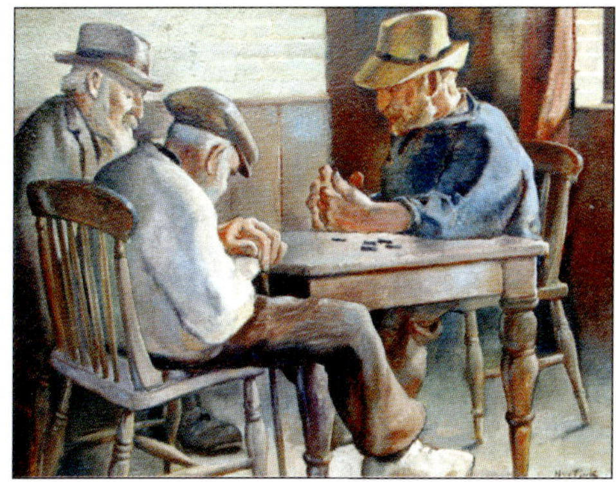

'The Card Players' an oil painting by Horace Tuck now hanging in the Village Hall in Upper Sheringham. (photo David Cooper)

21

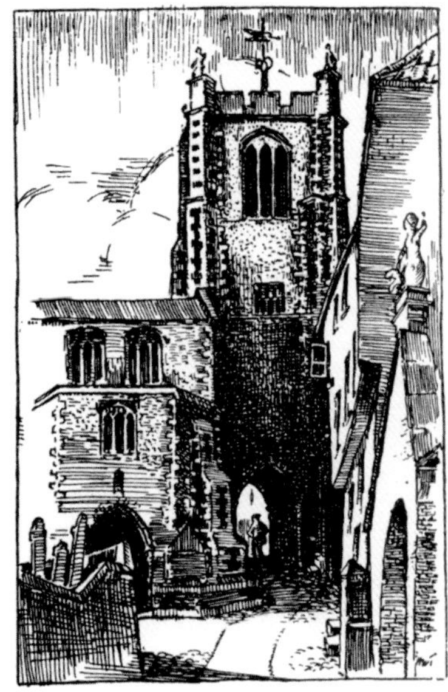

St John's Maddermarket Alley, *from* Norwich - A Book of Drawings, *by Horace Tuck, published in 1932.*

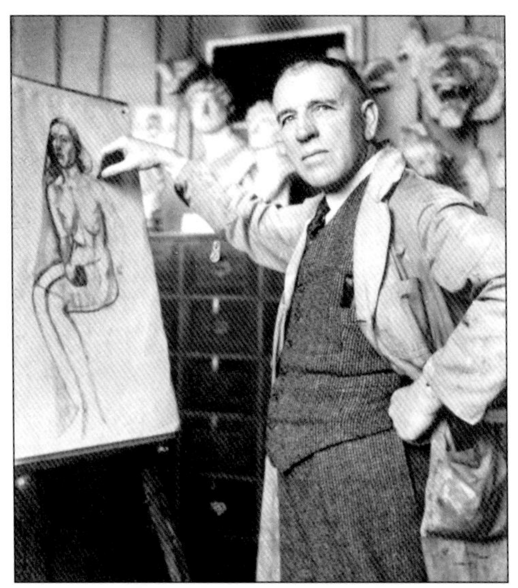

Horace Tuck (1876-1951)

forebear of Tuck's. Tuck also illustrated a book *Inns and Taverns of Old Norwich* and designed locally related ephemera. Hundreds, if not thousands, of Norfolk schoolchildren will have been presented with a Tuck 'original' in the form of a swimming certificate.

Tuck's obituary, written in February 1952 by his colleague and friend C.W. Hobbis, provides us with a succinct pen portrait of Horace Tuck, written by one who knew him well both as a friend and an artist:

> *Mr Horace Walter Tuck of Far End, Knowle Road, Sheringham, died in Cromer Hospital, aged 75. As a teacher of art and as an artist he was well known in Norwich and throughout Norfolk. He moved to Sheringham on his retirement in 1939 after nearly 30 years as a teacher of painting at Norwich Art School. He also lectured on the teaching of art of the Norwich Training College. His work was widely shown in the city. Before the war he held successful London exhibitions. His chief interest in painting was to capture the Norfolk scene.*
>
> *He was born and educated in Norwich, His interest in art has been shared by his wife, Mrs Elizabeth Mary Tuck, who was one of his pupils at the Art School. They were married in 1910.*
>
> *In an appreciation C.W.H. writes: By the passing of Horace Tuck many in this city and county have lost a friend whose memory they will ever cherish. We shall remember him for many things; his lovable qualities of heart and mind which made for rich companionship; his sparkling wit and never-failing good humour; his gentle spirit which looked out on a world with understanding and appreciation of its varied beauties in the common things in life in which, surely, he was akin to Rupert Brooke in his lines 'These I have loved.'*
>
> *To be with him was a stimulating experience, for wit and wisdom flowed easily from his lips and his fund of reminiscences and ability to quote apt sayings made time spent in his company memorable. Perhaps because of all this his teaching and example in the School of Art and other schools is of abiding worth to the great number of students who came under his influence.*
>
> *In his retirement from teaching it was quoted that 'Youth is a state of mind, not a time of life.' By such reckoning he was till young. Painter friend, colleague, we are the better for his life among us. Though he has gone, his spirit will live on.*

And thus we have a portrait of this talented painter; a kindly and sensitive man who was held in great affection by his family, those with whom he taught, and his students. The paintings we have in hand help us to build a picture of an artist for whom the Norfolk landscape remained a principal subject and abiding passion. That we can call his paintings 'lost' landscapes is due to more than a sentimental yearning for times past. He captured through his art a sense of place more telling than any photograph, for his paintings contain more than just a record of a place. Indeed, as Hobbis had hoped, Tuck's spirit does live on in his paintings.

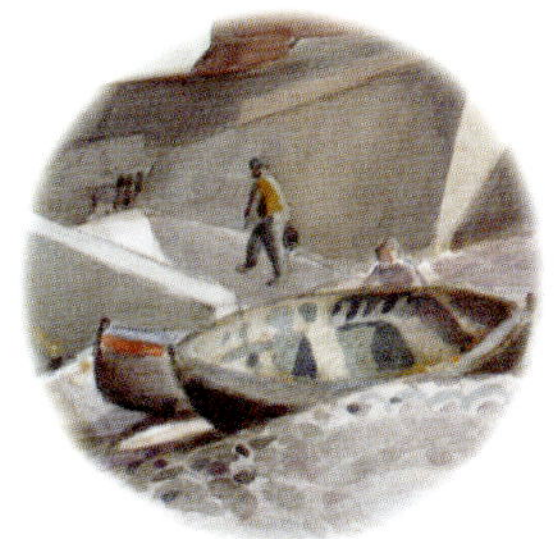

A Memoir of Horace Tuck

by his Great Niece Jennifer Tuck

I suppose, having recently joined the 'selective gathering' of pensioners, I am entitled to look back on life and to my childhood. A wonderful childhood I had with devoted parents who, as I recall, showed me the finer things of life, including art.

My father, Stephen Austin Tuck, and my mother, Margaret Ellen Tuck, introduced me to art at a very early age. My father's uncle was an artist of what has become to be known as the Late Norwich School, Horace Walter Tuck. I remember him well with his wife, Aunt Bessie, living at Far End, Knowle Road, Sheringham where I spent hours and hours as a young child until his death in 1951. He was known to me as Uncle Horry and he taught me so much about art, life and people in and around North Norfolk that I suspect I would not have otherwise known. My father was particularly close to him, being very interested in art, as was his father, my grandfather. We all spent a lot of time with Uncle Horry and Aunt Bessie; there was never time to be bored we were always so busy and interested, and life seemed such fun.

I remember Uncle Horry as a man with lovely sparkly eyes, even when he thought I wasn't looking at him. He was a quiet man who always seemed deep in thought, moving quietly about the house. There seemed to be lots of times when we needed to be quiet but lots of times of laughter as well. He smoked a pipe and sat in his chair beside the open hearth. Next to him, beside his chair on the other side, was a bookcase running several feet along the wall towards the kitchen. On the bottom shelf were books that he kept especially for me. I remember when he sat in his chair after painting or coming in from his workshop I would go to these books to choose my 'favourite' of the day. He would smile and then lift his head and quietly laugh as I clambered on to his lap with my book. Aunt Bessie would bring tea and cakes for the 'grown ups' whilst he and I would get on with the urgent matter in hand – the book. I think I must have fallen asleep on his lap sometimes as I remember being woken up and told it was time to go home. He had a long brown heavy cotton coat that he used to wear. When he'd finished work for the day he would undo the brown buttons down the front but keep it on whilst he sat down for his cup of tea. I recall that it was this large brown coat that I used to curl up into on his lap. It was a donkey-brown colour and very cuddly.

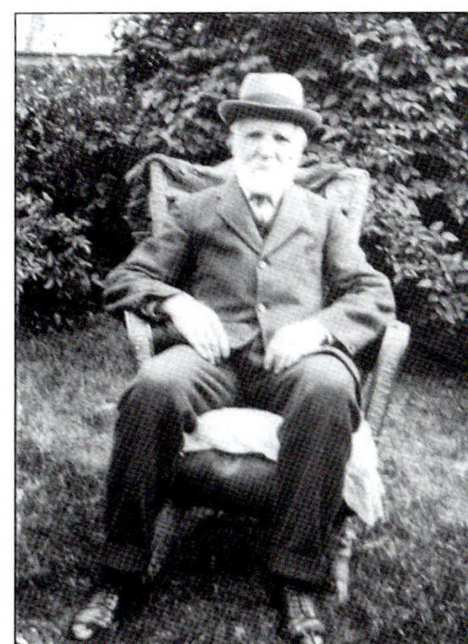

Horace's father, Austin Tuck, in his later years.

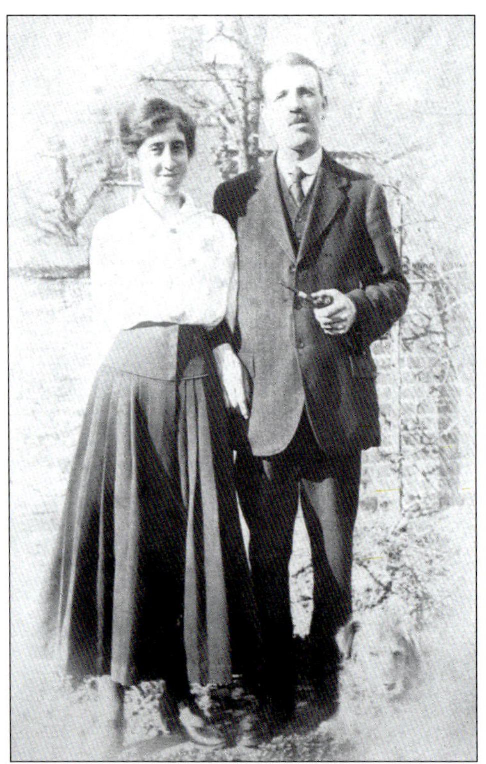

Horace and Bessie Tuck (Lena Pye)

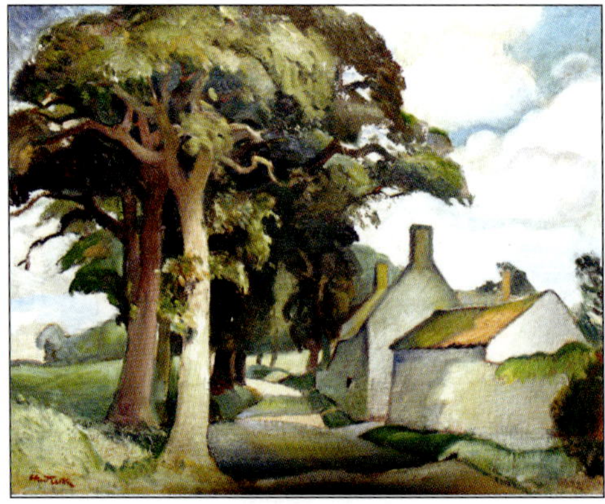

'Light bursting through the trees' - a painting by Horace Tuck now owned by his great niece, Jennifer.

In my younger years Aunt Bessie would also keep me amused. Whilst Uncle Horry was working, either out painting or in his workshop; she would let me help her cook cakes for whoever was around at the time for afternoon tea. The kitchen was plain and stark, but practical, with everything in its place. There was a butler sink and wooden draining board with the worktop to the right and shelves underneath. To cover the shelves and keep everything clean she had made some gingham curtains, I'm sure they were green gingham that hung on expanding wire, with very neat and perfect gathering at the top. We would get the mixing bowl and ingredients out and in the earlier years I was given a stool to stand on so that I could reach. Goodness, that wonderful day when I didn't need the stool anymore, I really felt I had grown up. I think mostly we cooked buns as I could spoon the mixture out with a teaspoon. Latterly we went on to bigger and better things like cheese straws, scones, Norfolk rusks and Norfolk shortcakes, recipes that I use to this day. When the cakes came out of the oven we'd cool them before arranging them on a plate. I would proudly carry the plate through to the sitting room for afternoon tea followed by Aunt Bessie with the tea tray; I hadn't graduated to that yet. The whole gathering, however many there were that day, said they were the best buns and cakes they had ever tasted. They said that every time, and I remember thinking to myself, even as a youngster, that my cakes must be getting better and better, not realizing, then, that it was really only so because Aunt Bessie was telling me how to cook, and she did most of it anyway. I think that between them my mother and Aunt Bessie were responsible for my cooking today, working as a confectioner. My mother took on where Aunt Bessie left off and for that I will always be so very grateful to both of them.

I saw a lot of Uncle Horry and Aunt Bessie over the years. My father had an old Lanchester car which made it very easy to travel back and forth. My father always took the back lanes to 'everywhere' so it took forever and so many times I'd ask, in anticipation, if we were there yet. At times I would stay overnight at Far End with my mother whilst my father returned home to go to work. Each day I'd either help with the cooking or watch Uncle Horry at work. He would paint in 'the field', either on his own or in company, returning home later on to do more work on that particular canvas. I would watch him either in his workshop or in the garden. I'd stay completely silent as my father had drummed into me that I could watch but not move or make a noise to disturb him; father was very strict. Often he'd see me watching and with a twinkle in his eye he'd ask if I'd like to come closer to see him match his colours. In a very quiet way he had a vitality of enthusiasm about his work. It seemed to radiate from him. He described to me about light bursting through the trees. How light burst through the branches of a tree and bounced to the ground sitting there for while, as though gathering its thoughts, before bouncing back up again. I now know that he was describing the imprisonment of light and was teaching me as a child. There seemed so much to learn from Uncle Horry that later on I was allowed to stay at Far End on my own, the very first place that I'd stayed on my own. I always felt completely happy there in their warmth and safety. Thinking back maybe, as a childless couple, they liked to have a youngster around and I'm sure my mother must have enjoyed a bit of peace and quiet at home for a change. Bedtime was always fun; Aunt Bessie would read me a story in bed and then we'd look out of the window over the wood through the pretty curtains with their little flowers. I'd pull the curtains and snuggle down for the night. Often owls would hoot and I'd pull the covers further up over my head. When I woke the next day, after dressing, Aunt Bessie would plait my hair. I always considered that she did it better than my mother, probably because it was just different. After breakfast she would take me to see some of Uncle Horry's paintings and carvings. She, too, was a quiet lady, immaculately dressed with her white hair tied neatly back in a bun. She had an air of quiet and friendly confidence about her which seemed to pull me close to her. I always remember her wearing pleated skirts and a cardigan with a crisp collared blouse underneath, or an immaculate dress in the summer. My mother, later in life, had told me that Aunt Bessie had said to her, some years earlier, that she always regretted her economies and never her extravagances in life. From my own observations Uncle Horry and Aunt Bessie didn't have much and lived very frugally, but what they did have was very good.

I loved it there as a child. Aunt Bessie was so proud of Uncle Horry's work. I would hold her hand as we went through the little side gate into the wood. How different it was in daylight with lots of wildflowers and trees. My father was excellent at identifying wild-flowers, there were hardly any in that wooded area that I didn't know and today I look at them and think of the long hot days in the wood at Far End. Later on, when I too began to paint, it was mainly of wildflowers.

Uncle Horry's woodcarvings were another example of his talent. I watched him carve nude ladies, a Madonna and child and lots of others, but best of all was a little horse and cart. It all started with a fairly rough block of wood and I was amazed as the cart began to be carved and take shape. He was forever picking it up and doing some more to it and putting it back down again. Slowly, but surely, the cart had taken shape and then he began with one wheel and then the other. On all my subsequent visits I couldn't wait to be told I could go to see how the cart was coming on. Lo and behold, on one visit the horse was beginning to take shape. This seemed like endless fun for me and now the cart was becoming more important to me, on my visits, than my beloved bookshelf. The horse was eventually finished, with just the little block left on top of the cart where a man was to be carved. We had a bad winter that year and could not visit so often. Spring came and off we all went to Far End. I rushed to the cart; the little man had barely been started. I almost cried, although I now realise that it had been put aside for other work.

Uncle Horry seemed to have many painting friends, some of whom I knew and some I didn't. One in particular I remember who, later, became Sir Alfred Munnings. My grand-father, Alfred Austin Tuck (Uncle Horry's eldest brother), worked at Page Bros, in Norwich, as a lithographer with Alfred Munnings. Both were on 5-year apprenticeships. To save confusion of both being named Alfred, Alfred Munnings became known to all as AJ, his initials. I always knew him as AJ. He was a lovely man but there was nothing quiet about him. He and my grandfather were great friends who spent time together away from work. The major client of Page Bros, at the time, was Caleys, the chocolate manufacturer in Norwich. My grandfather and AJ did labels, sketching and advertising work for them,

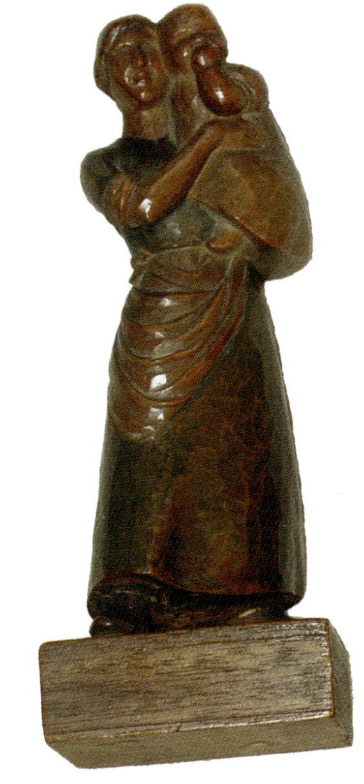

Limewood carving 'Mother and Child'. Tuck often coloured these carvings, as here. (Jennifer Tuck)

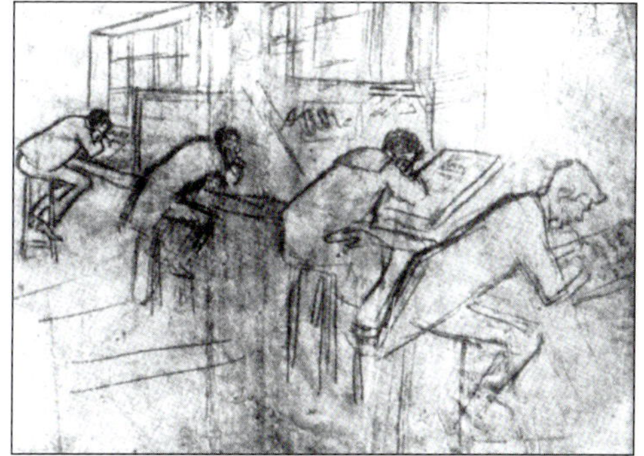

The artists' room at Page Bros - from a sketch made by Alfred Munnings.

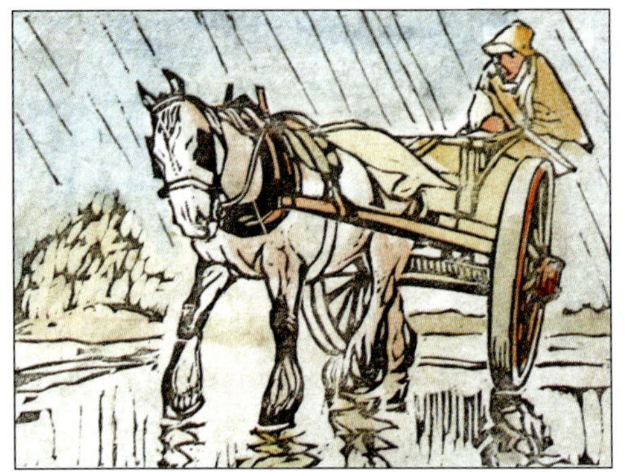

A favourite motif in Tuck's work, the horse and two wheeled-cart, a coloured woodcut. Tuck's great niece recalls 'He did many drawings of horses; the Munnings' influence coming in. His 'Bible' was Stubbs' The Anatomy of the Horse, *the ever-faithful copy tucked under his arm. I remember the old battered copy, I was even allowed to try to mend it for him.'* (Jennifer Tuck)

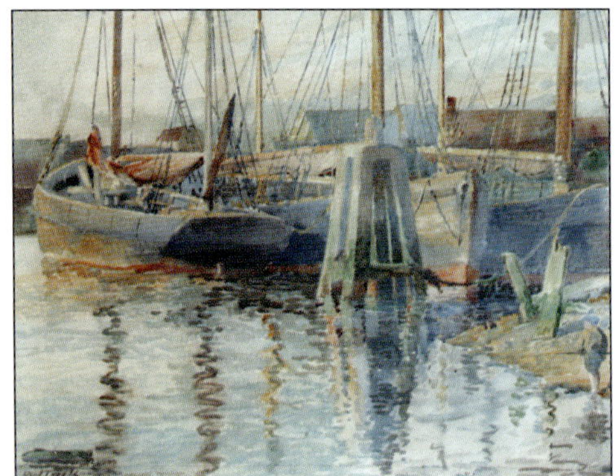

'Don't forget the little man,' - using a figure to balance the painting. (Jennifer Tuck)

amongst other things. One day, bored during a lunch hour, AJ was doodling on a piece of board, creating a man wearing a red coat seated at a table sampling a sauce bottle. When finished he chucked it on the floor in a corner, as scrap, before getting on with the afternoon's work. My grandfather, the story goes, picked it up at the end of the day and took it home thinking that he liked the doodle and that, in time, 'AJ was going places' and he'd like to have a keepsake. The drawing was later framed, very basically, and was passed down through the family still in its original frame.

My grandfather and my father had always painted as a hobby, mainly watercolours. They painted together, particularly in the Sheringham area, where they joined together with Uncle Horry. My grandfather had introduced AJ to Uncle Horry (the two were also contemporaries at Norwich Art School) and several times all four of them painted together, either at Far End or they went out to paint in the surrounding area. I was told that Roughton, near Cromer, seemed to be a special spot as did the quaysides at Great Yarmouth and Lowestoft. AJ only had sight in one eye and, through an earlier part of his career, had enlisted the services of a young Romany lad called Shrimp. Shrimp used to mount horses for AJ to paint. Mounted and with reins in one hand he would then extend his other arm to the front pointing at AJ. Then he would raise his thumb upwards so that AJ could centre his paintings.

I recall being allowed to watch the artists at work. There were the wonderful silences that seemed to go on forever and then there would be such laughter. The silences I shall never forget as everything seemed so still, the odd leaf fluttered down and the birds sang, just the sighs and the brush strokes and the odd grunt from time to time. AJ would raise his voice and shout for Shrimp, who'd long since disappeared to pastures new, saying that he couldn't work without him. Again laughter and ridicule. On occasions it became very raucous with AJ resorting to language that I'd never heard before. At that time Aunt Bessie and my mother would hastily collect me and I'd be taken out of the way.

It was fun watching them all paint together and they found time, between them, to teach me a few basics. The light on the backs of the horses was always the same colour, whatever colour the horse, picking up the light from the sky. The book that most of them seemed to use for reference was Stubbs' *The Anatomy of the Horse*. They called it their Bible. Uncle Horry's copy was getting very battered and one rainy afternoon I was allowed to help Aunt Bessie re-cover it. They also told me about 'balance', which they explained to me as 'the little man'. I was told that no matter how big the subject, the painting had to be balanced. Many of their paintings were balanced by a small figure, standing to one side or on a boat fishing, in the foreground. Even a dominant shoreline was sometimes used. These 'little men' are spotted in Uncle Horry's work particularly his paintings of boats. I was also told that a signature was only used as balance if you were very desperate. Laughter and a chorus of 'don't forget the little man' have remained in my mind ever since.

Another of his great friends was Norman Crosse. Around the same age as Uncle Horry, they painted together frequently and produced work that seemed almost identical. They both loved wherries. Windmills were another favourite. A painting owned by my father was of a windmill at the top of a hill with a horse and cart steadily climbing towards it. My father said that he had watched the horse and cart going up that hill for 70 years and it hadn't got there yet! I think that's something I shall be telling my children before long. Some of the paintings I didn't understand at the time. There always seemed to be a lot of sky and not so much picture, which as a child I decided I would rather have seen.

Obviously ignorance was bliss and later it became known to me that this was the Dutch influence on The Norwich School with their typical low skylines. There were other subjects of Uncle Horry's work that I'd not seen for myself before. I was quite amused by his painting of the Scottish fishergirls (see page 60). My father and mother took me to Great Yarmouth in the autumn one year where I could see these women for myself. They were the Scottish fishergirls, from Aberdeen, who arrived in Great Yarmouth during the herring fishing season and stood all day on the quayside behind the big troughs, bundled in their warm clothes with skirts down to the ground, gutting the fish with their bare hands. They were so fast that I could hardly see what they were doing. Once or twice a herring would be dropped and slip on to the ground. My father let me go to pick one up after a fishergirl had signalled that I could. I recall the absolute coldness and slipperiness of the herring and wondered how on earth these women could work bare-handed in the freezing conditions. We'd take the herring home in a bag, they were really big, and have it between us with bread and butter for our tea. At the end of the season the Scottish fishergirls disappeared as quickly as they had come. I didn't go with Uncle Horry to Great Yarmouth when he did these paintings but do recall him finishing one at home.

Uncle Horry had a great passion for ginger biscuits. My maternal grandfather, Ernest Morgan Pert, I called him 'Pip pa', was a Master Grocer and had a shop in Rupert Street, Norwich, long ago demolished to make room for the then 'new' Norfolk and Norwich Hospital. I went, with my mother, once a week on the No.84 bus to see my Grandfather at his shop. On entering the shop by its corner door, on the junction of the street, I was faced by the large curved wooden counter, underneath which was an array of big square biscuit tins. Grandfather, on seeing us, would come out of his office at the back of the shop to greet us. We'd then be taken back to his office where he and my mother would catch up on all the news. He would draw me pictures of elephants, goodness knows why, and they would always make me laugh as they all seemed so different. Later, he would give me two paper bags, one large and one small, to take to the biscuit tins. The large bag I was allowed to fill with as many broken biscuits that I could find, to take home for us to eat, and the smaller bag I could fill with ten whole, undamaged ginger biscuits. These were for me to take to Uncle Horry as they were his favourites and Pip pa always appreciated that I liked to take something when I went to see him and Aunt Bessie.

As I got a bit older I seemed to spend more and more time at Far End, in fact more time than with my own grandparents. My grandmother, Emma Tuck, to say the least, was a very cantankerous person and in my eyes, as a youngster, very fearsome. Nothing was ever right for her and I think that even my grandfather, a complete gentleman, enjoyed

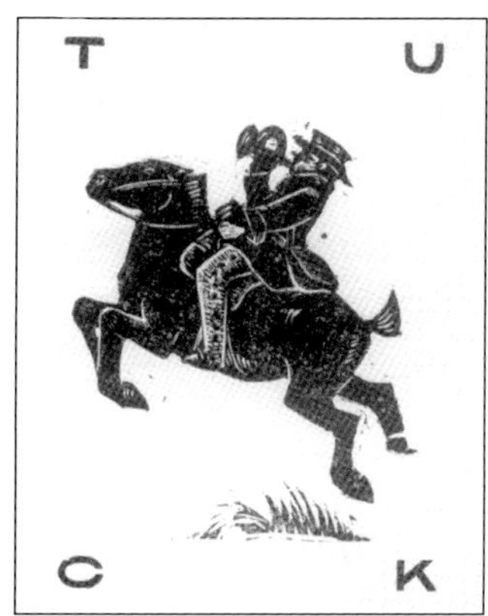

A Horace Tuck design for use on envelopes by Stephen Tuck, a keen philatelist.

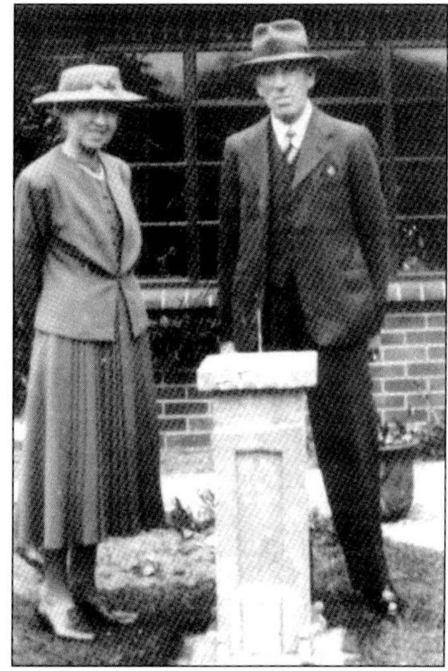

Horace and Bessie at the Tuck home 'Far End', Knowle Road in Sheringham.

his 'escape' to Far End. Uncle Horry and Aunt Bessie were such a close couple with a lovely home. Aunt Bessie was a pillar of the church, at Beeston Regis, near Sheringham. We'd walk there, sometimes, with her. It was beautiful there right close to the sea. The sound of the sea was not very familiar to me so I was always excited when Uncle Horry took me painting nearby, especially at Blakeney when the tide came rushing in. I was fascinated. After going to church we'd walk further to the 'Hump' at Sheringham. This is a large hill overlooking the sea that can be seen for miles around.

Aunt Bessie took a very special interest in Uncle Horry's painting. She encouraged him endlessly and painted a number of watercolours herself. These were almost in the same mould as those of his. He stood behind her and helped her, never criticising always encouraging. They made Christmas cards together from his linocuts and woodcuts. The one he made in 1934, when they lived in Branksome Road, Norwich, was always remembered as a special one. Uncle Horry had forgotten to carve his initials back to front that year for the card, instead, putting them the normal way round. As a result, when printed, they were back to front (see page 34). The card was still sent out that year for Christmas surmising that no one would notice, but my father, who never missed anything, was highly amused and thought of it as one of life's little idiosyncrasies. He told many a time of how he 'ribbed' Uncle Horry and through the years it had become a bit of a family joke. I get that card out sometimes and chuckle to myself just as my father did. He also, from time to time, provided book illustrations in woodcut and linocut.

The little cart hadn't developed any further but new ventures appeared in the workshop. Uncle Horry showed me his carvings with coloured waxes on them. Dull colours they were, but they gave his carvings a whole new look, adding depth and a more complete finish. I was mesmerised by this but still looked longingly at the little cart. When would it be finished? Many of his paintings, both watercolours and oils, together with linocuts, woodcuts, etchings and lithographs, had the cart in them and it became a recurring motif in his work.

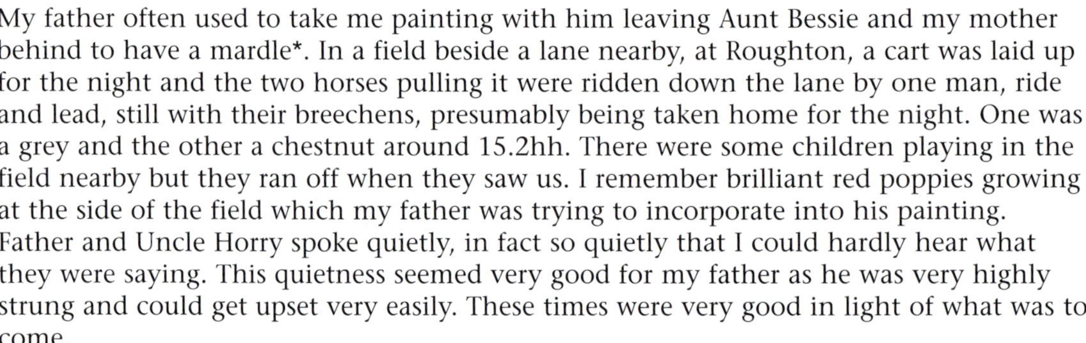

My father often used to take me painting with him leaving Aunt Bessie and my mother behind to have a mardle*. In a field beside a lane nearby, at Roughton, a cart was laid up for the night and the two horses pulling it were ridden down the lane by one man, ride and lead, still with their breechens, presumably being taken home for the night. One was a grey and the other a chestnut around 15.2hh. There were some children playing in the field nearby but they ran off when they saw us. I remember brilliant red poppies growing at the side of the field which my father was trying to incorporate into his painting. Father and Uncle Horry spoke quietly, in fact so quietly that I could hardly hear what they were saying. This quietness seemed very good for my father as he was very highly strung and could get upset very easily. These times were very good in light of what was to come.

On a lighter side it wasn't all 'art' in its various guises; there were other pastimes with which Uncle Horry and Aunt Bessie kept me busy. We had endless fun on the beach with

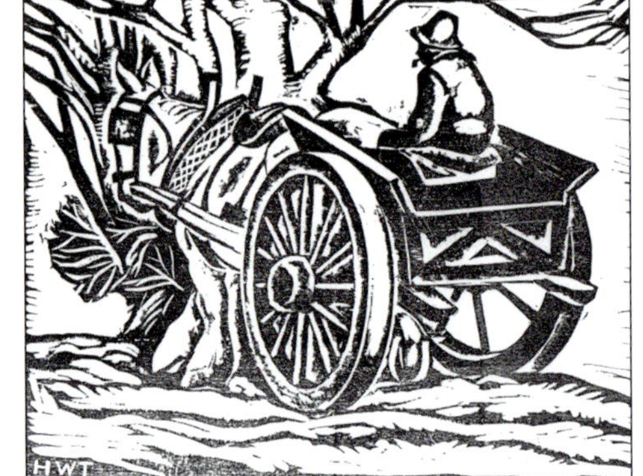

The Carter - linocut (Jennifer Tuck)

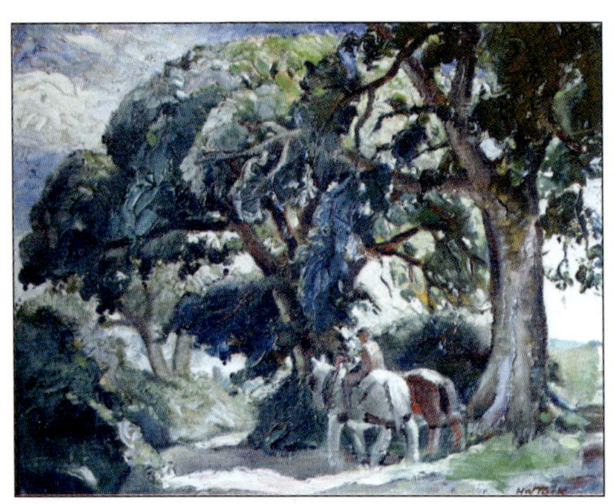

'A grey and a chestnut...' (Jennifer Tuck)

*mardle - Norfolk dialect for a natter or conversation.

my ball. Sheringham had a very stony beach so we sometimes went farther afield. Being a youngster I didn't run that fast nor, being older, did they, so I remember it was my father who was always the runner of the day especially when the ball didn't go where it should have done. And so off ran my father followed in hot pursuit by me, returning to find that the others were all standing in the same spot laughing and making no effort at all. I paddled in the sea with my father and Uncle Horry with trousers rolled up to their knees. We splashed in the small waves all entering into the spirit of it. I was taken for lots of walks in the woods where we'd kicked leaves and made a swishing sound, but the wood beside Far End was the most special of all. We'd play 'hide and seek', I always got found and it seemed it was me who did all the 'seeking' to no avail. They were all very good at it. I was taken to the very edge of the wood from the centre where I could see underneath the trees, to where, I was lead to believe, the fairies lived.

When Uncle Horry and Aunt Bessie came to visit us at home in Sprowston, Norwich, where my parents had their house built in 1926, we'd invariably go to Mousehold Heath nearby. This was a very large wood and one part of it was always my favourite. There were a series of little hills, which seemed huge to me in those days, which became known to me as the 'wheezy bumps'. Here we'd run up and down, at least my father and I did, whilst the rest of the gathering, especially my mother and Uncle Horry, made a very weak attempt at it.

Returning home Aunt Bessie, my mother and I would cook scones, mostly, and then, when cool, we'd cut them in half. The tray of tea, milk and china would be carried by my mother, followed by Aunt Bessie with the plate of warm scones and butter, whilst I would follow on behind with a green jam pot, with a silver spoon, full of my mother's home-made raspberry jam. We carried them down the garden to a part known as the 'sunk' garden. My father had made a long wooden seat and had dug out a pond that had a few fish and plants, overhung by a large apple tree laden with 'Lady Sudeley' apples. The apples were beautifully juicy and we all ate one after the scones on that particular day. My father fetched a bag and filled it with these apples for Uncle Horry and Aunt Bessie to take home. There were so many of them and they didn't store very well so my father was pleased to be able to give them away, and Aunt Bessie always knew how to make mouth-watering delicacies out of anything.

In Norwich, one Christmas time, Uncle Horry and Aunt Bessie joined us. We looked at the Christmas lights and the bright shop windows. Carols were being sung on Jarrolds' Corner being accompanied by members of the Norwich Salvation Army band. We, and a number of other people, joined in the carols; it seemed like magic. Uncle Horry was very taken by the band, people wandered away between carols while others arrived, but he just stood there for ages, deep in thought.

A number of features in Uncle Horry's work reflect the date and times of his paintings, most of which he left undated. At the beginning of the Second World War most of the signposts in Norfolk were painted white. This was done so that if the Germans landed at night they couldn't find where they were, without the greatest of difficulty. Several

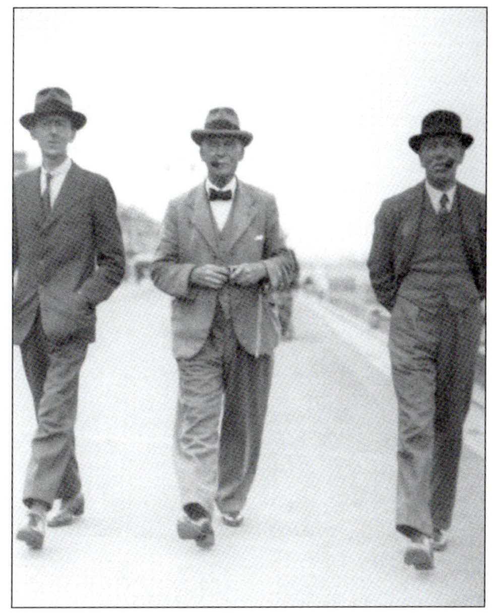

Three Tuck painters on Sheringham seafront. From left: Stephen Tuck, Alfred Tuck (HWT's eldest brother), and Horace. (Jennifer Tuck)

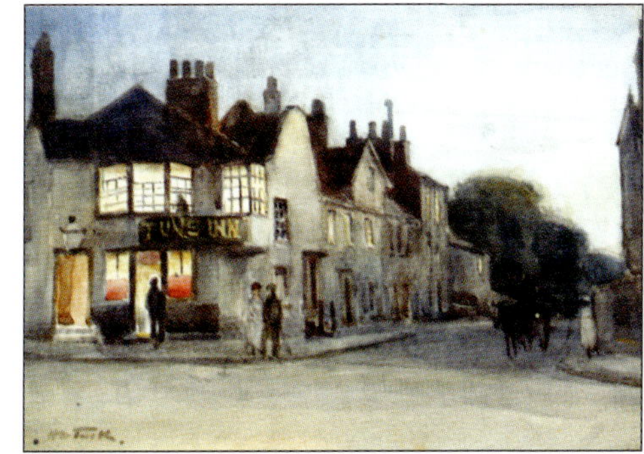

'The bright shop windows ' - the Tuns Inn, Norwich. (Victoria Fitzgerald-Lambard)

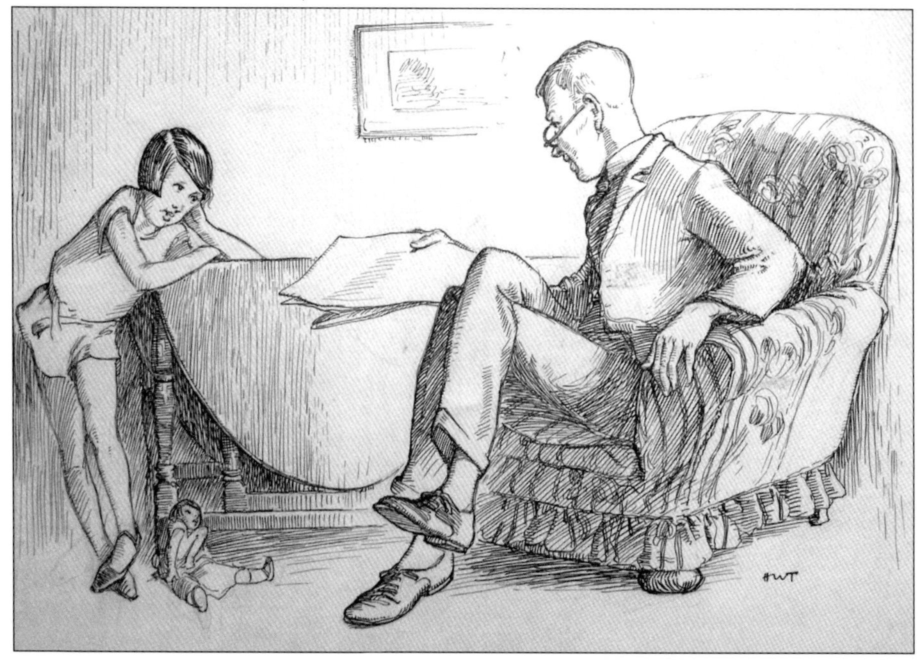

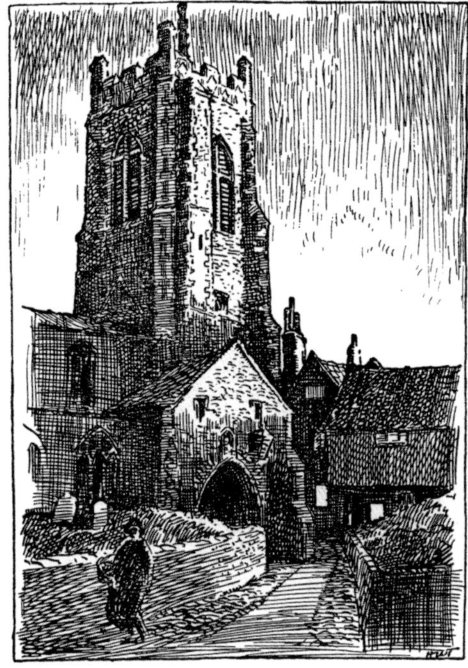

Tombland - from Norwich: A Book of
Drawings *by Horace Tuck, 1932.*

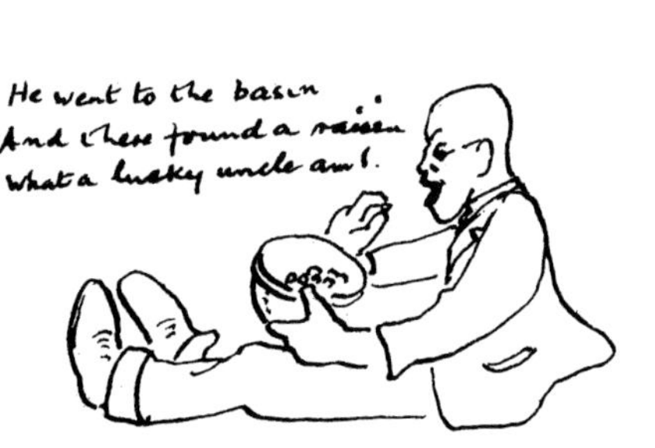

paintings, in the collection today, show these blanked-out signposts, which, well into my childhood after the war, remained white. Due to the number of airbases in the area Norfolk was one of the last counties in the country to have the names painted back on them in black. I was taken by my parents, well into the 1950s, to little villages in the Coltishall area where they remained unpainted for many a year.

Uncle Horry not only painted and carved scenes of our countryside but also used 'life' models as well. I sat for him a few times. Once I recall leaning on an old table and getting very uncomfortable. My father was asleep in a chair nearby and, feeling I couldn't stand being so stiff any more, I got up and raced over to him, jumping on him whilst he was still asleep. Needless to say I didn't do that again! Uncle Horry retrieved me and I was sat down again watching, out of the corner of my eye, my father still fuming. Uncle Horry was so kind to me in his very quiet way, so I didn't mind getting uncomfortable again whilst he resumed his work.

Between visits, which were less frequent now with school very much in the way, Aunt Bessie would write to me. They were mostly two-page letters, back and front, about nothing in particular, but at the bottom of the second page there was always a doodle with a little rhyme. Each time she'd written she would pass the letter to Uncle Horry who would draw the doodle for her. These made me laugh and I proudly showed them to my mother and father each time they arrived. This obviously rubbed off on my father, who, when stationed away, sent me postcards with doodles and a message. Life was really great, there always seemed to be someone, somewhere, thinking about me.

Uncle Horry had several holidays away from Far End, both with friends and without. Colin Cushing, a friend of many years, was a lithographic artist of considerable ability. He used a photo-process method, a craft that today is little applied. He was stationed at Montreuil-Sur-Mer, France during the 1914–1918 war and married a French girl. They lived in a cottage in the village, often painted by him and Uncle Horry on his visits. The last painting of Colin's that came into Uncle Horry's possession, of this cottage, was dated around 1925. While in Norfolk they frequently painted together on the Cley marshes, and one particular scene is of two Norfolk windmills, again with that low skyline. Colin died when still a young man.

Devon and Somerset were other counties Uncle Horry loved; he visited AJ at his home on Exmoor. A lovely country spot near Lynton was a favourite for them, and I recall a watercolour of Clovelly, of a dun-coloured donkey climbing up the steep hill from the harbour.

Wherever Uncle Horry used to be he was always tidily dressed in a check shirt and tie. We met him in various places locally, which was always fun; sometimes he'd bring a small canvas of a place he had painted on holiday and tell us all about it. One, in particular, was a pub in Surrey where he had stayed.

Uncle Horry was an artist of immeasurable talent and not only painted for himself, but also taught at Norwich School of Art. Some of his students remember him today. Frank Duffield was a name he spoke of frequently. I have only seen one of his paintings but it definitely has Uncle Horry's influence. Another name that springs to mind is that of Ralph Tetley, who, until his death in February 1985, lived with his wife in Wroxham, Norfolk, a popular boating and yachting area just a few miles from Norwich.

In the 1980s my father commissioned Tetley to paint a watercolour of Britannia Class Locomotive No 10013 'Oliver Cromwell' leaving Norwich Thorpe station for Liverpool Street, London. My son's name is Oliver and it was for this reason that the work was commissioned. Ralph Tetley's widow gave this watercolour to my father on 24 August 1985, a day before my son's birthday, six months after her husband had died. My father had always appreciated this gesture and the painting, greatly treasured, is with my son to this day.

My father was another of Uncle Horry's students, attending life classes. My father, in such close contact with him, also had many private lessons in and around Norfolk. They visited the Norfolk Broads together from which lithographs, sketches and paintings of trading wherries emerged. At Great Yarmouth they painted drifters from the quay and one of my father's watercolours, of drifters, was hanging at Norwich School of Art for many years in the 1920s. At Tombland, Norwich, they painted the scene of a horse and carriage trundling past the Samson and Hercules, in Pigg Lane, where the River Wensum flowed under the bridge. They also captured the Tuns Inn with its warm, welcoming lights at the top of Grape's Hill at the junction with Earlham Road. My father always regarded Uncle Horry as his mentor to his dying day.

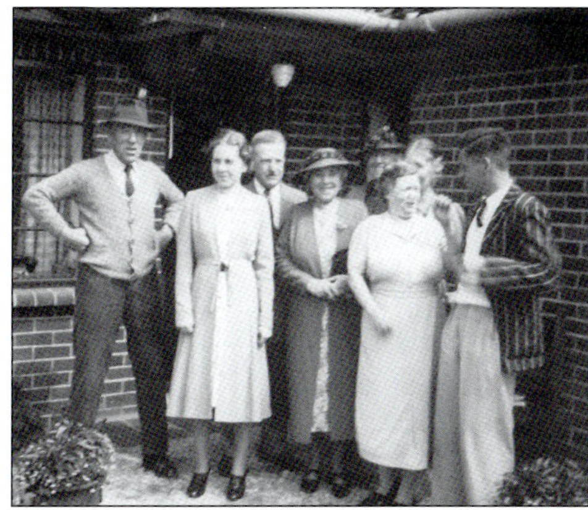

'Always tidily dressed in a shirt and tie' - Horace Tuck (far left), and front row from left: Lena Pye (HWT's niece); Lena Cole (née Tuck), HWT's sister (Lena Pye's mother); Elsie (Harry Tuck's wife and HWT's sister-in-law); Charles Taylor Cole (Peter), HWT's nephew and Liz Keevill's father, wearing his Goldsmiths' blazer (he was a student there at the time). Back row from left: Harry (HWT's brother); Nellie Boston (HWT's sister); and (partly hidden) Bessie Tuck. (Lena Pye)

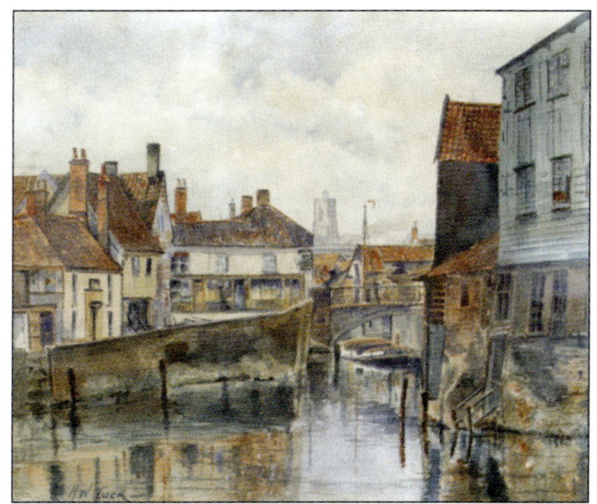

Pigg Lane, Norwich. (Jennifer Tuck)

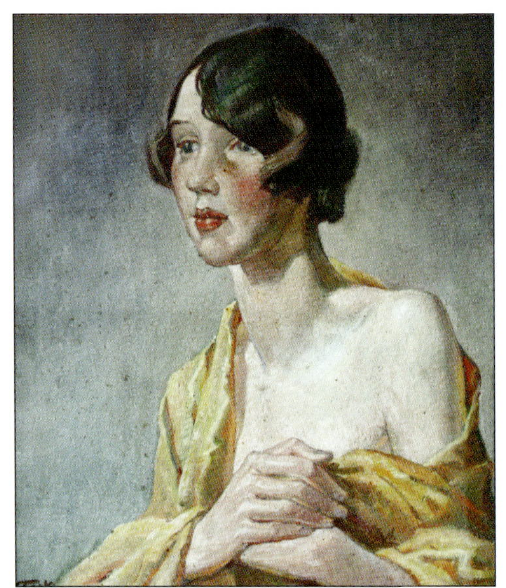

The Yellow Wrap *(tempera on canvas)*
by Horace Tuck. A label on the verso of
the portrait reads 'Royal Academy
Exhibition 1930 - James Bourlet & Sons
Ltd, Nassau Street, London. II The
Yellow Wrap, Horace W. Tuck, 24
Branksome Road, Norwich.'

One of Uncle Horry's first loves was sepia drawings. This inspiration came from the works of one of his illustrious Norfolk predecessors, John Sell Cotman, who died in 1842. Horace used this medium to capture towns and buildings in Normandy, and one in particular springs to mind, of the chapel on the hill at St Quentin. He only did the sepia drawings very infrequently, a process now that seems quite remote.

Uncle Horry taught at Norwich School of Art and exhibited there. He worked tirelessly for The Norwich Art Circle and a number of his works are part of the permanent collection at Norwich Castle Museum. It was his pride and joy when he was asked to exhibit at The Royal Academy, London, a high accolade for any painter. His painting 'The Yellow Wrap' was 'hung on the line' in the 1930 exhibition, but being a very modest man he just accepted it all in his stride. Aunt Bessie, my grandfather and my father were so proud of him. Over the years my father recalled this moment with such pride, always saying that 'Uncle Horry would come into his own one day'.

Far End will always have a special place in my heart. The place where I had such fun as a child, as well as all the things taught to me by Uncle Horry and Aunt Bessie. Then, at the start of 1951 my father was beginning to get very uptight with life. I didn't really appreciate what was really going on at the time as I think most of it was kept from me. Apparently he had a major breakdown earlier in life, from which due to the kindness, care and support of my mother, Aunt Bessie and Uncle Horry, he managed to recover. This time it was to happen again, although to a much lesser degree.

In November 1951 Uncle Horry died. I remember in my parent's bedroom, just below the bay window, was a window seat. My father sat on it sideways with his feet up, hugging his knees. I'd never seen him do this before. I remained in my room but I could see and hear the conversation. He said that 'the collection must stay together and never be split up'. He repeated it over and over. He told my mother that he had lost his mentor. He sat and cried; at that point my mother hustled me downstairs.

I don't really remember the day of the funeral, probably as I was not allowed to go. It was explained to me later, by my mother, recalling the funeral of her own mother in 1910, when she was just a little girl. It was a hot June day and my mother was dressed in a thick, full-length coat, hat, gloves and long buttoned boots. She was made to walk behind her mother's coffin, along with her father and two brothers and sister, up to and along Unthank Road, Norwich to the cemetery. She said she had never forgotten that day and in no way was I to be put through the same experience.

Later, in the early part of 1952, my grandfather died and granny Tuck came to live with us for six years until her death. I think that was where most of my beautiful childhood ended and the next chapter of my life began. We visited Far End whenever we could but the parting gesture of Aunt Bessie I shall remember to my dying day. My father, mother and I arrived late one morning. They were still sad occasions without Uncle Horry. Bessie met us at the gate and we walked up the path to the front door, the blue agapanthus in its

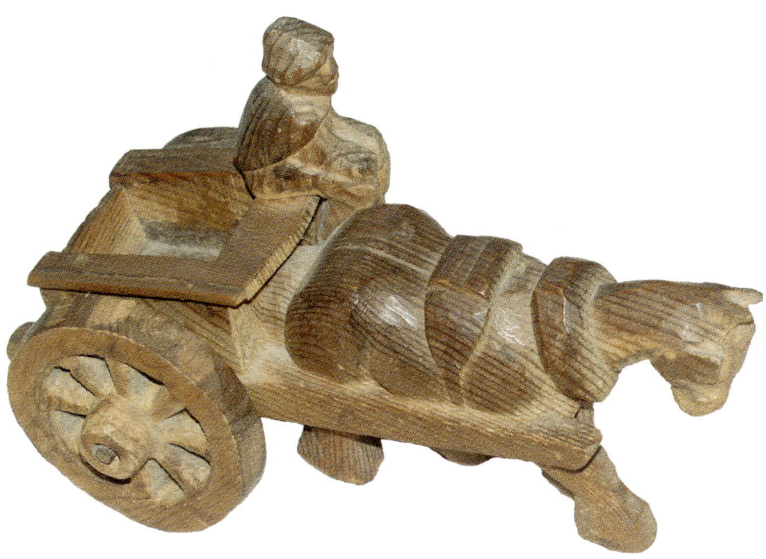

paramudre beside it. We spent the rest of the day there and as we got into my father's car to go home Aunt Bessie was holding a box with its lid a bit higgledy-piggledy and not fitting properly. It had paper sticking out of it too. She leant down and gave it to me, telling me to open it very carefully. To my utter amazement it was the little horse and cart that Uncle Horry had been carving all these years. I noticed the little man had progressed but his head was not completely finished. She told me that I must take it home to keep and that my father would finish carving the little man's head for me. I can't remember what I said to her, except I gave her a great big cuddle that I don't think I'd ever given anyone before. The box was placed on my lap in the car, still with its ill-fitting lid, and I kept very still all the way home. My father did finish the little man's head, in true Uncle Horry style, and it is with me to this day. That was an unforgettable memory.

Uncle Horry and Aunt Bessie were two treasures in my life, even more so, I think, than my own grandparents. They filled my young life with endless fun, charm and learning of the finer things. I shall always be indebted to them.

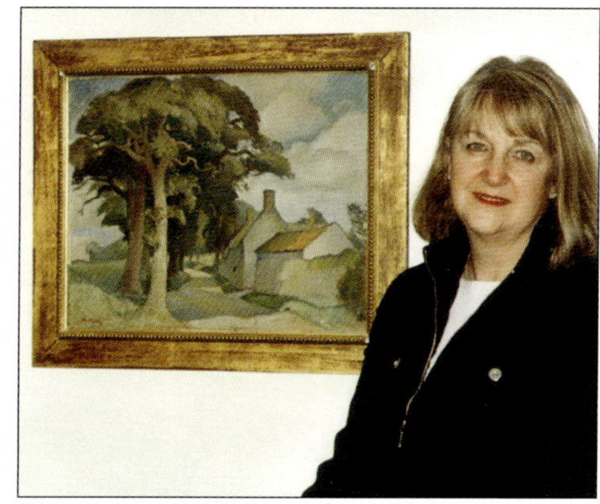

Jennifer Tuck.

**Jennifer Tuck
November 2005**

This memoir is dedicated with love
and thoughts for my father

STEPHEN AUSTIN TUCK

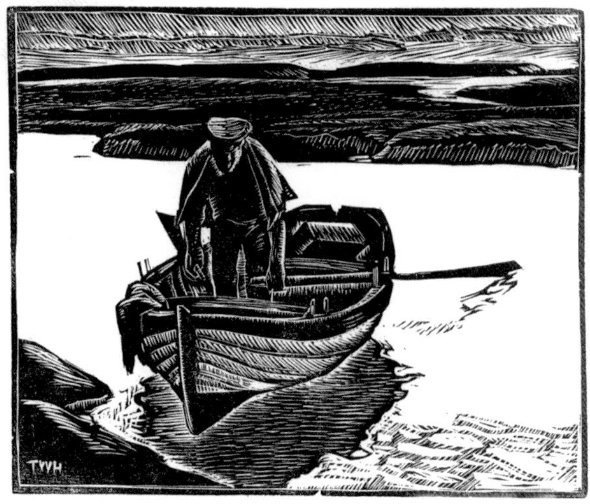

Morston - woodcut
(Jennifer Tuck)

Opposite: *Cley Mill.*
One of the most famous landmarks
on the north Norfollk Coast
oil on canvas

The Norfolk Paintings

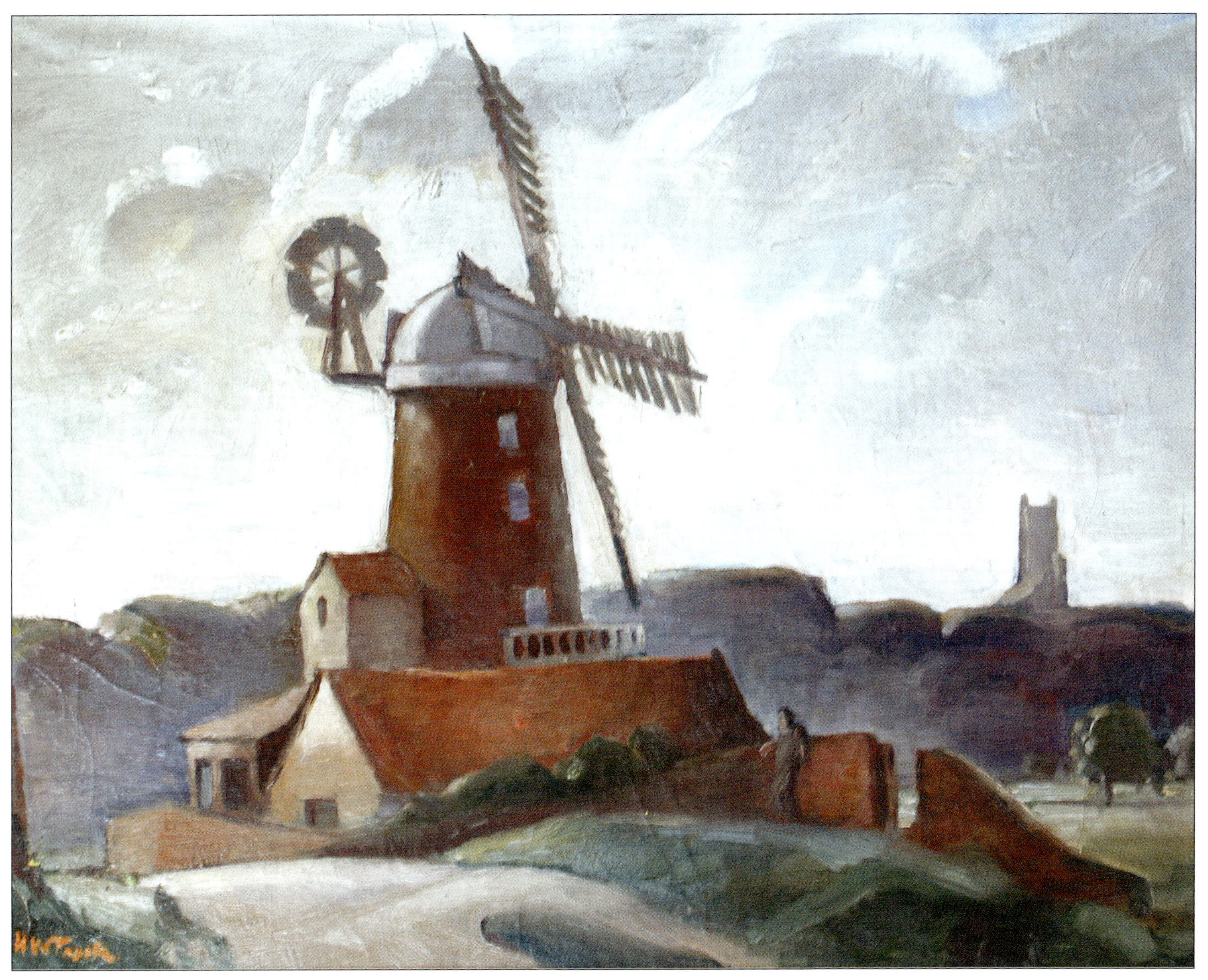

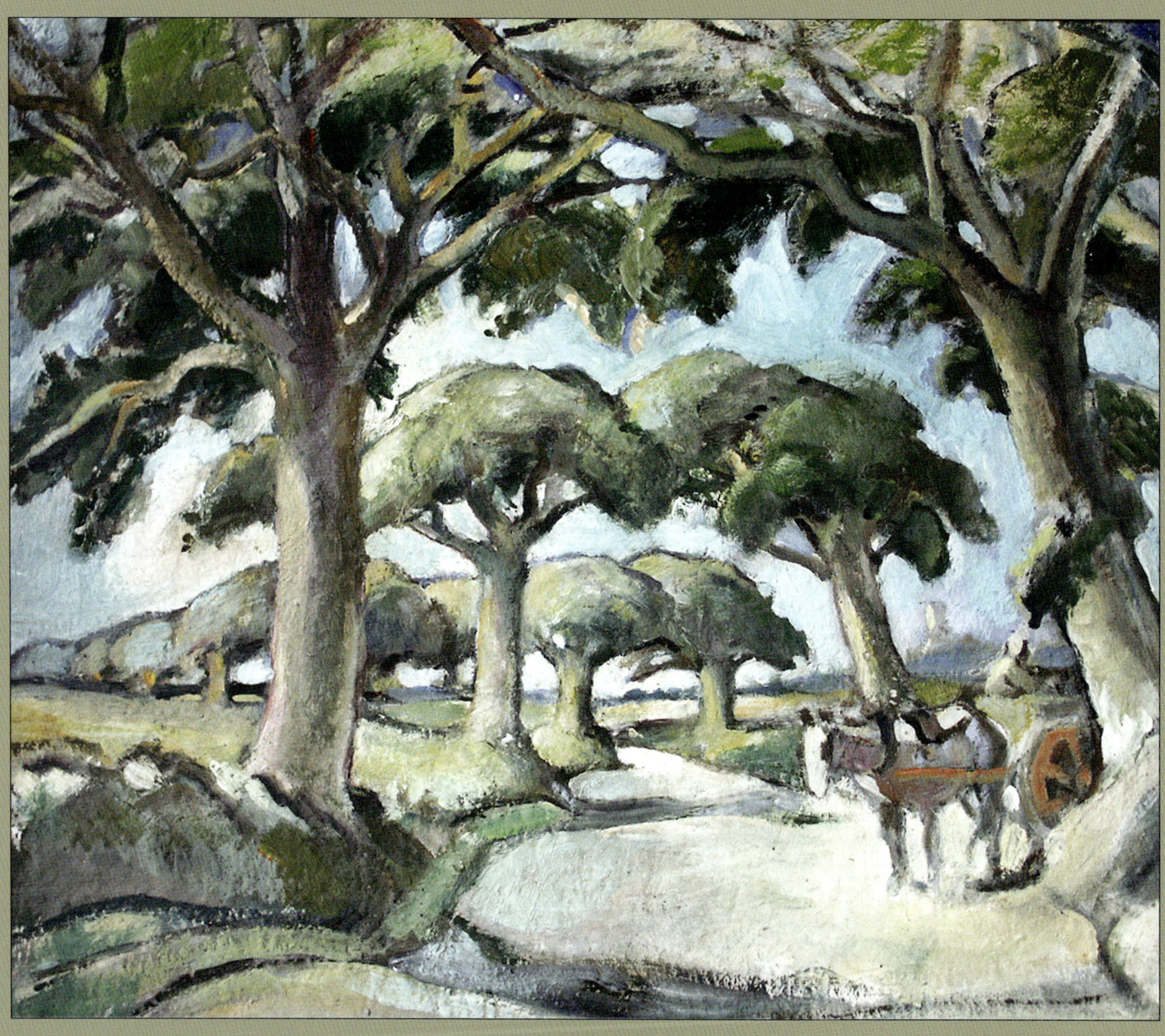

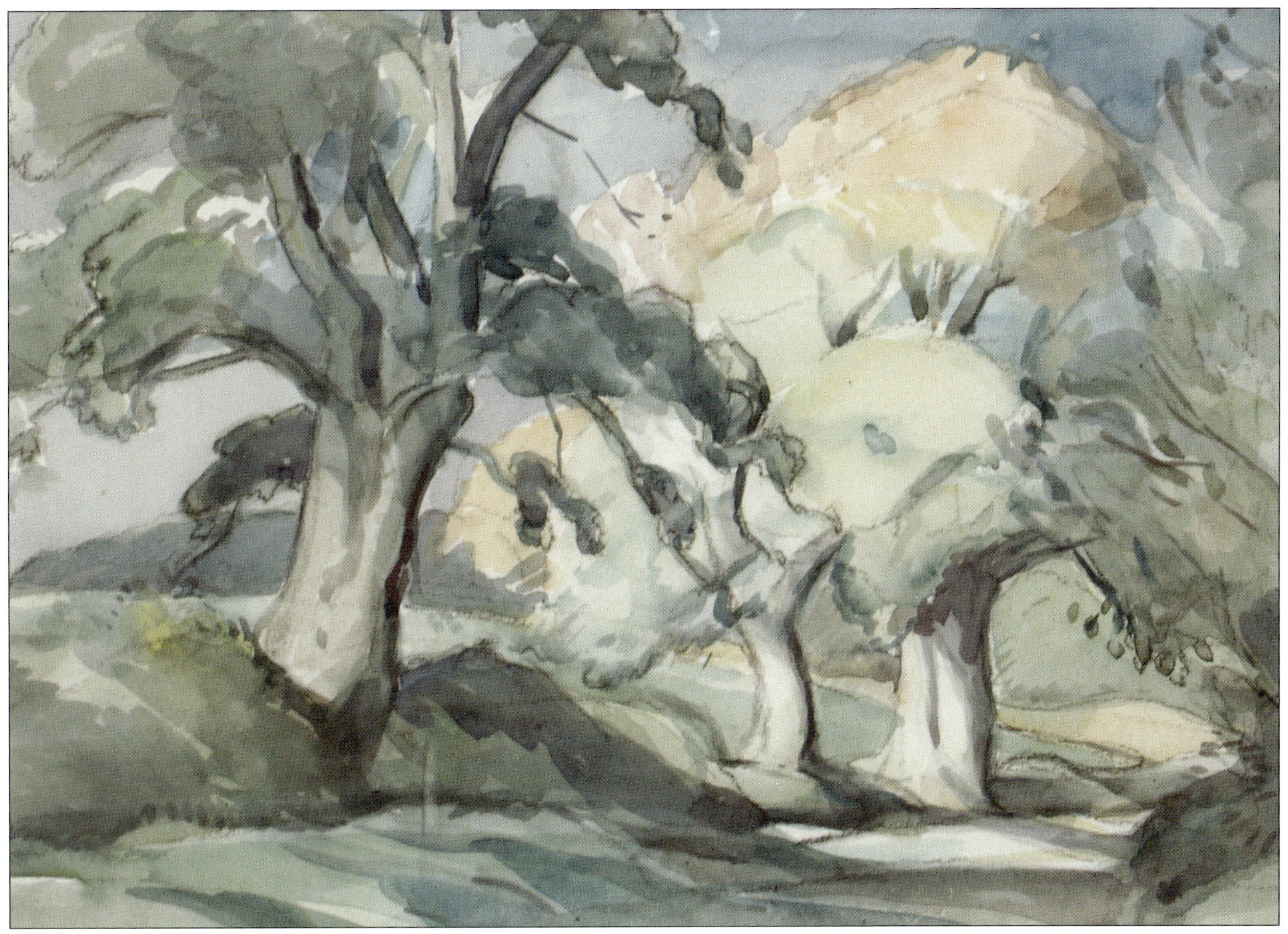

Avenue of Trees, Sheringham Hall Park Road
watercolour
14x10 inches

Opposite: *The Road to Blakeney*
oil on canvas
24x16 inches

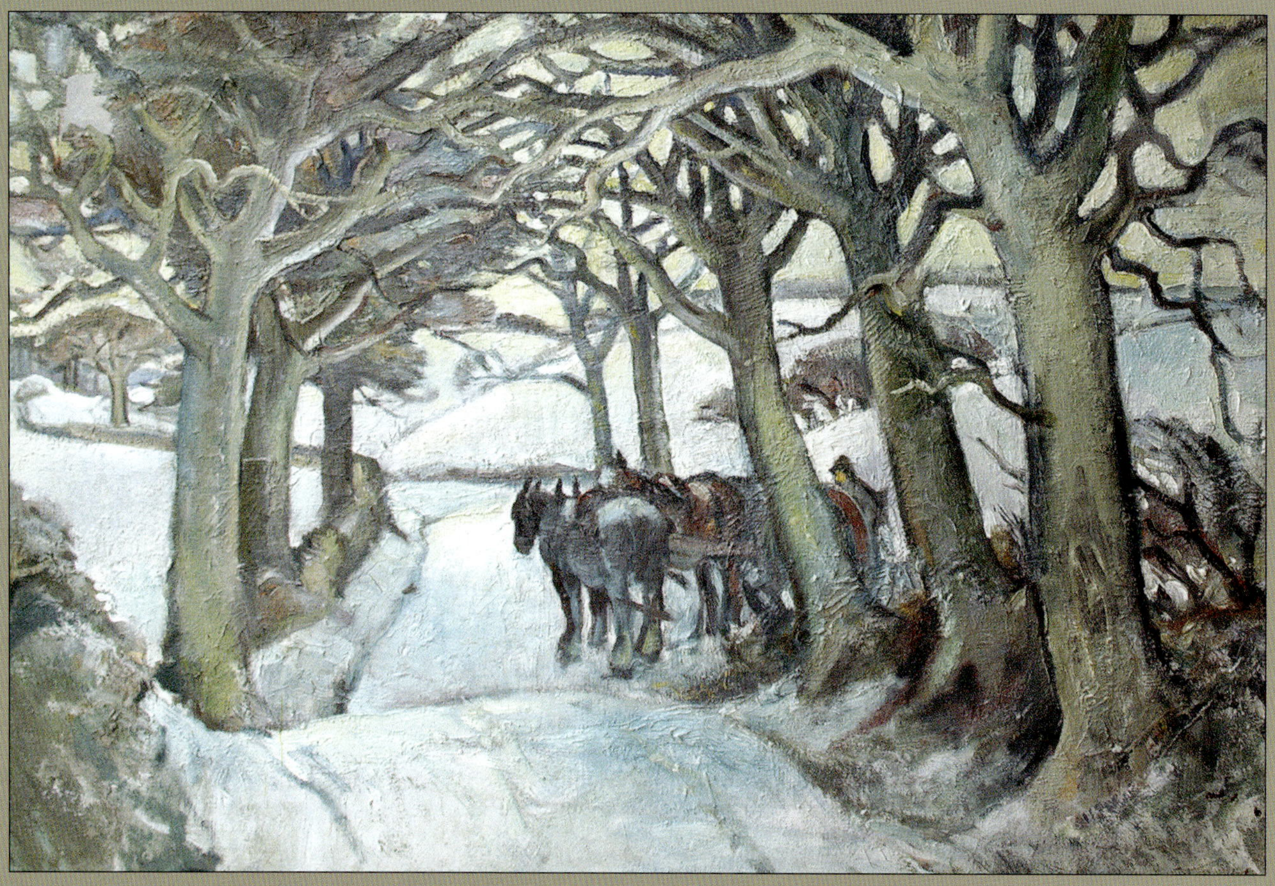

The Snowbound Road
oil on canvas
18x12 inches

Opposite: *The Village Inn. The Three Swallows*
Inn at Cley, with Blakeney in the background
oil on canvas
23x18 inches

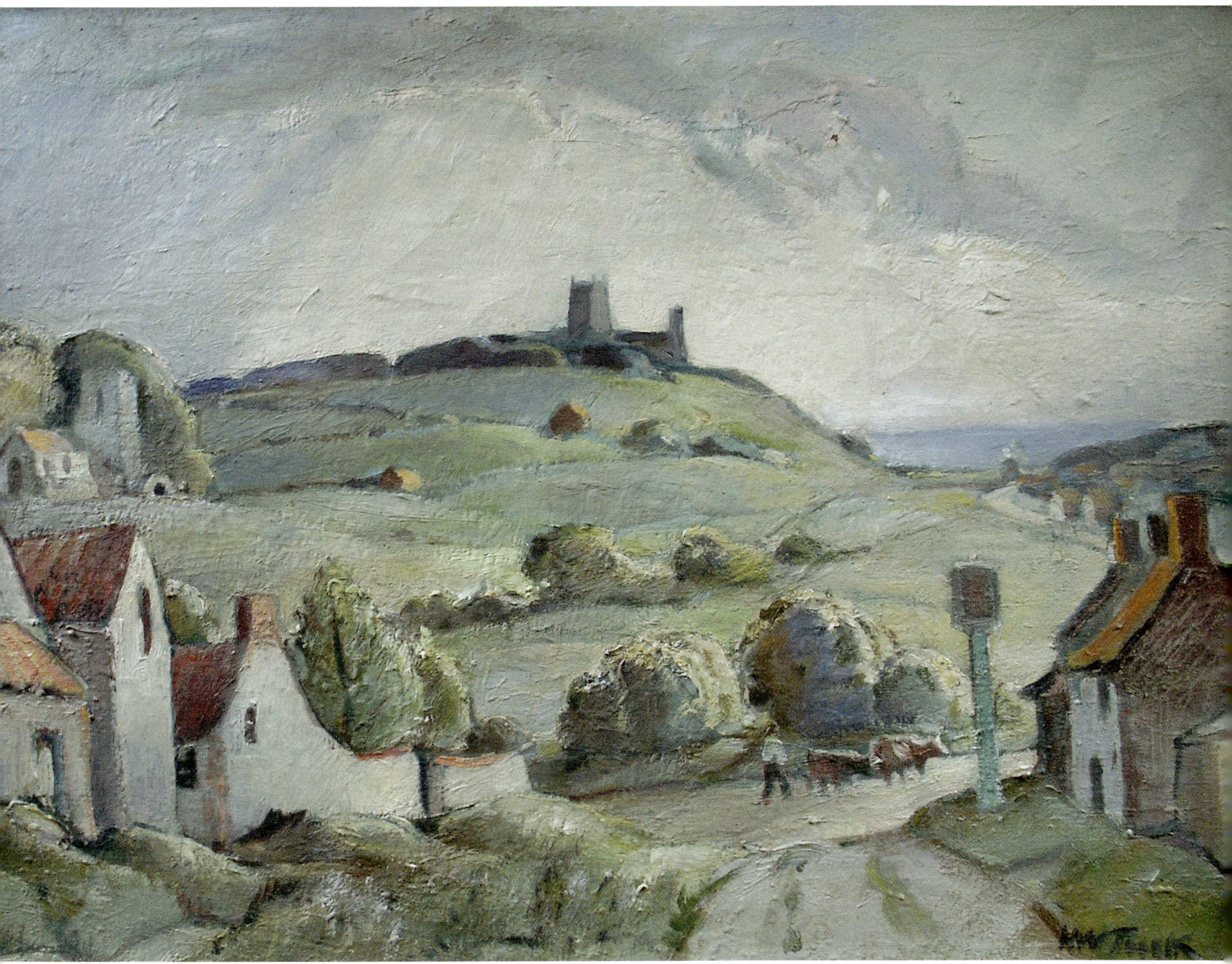

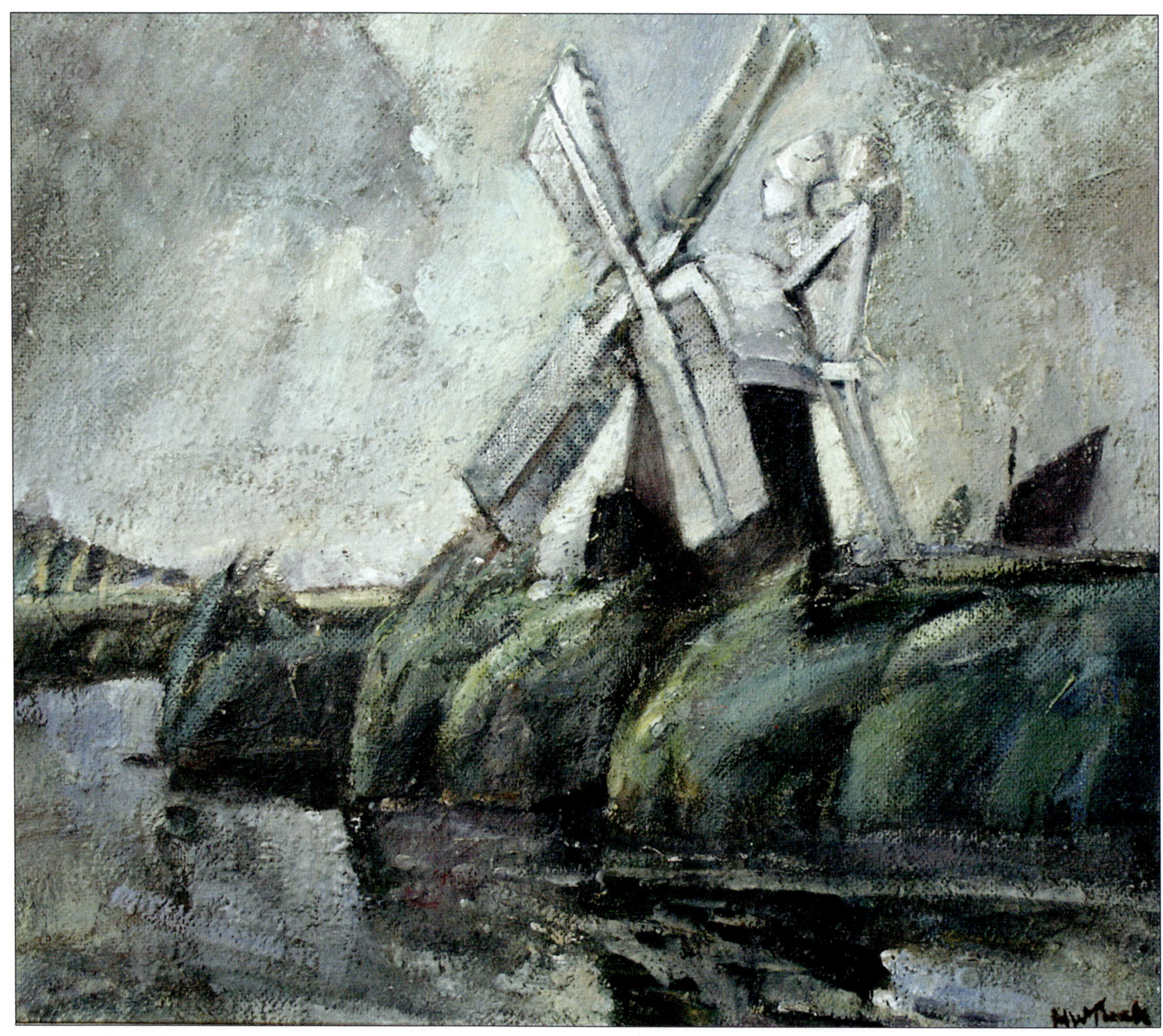

Sails. A windpump on the River Waveney
oil on canvas
17x14 inches

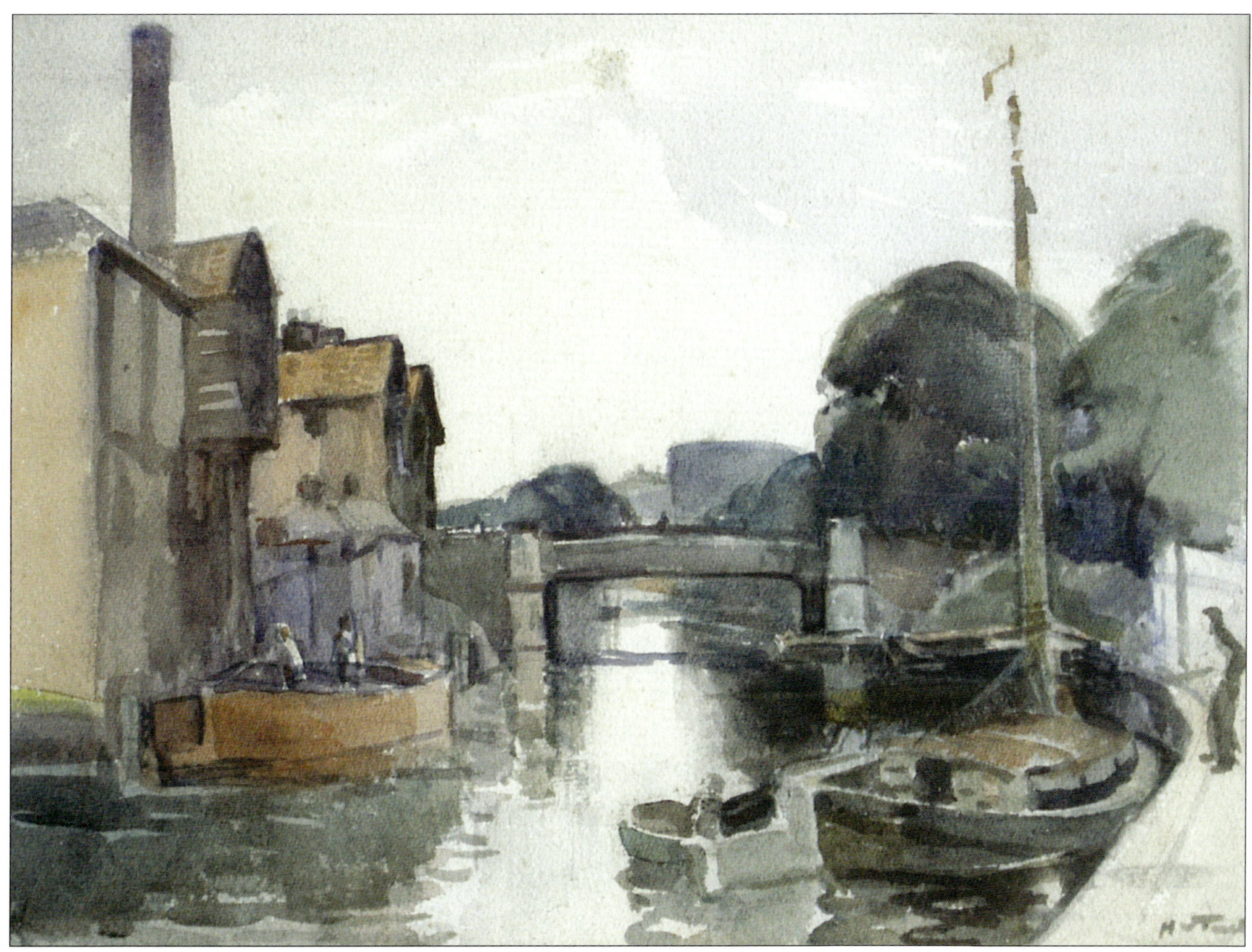

River Wensum, near Mills' Yard, Norwich.
watercolour
14x10 inches

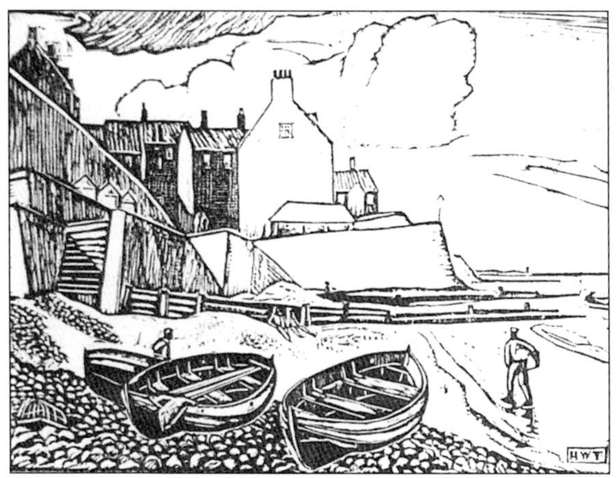

Sheringham
woodcut

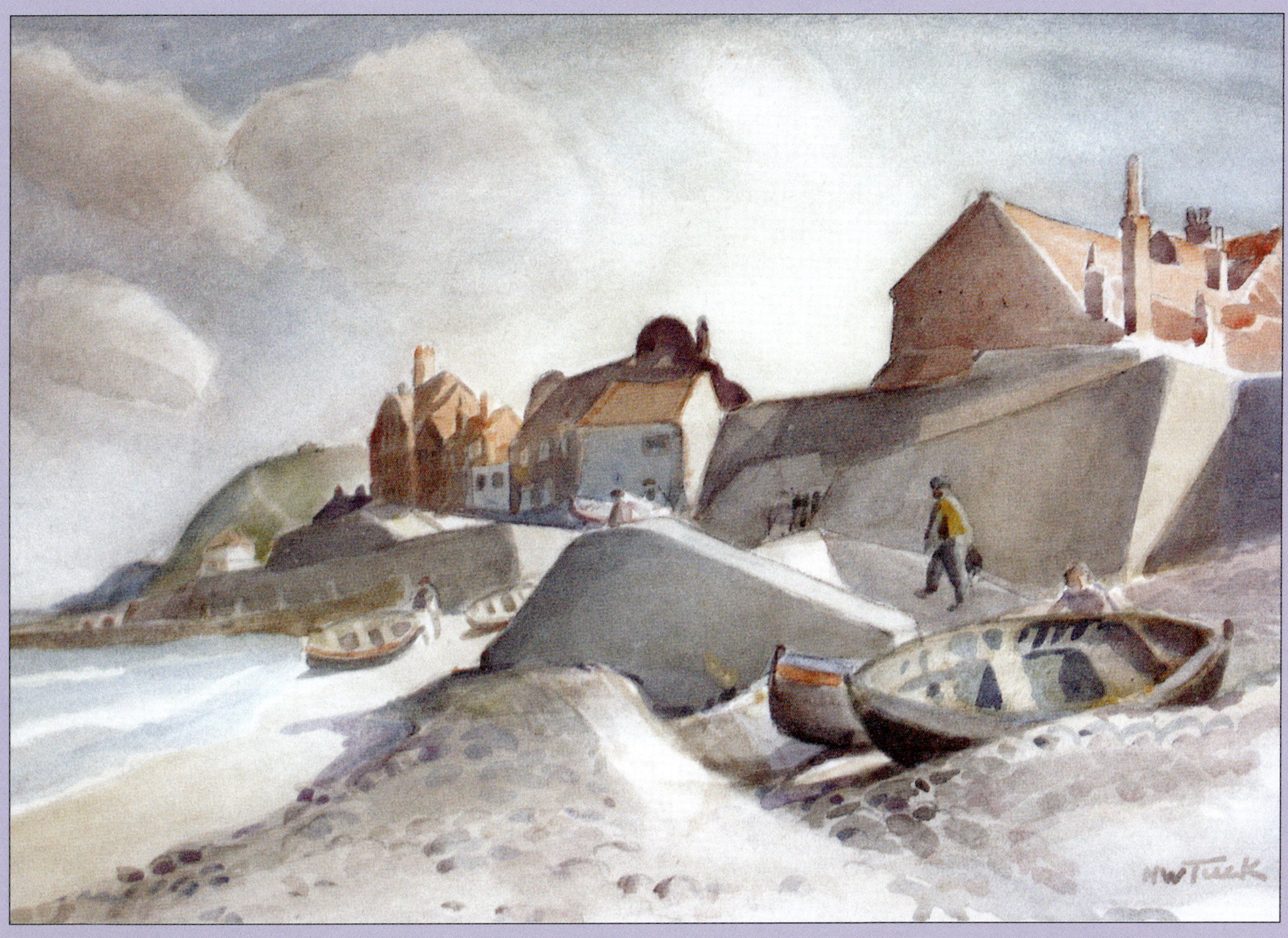

The Beach at Sheringham.
watercolour
12x8 inches

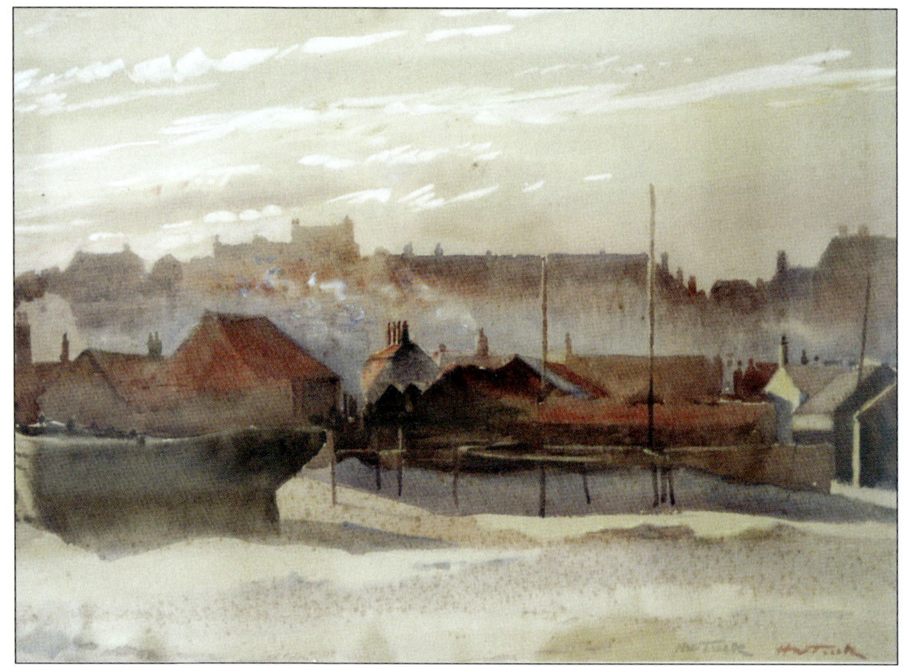

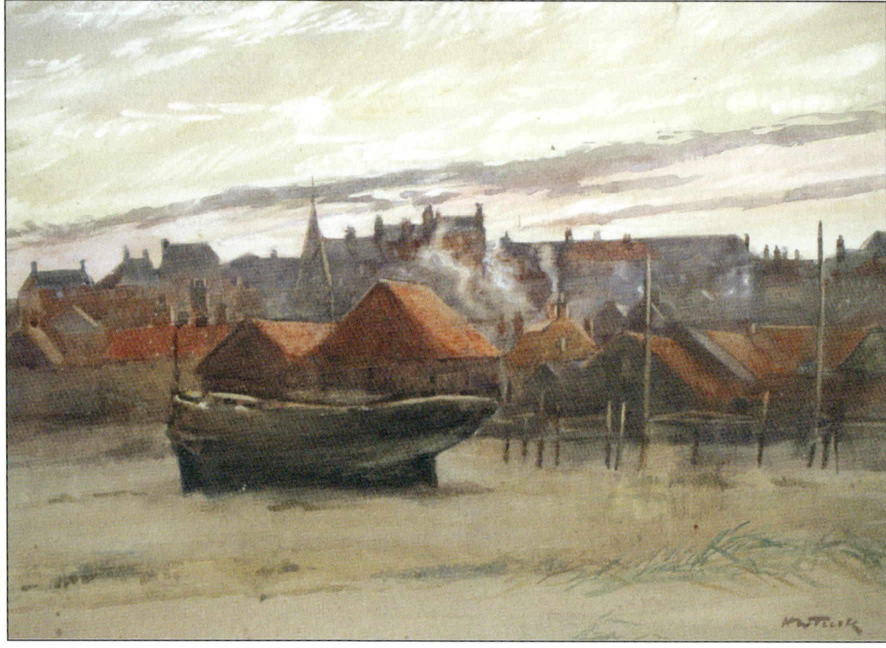

Low Tide. North Lowestoft
watercolour (pair)
18.5x13 inches

Opposite:
Blue Bridge
watercolour
12x8 inches

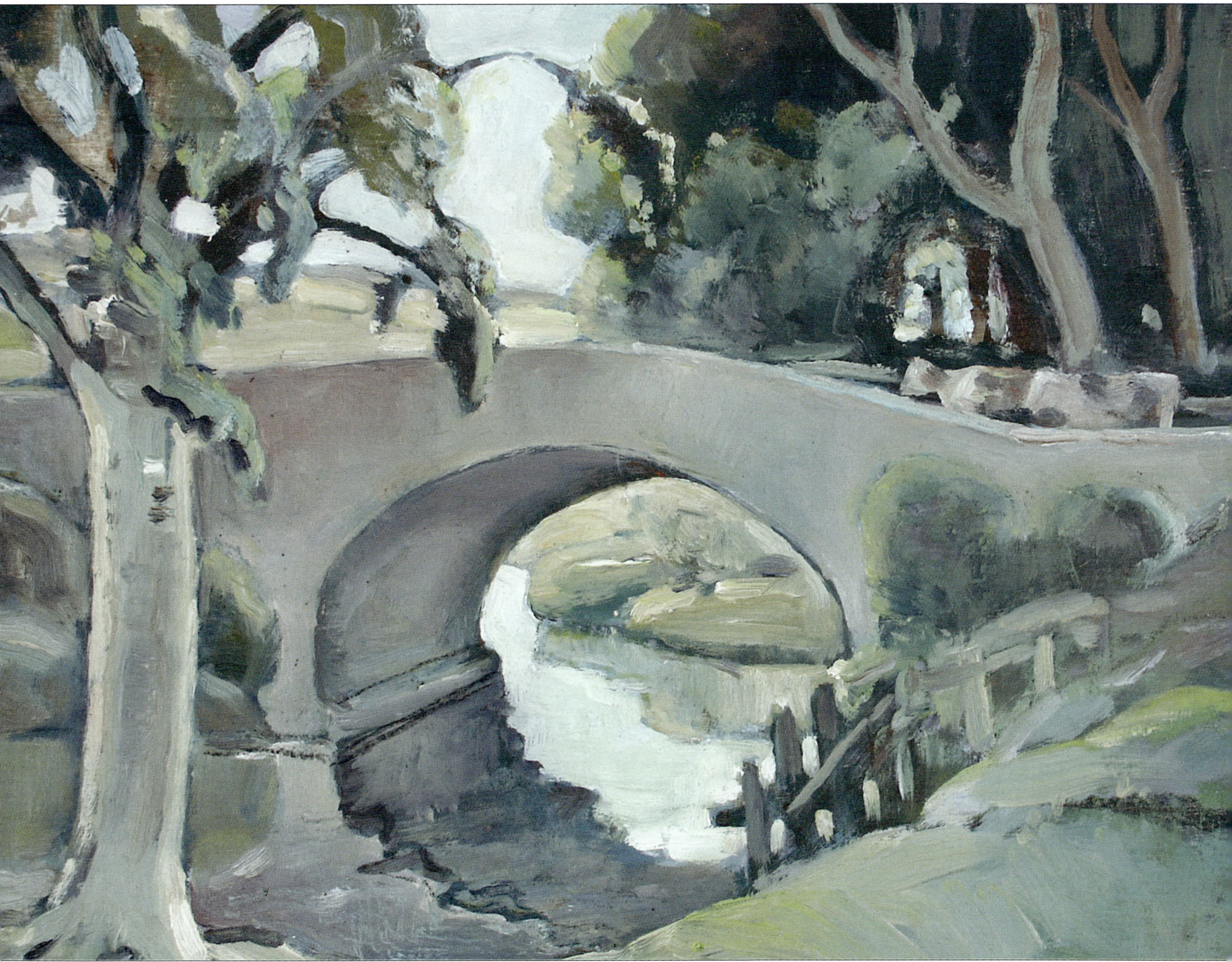

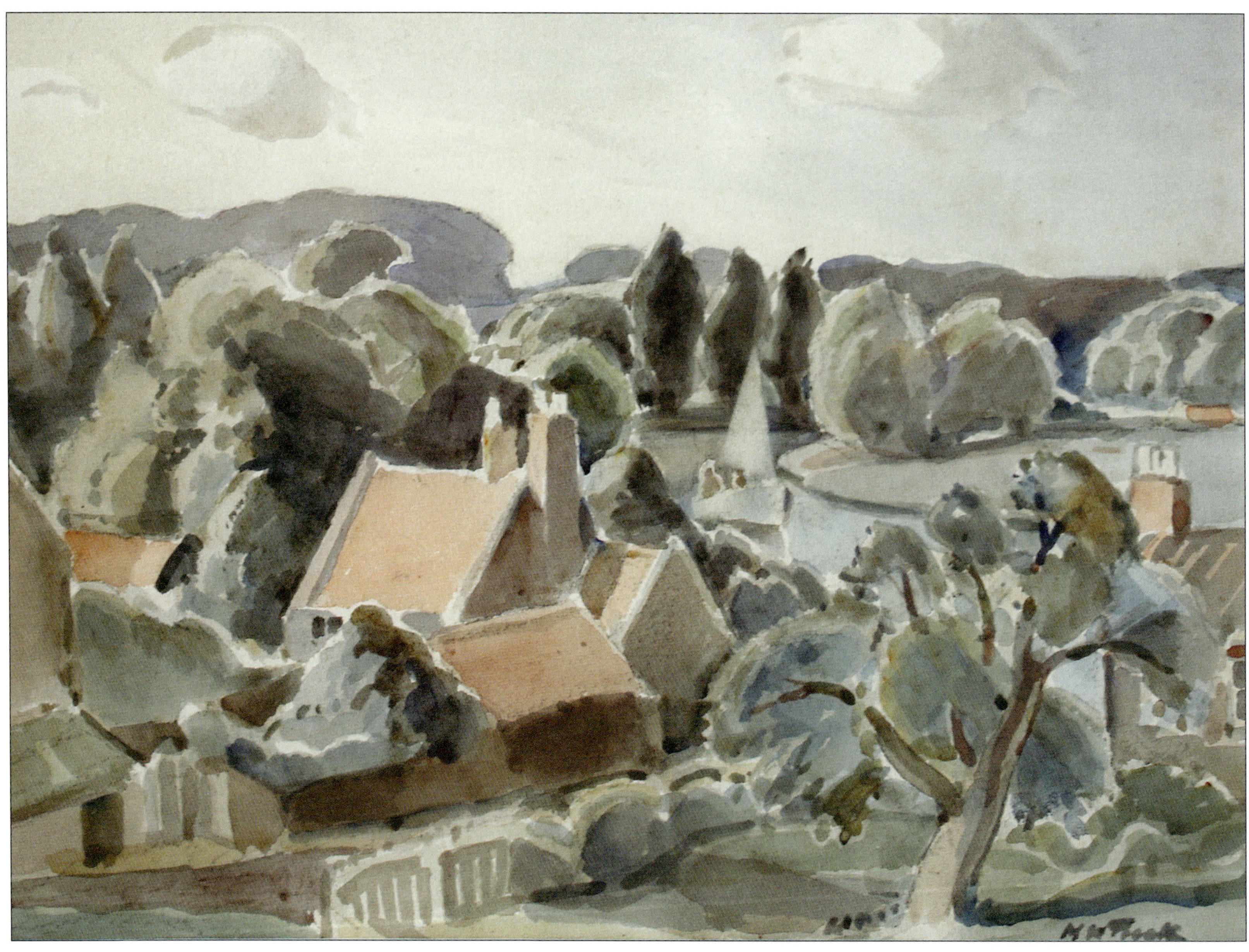

Little Boat, near Norwich
watercolour
14.5x11.5 inches

Opposite:
Homeward Bound
oil on canvas
12x14 inches

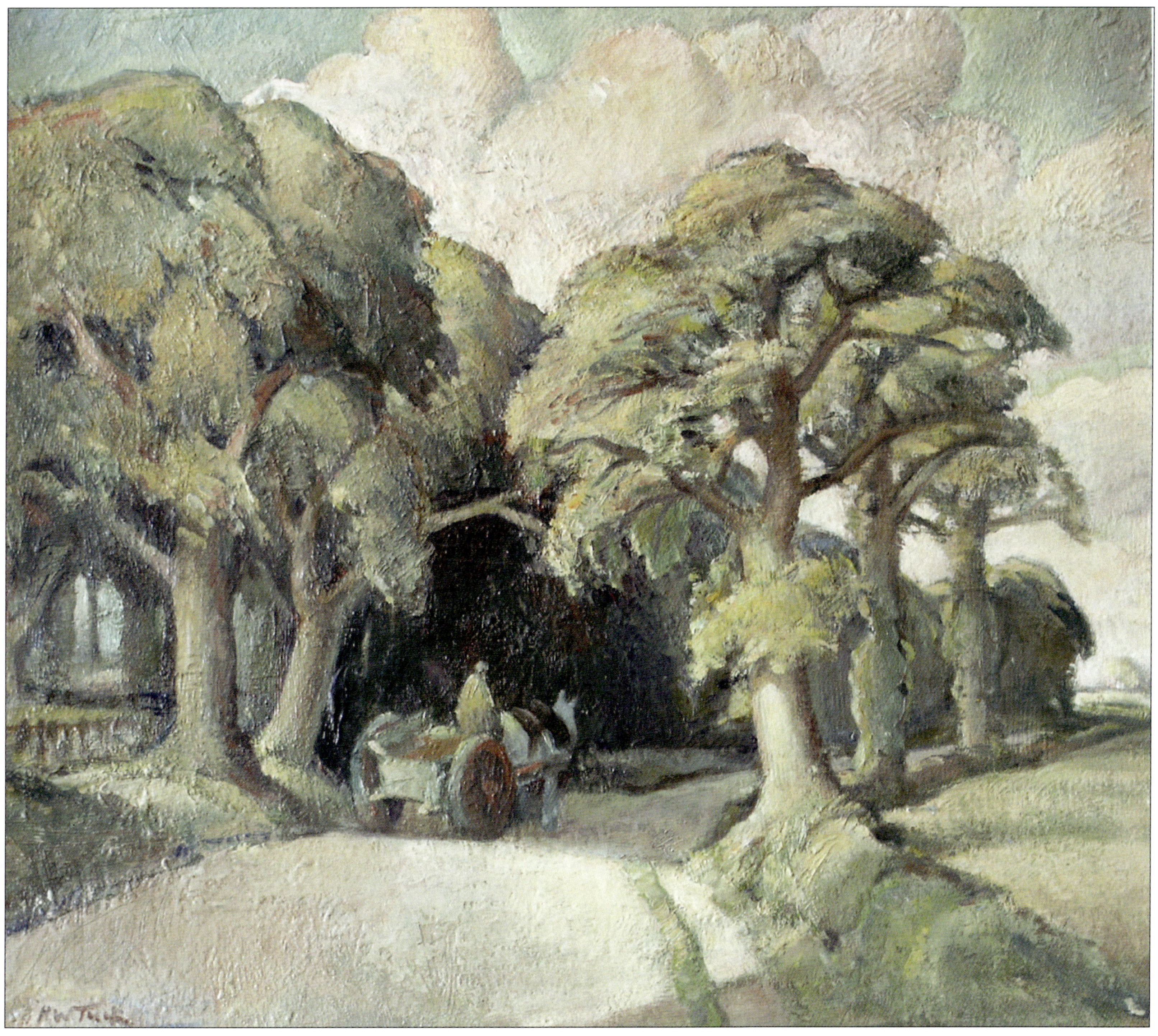

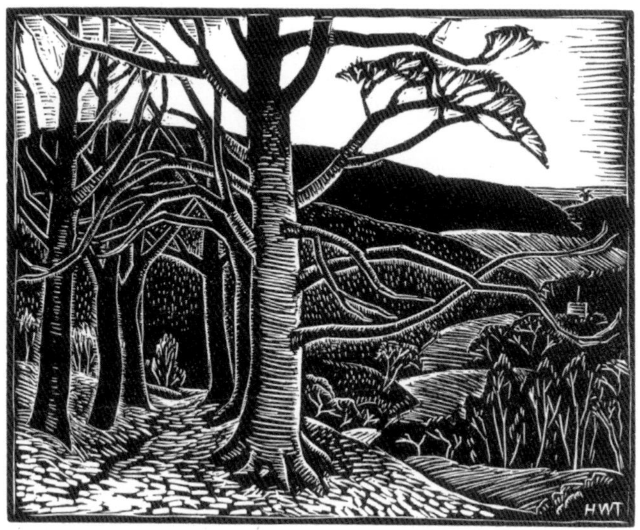

Copse
woodcut

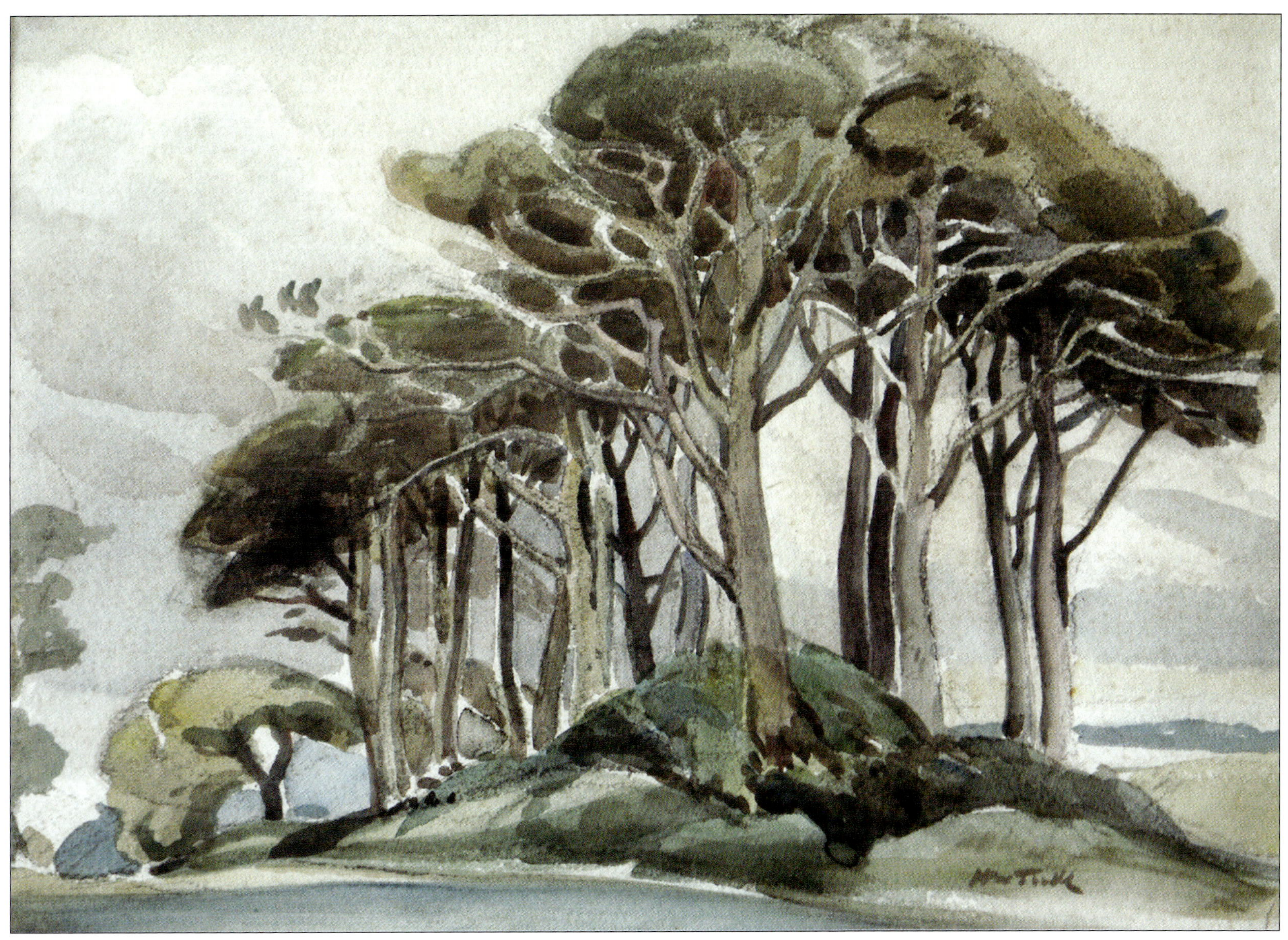

Copse on the Norfolk Coast
watercolour
14x10 inches

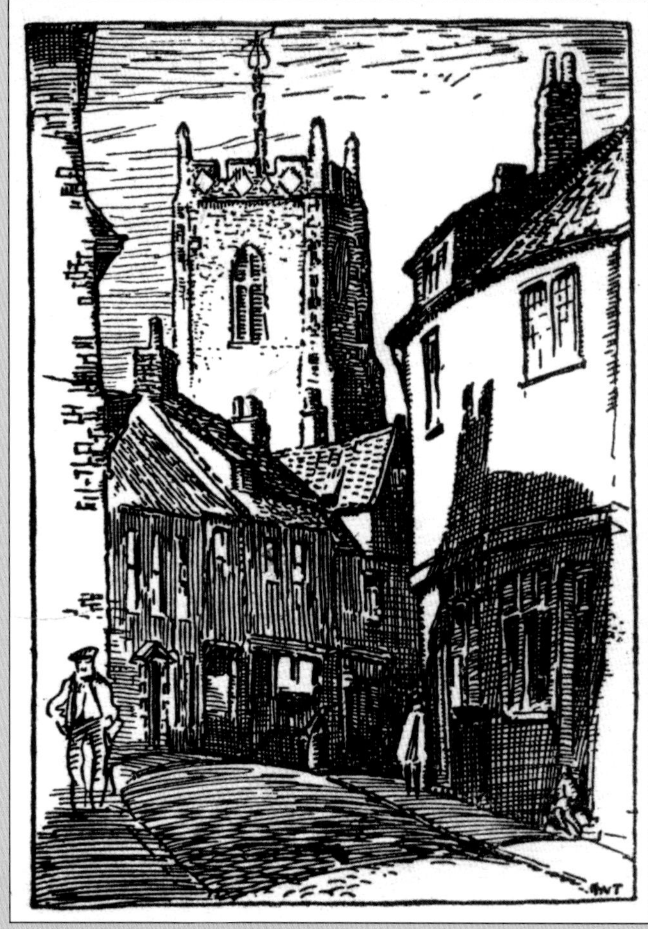

Prince's Street, Norwich
from *Norwich - A Book of Drawing, 1932*

Opposite:
Towards the Coast.
Wiveton Church and Bridge with
Blakeney Church in the background
watercolour
14.5x11 inches

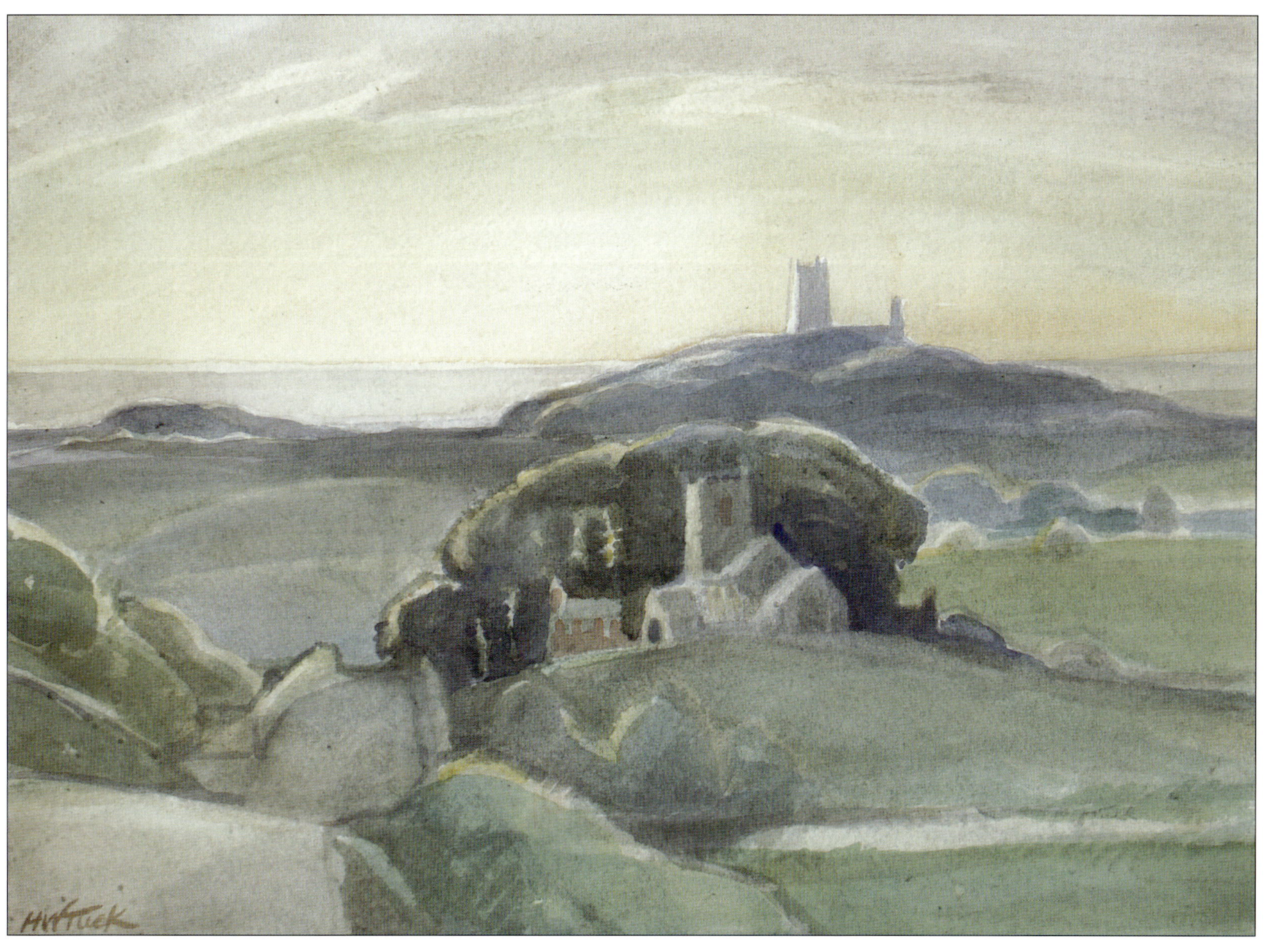

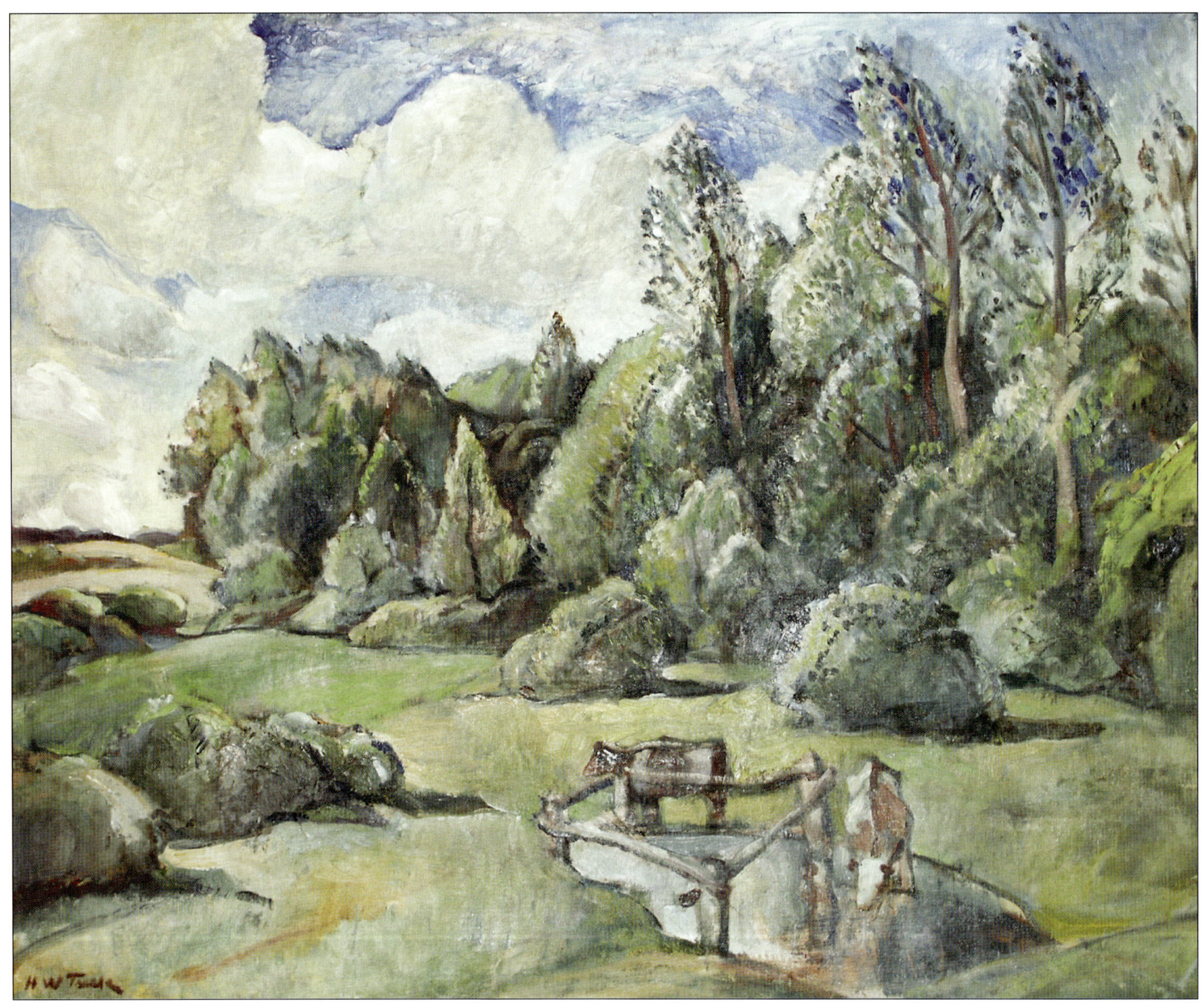

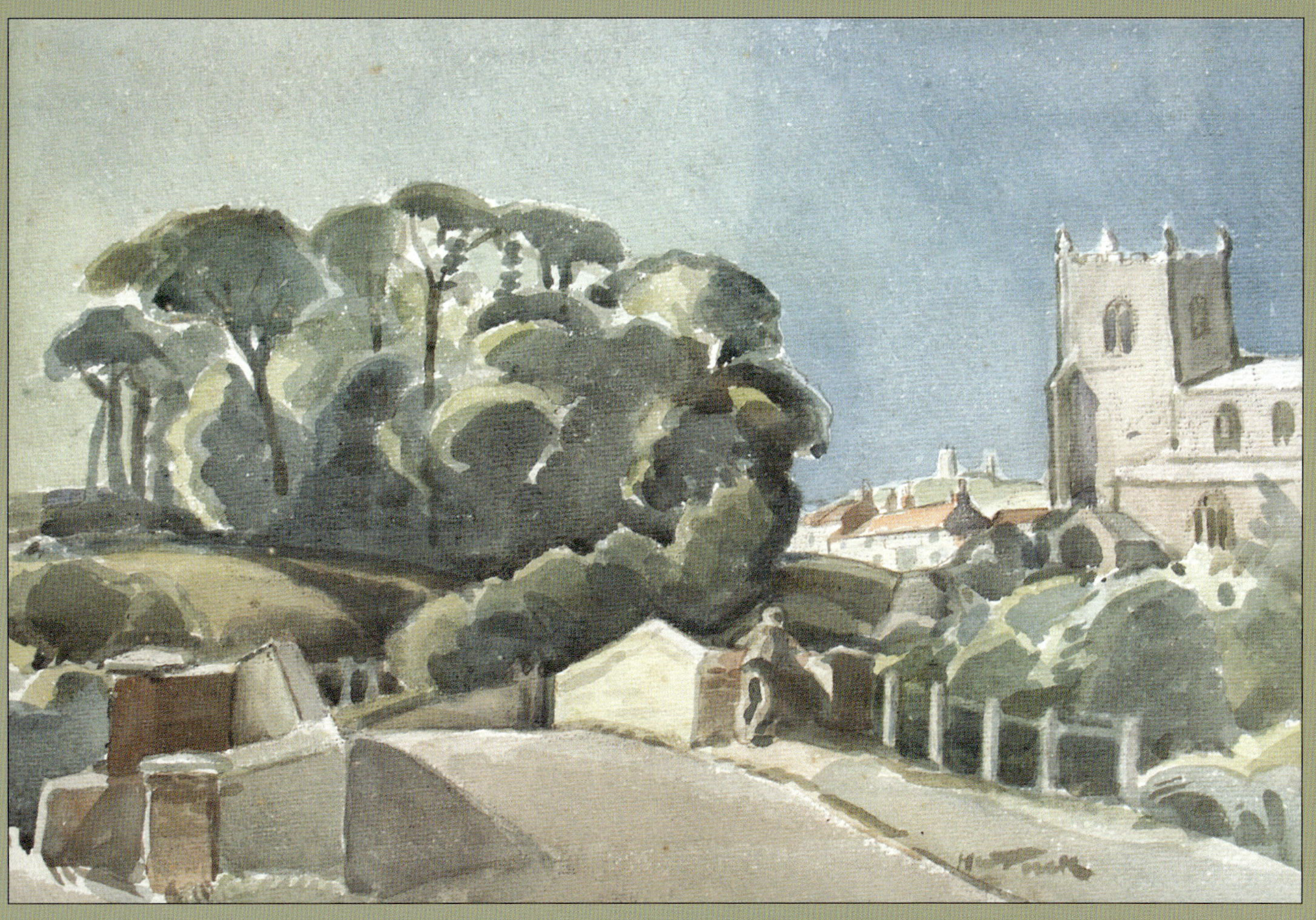

Opposite: *Cattle at the Pond, near Sheringham*
oil on canvas
29x23.5 inches

Wiveton Church and Bridge
watercolour
14.5x10.5 inches

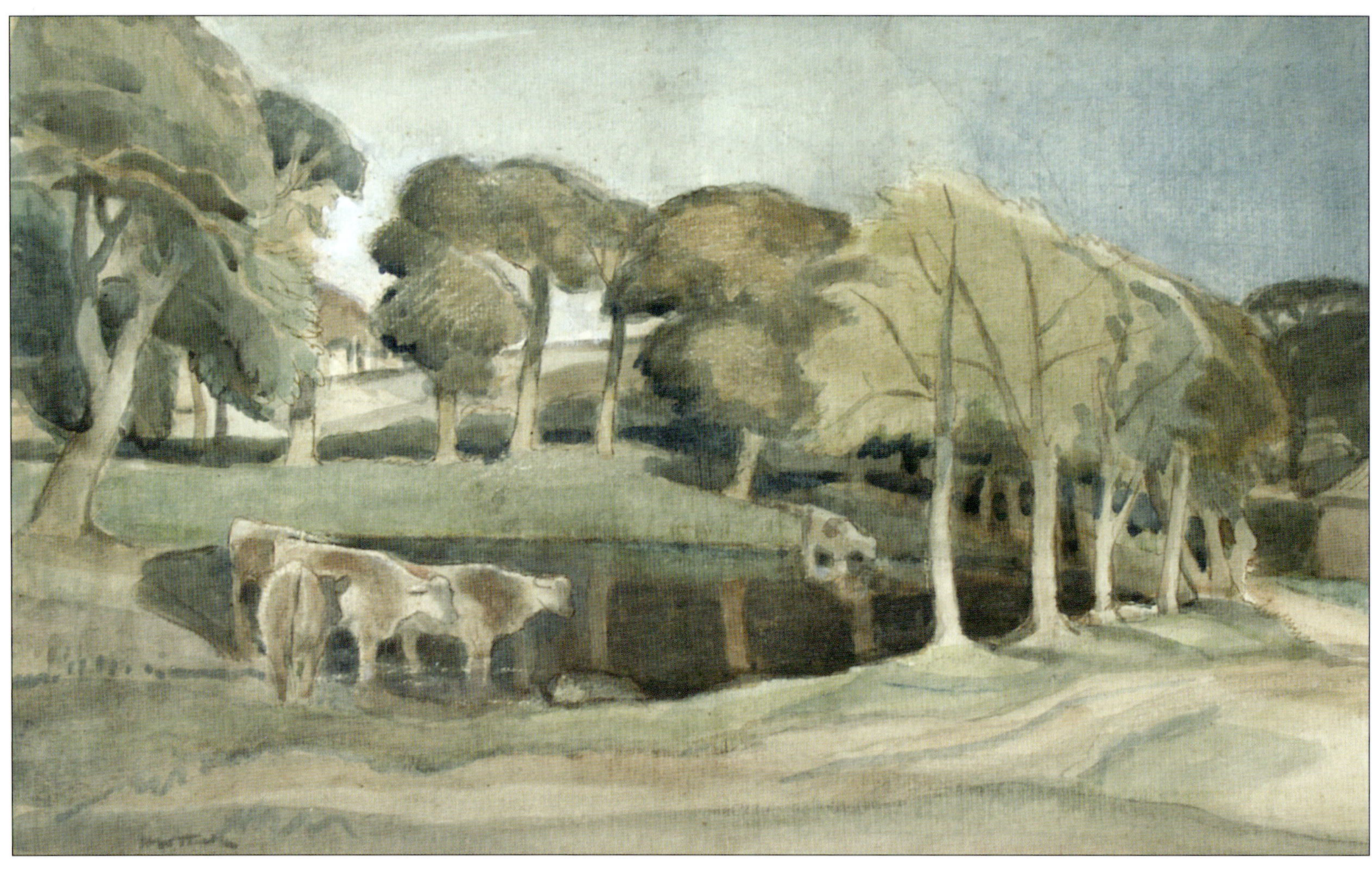

On a Norfolk Farm
watercolour
14x10 inches

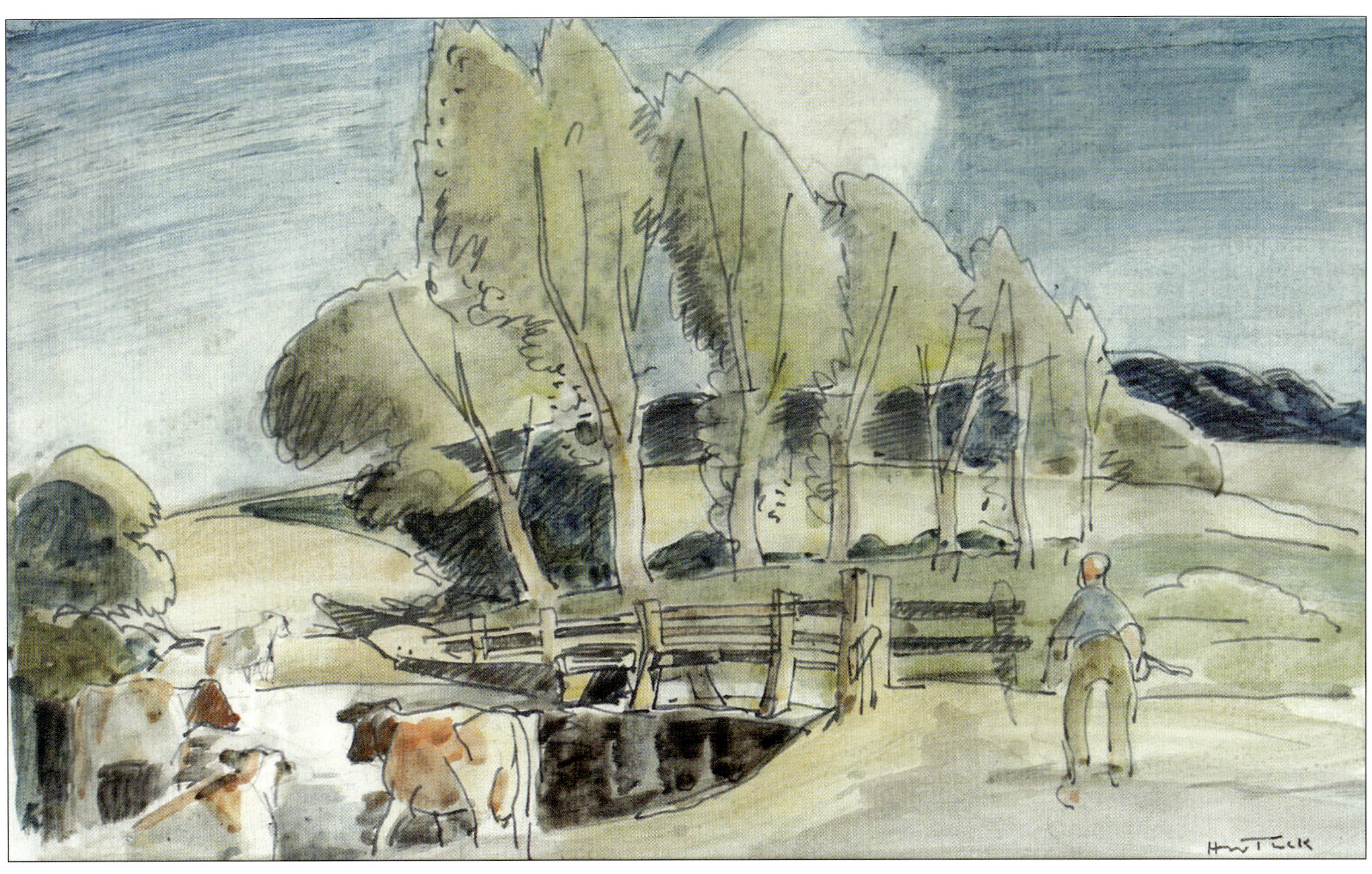

The Norfolk Farmer
watercolour/ink
10.5x7 inches

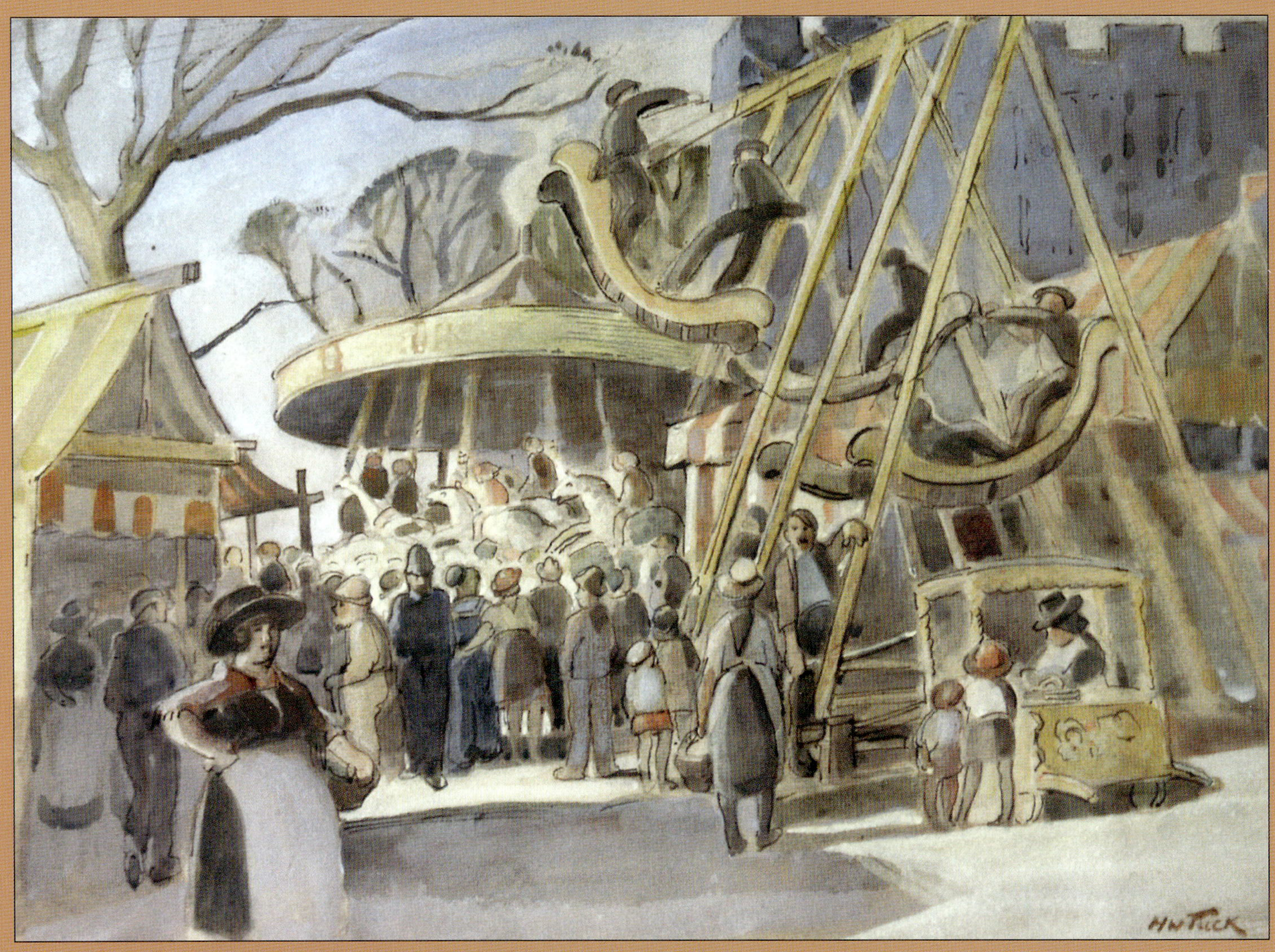

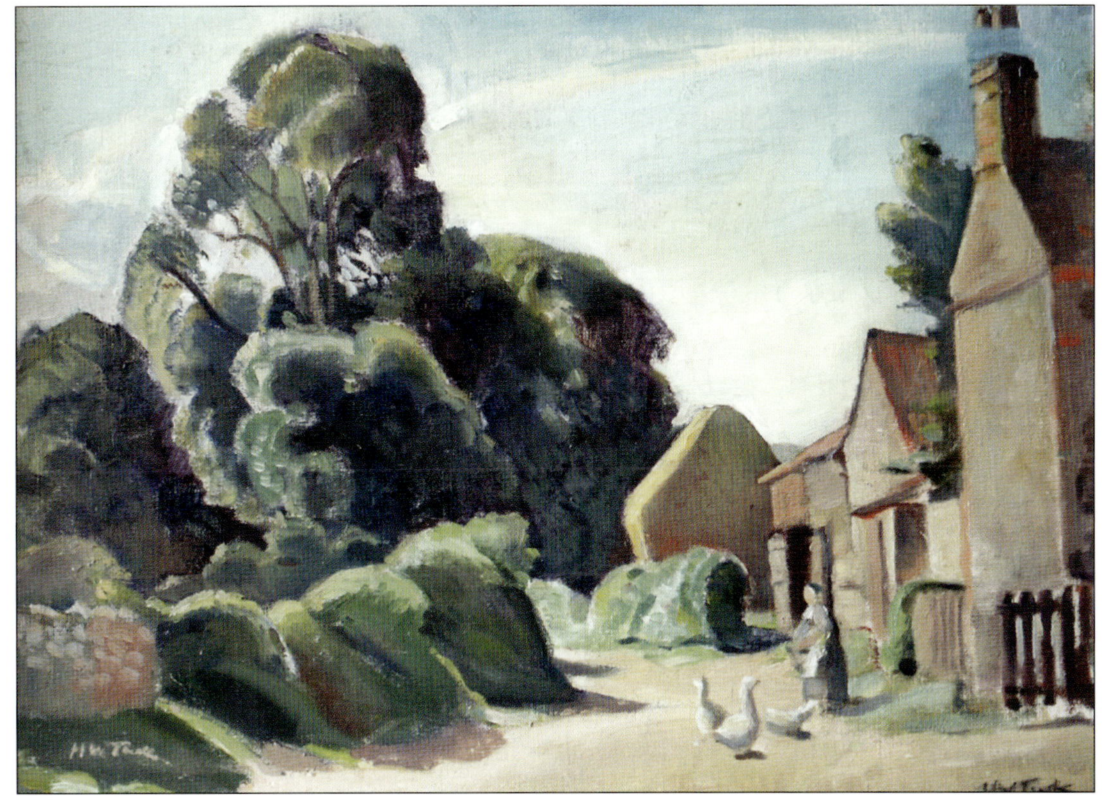

Feeding the Geese
oil on board
10x12 inches

Opposite: *Norwich Fair*
watercolour
15x10.5 inches
Held annually at Easter, the fair took place
on the old cattlemarket site behind the Castle.

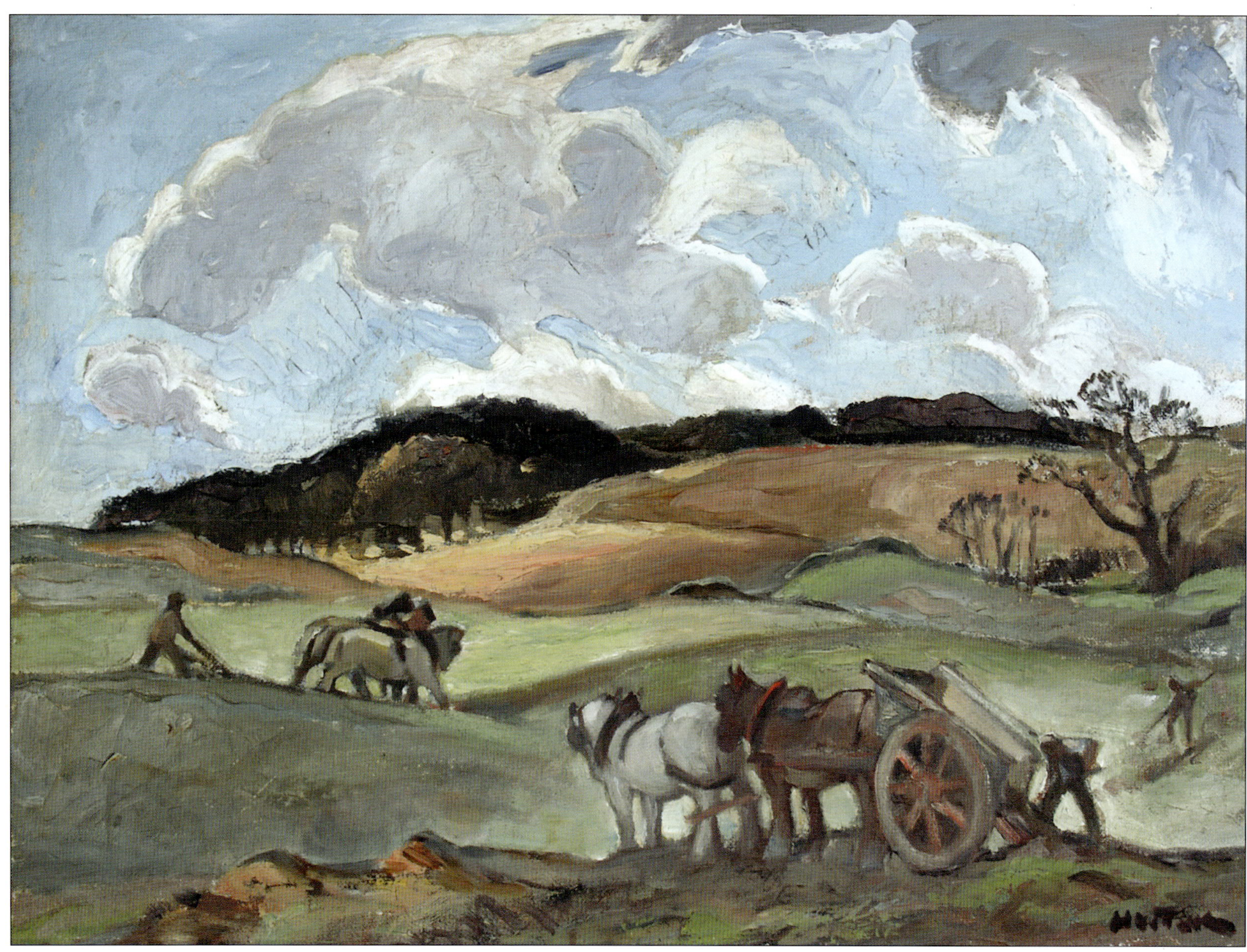

Spring Landscape.
Farmworkers near Sheringham
oil on canvas
18x14 inches

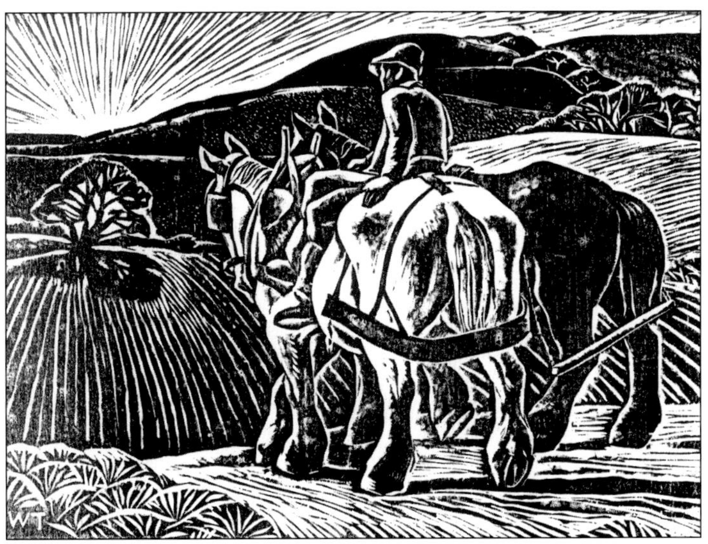

The Ploughteam
linocut
8x10 inches

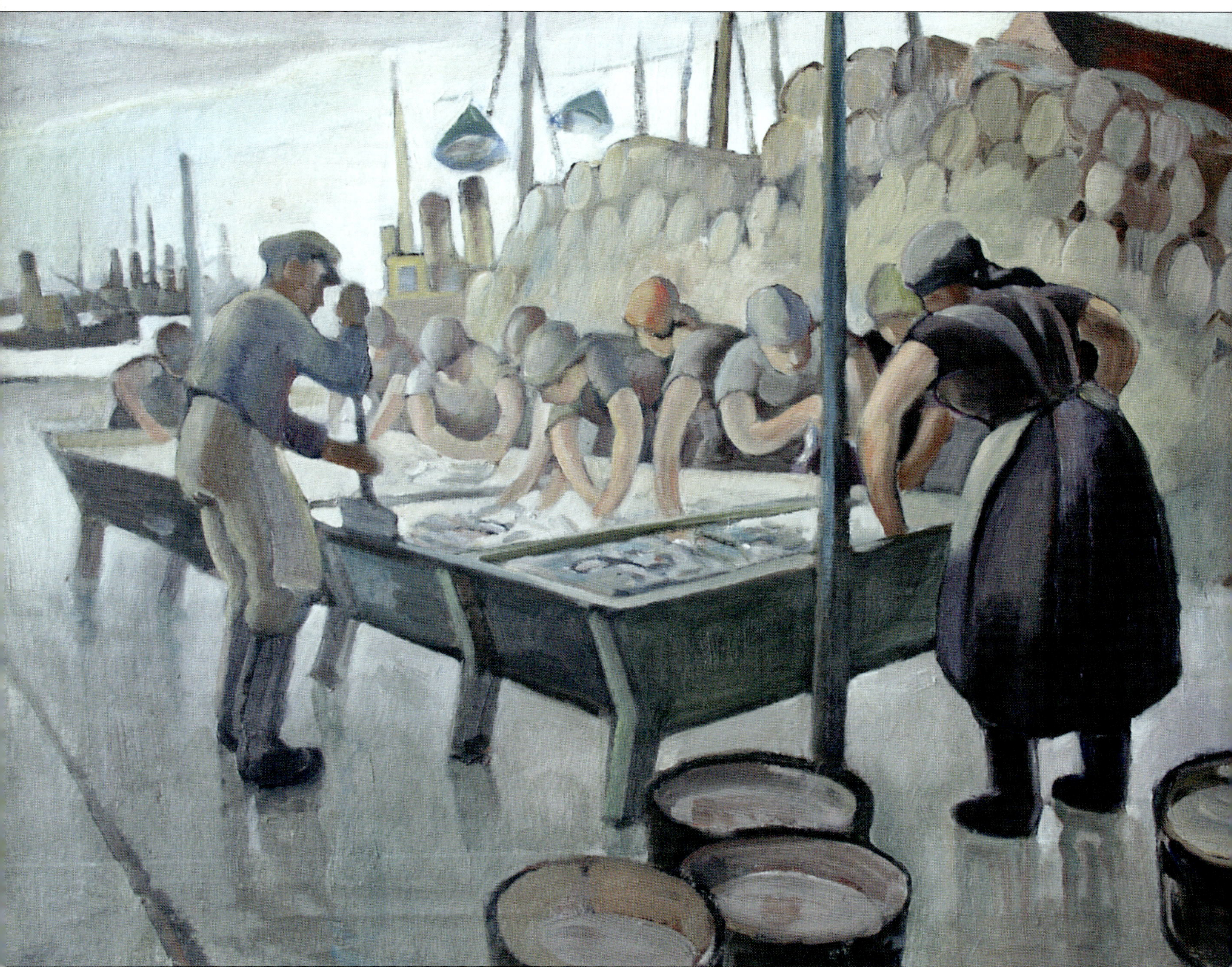

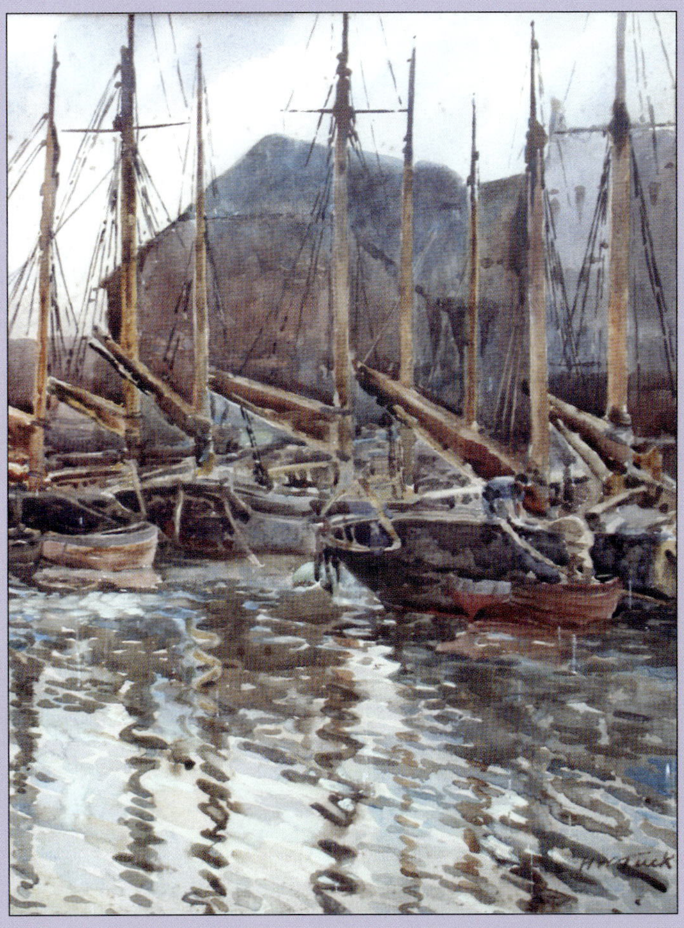

Boats at Rest - Lowestoft
watercolour
12.5x16 inches

Opposite:
Scottish Fishergirls, Great Yarmouth
oil on canvas
25.5x19.5 inches

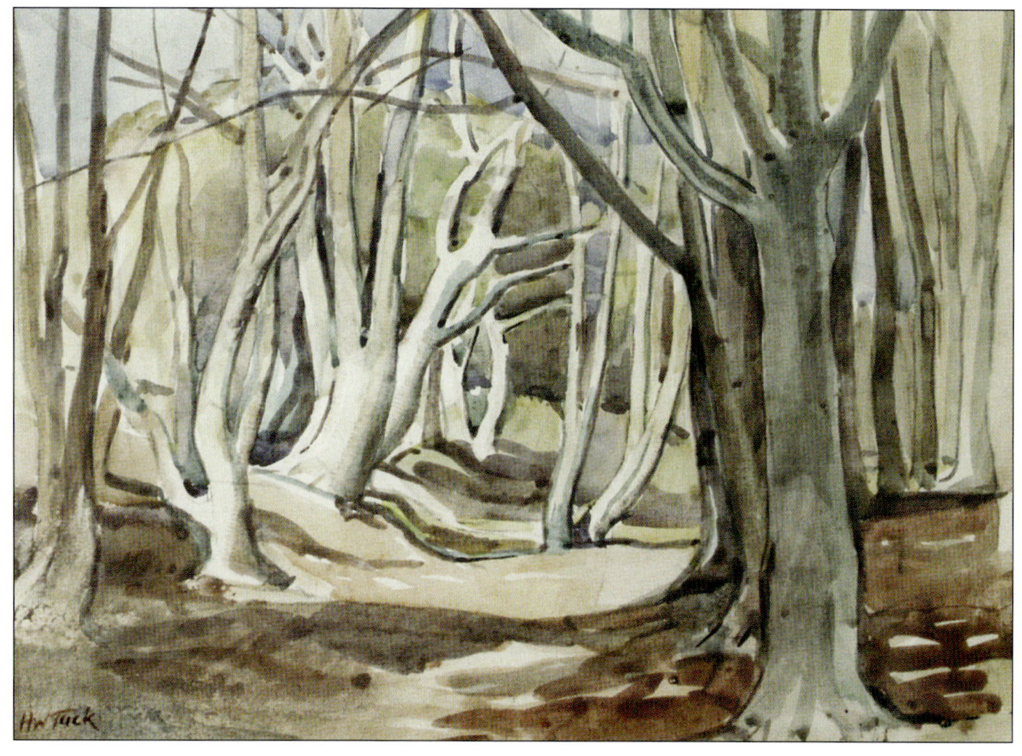

Lion's Mouth, Cromer Road, Sheringham
watercolour
15x11 inches

Opposite:
Illuminated Beech, near Sherringham
oil on canvas
20x16 inches

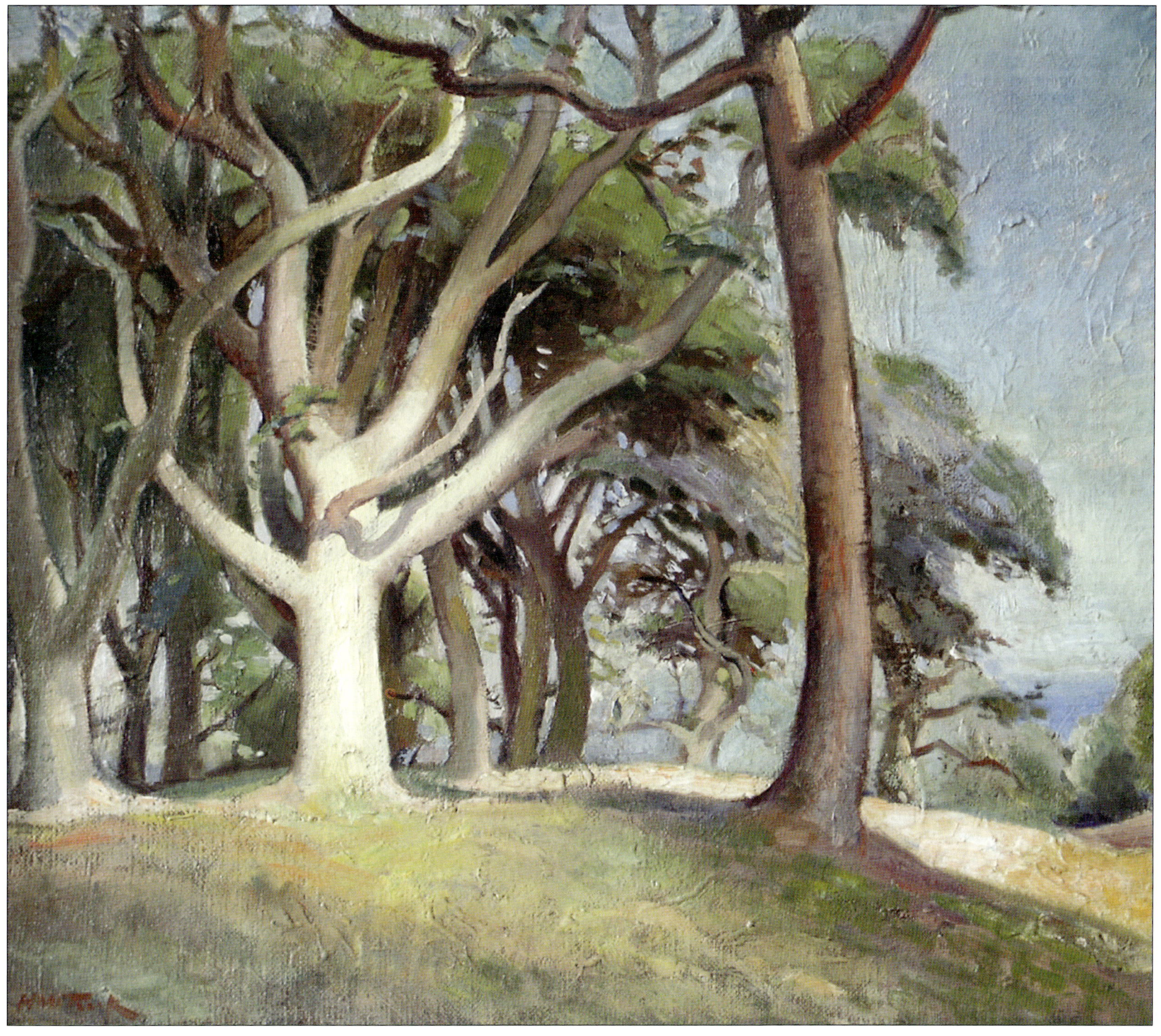

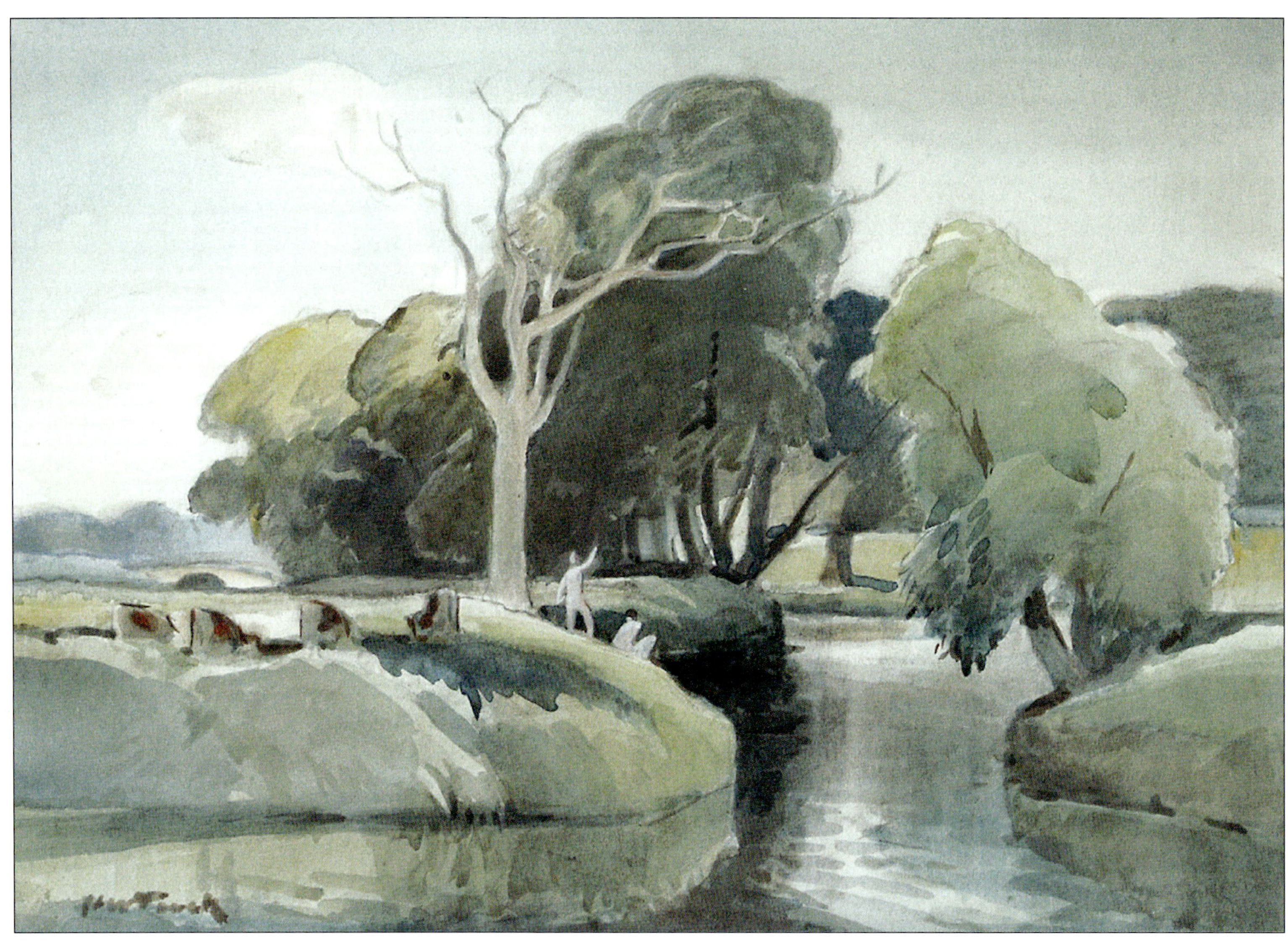

Fishing on the River Bure
watercolour
14x10 inches

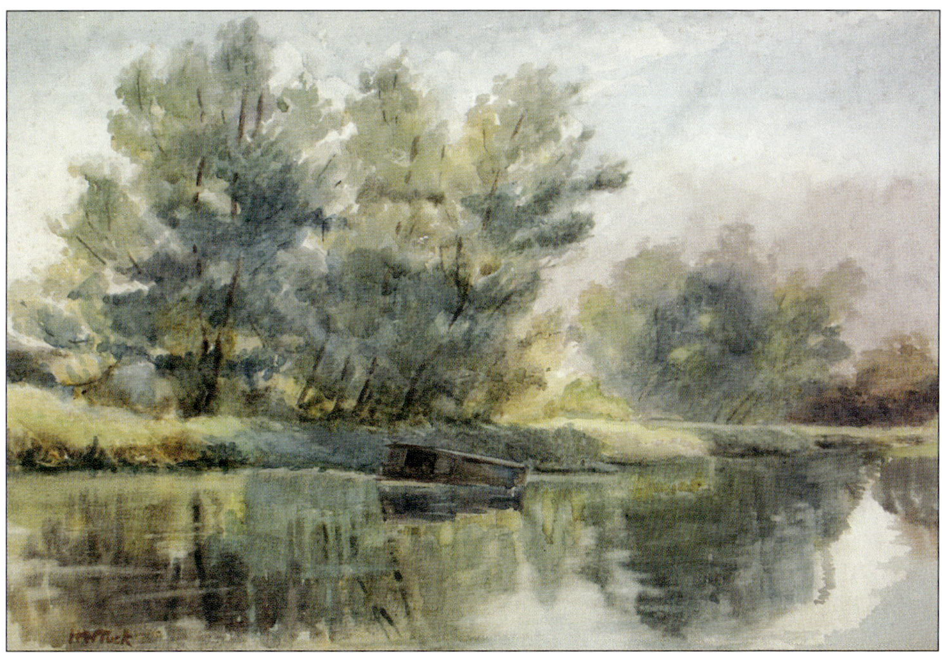

On the Broads
watercolour
15.5x10.5 inches

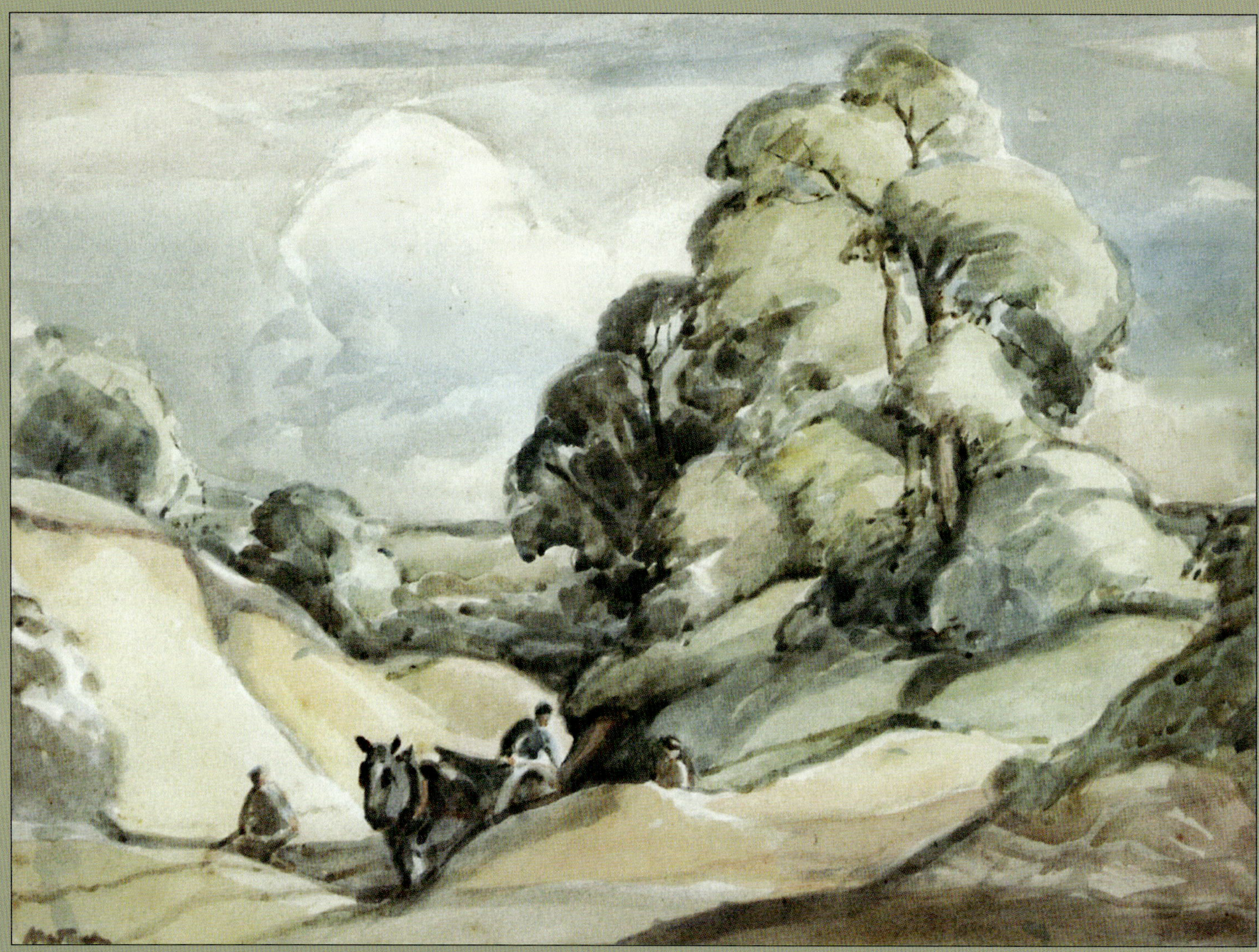

The Gravel Pit, Sheringham
watercolour
14.5x10.5 inches

Opposite: *The Village Inn*
oil on canvas
20x14 inches

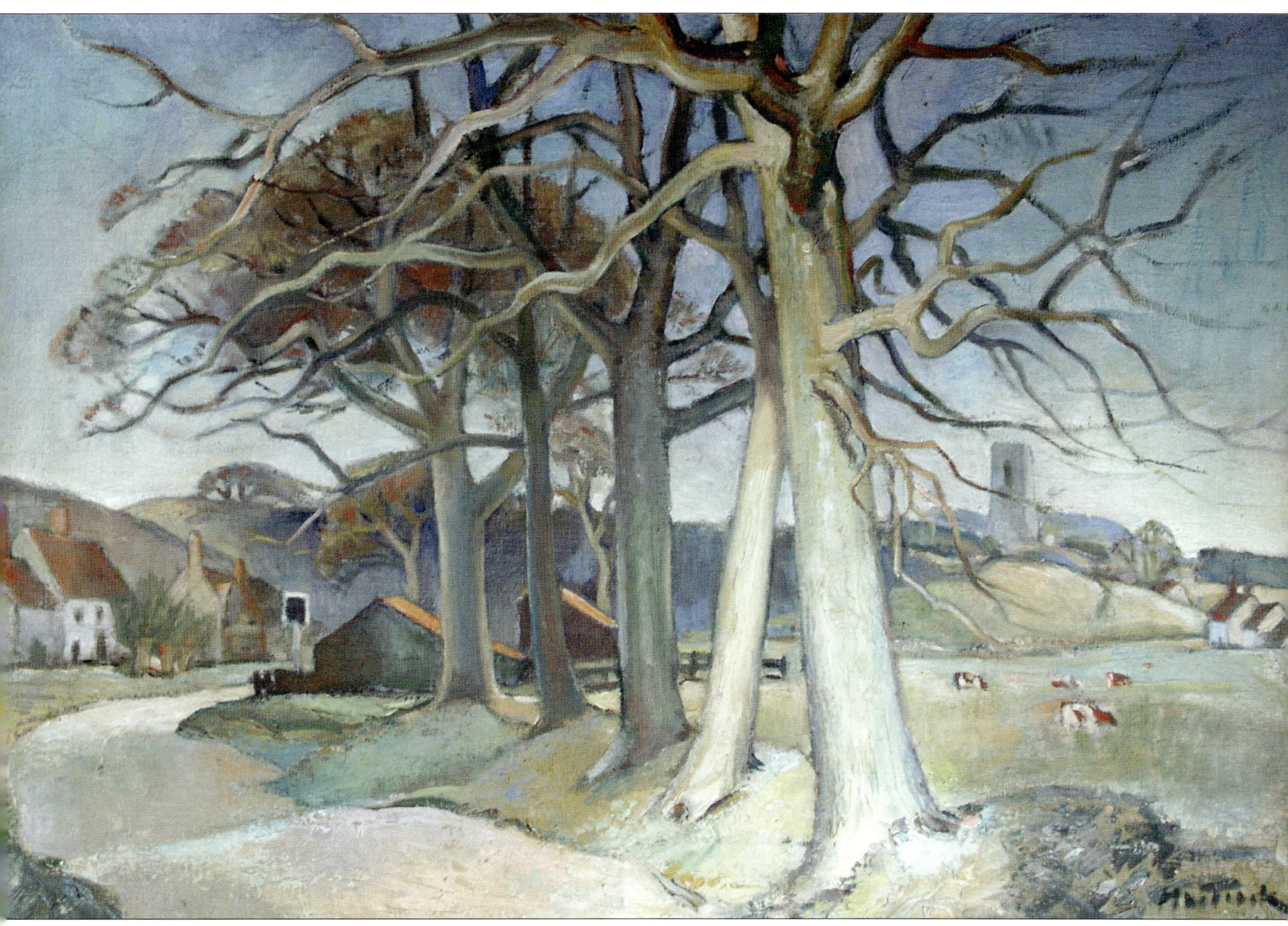

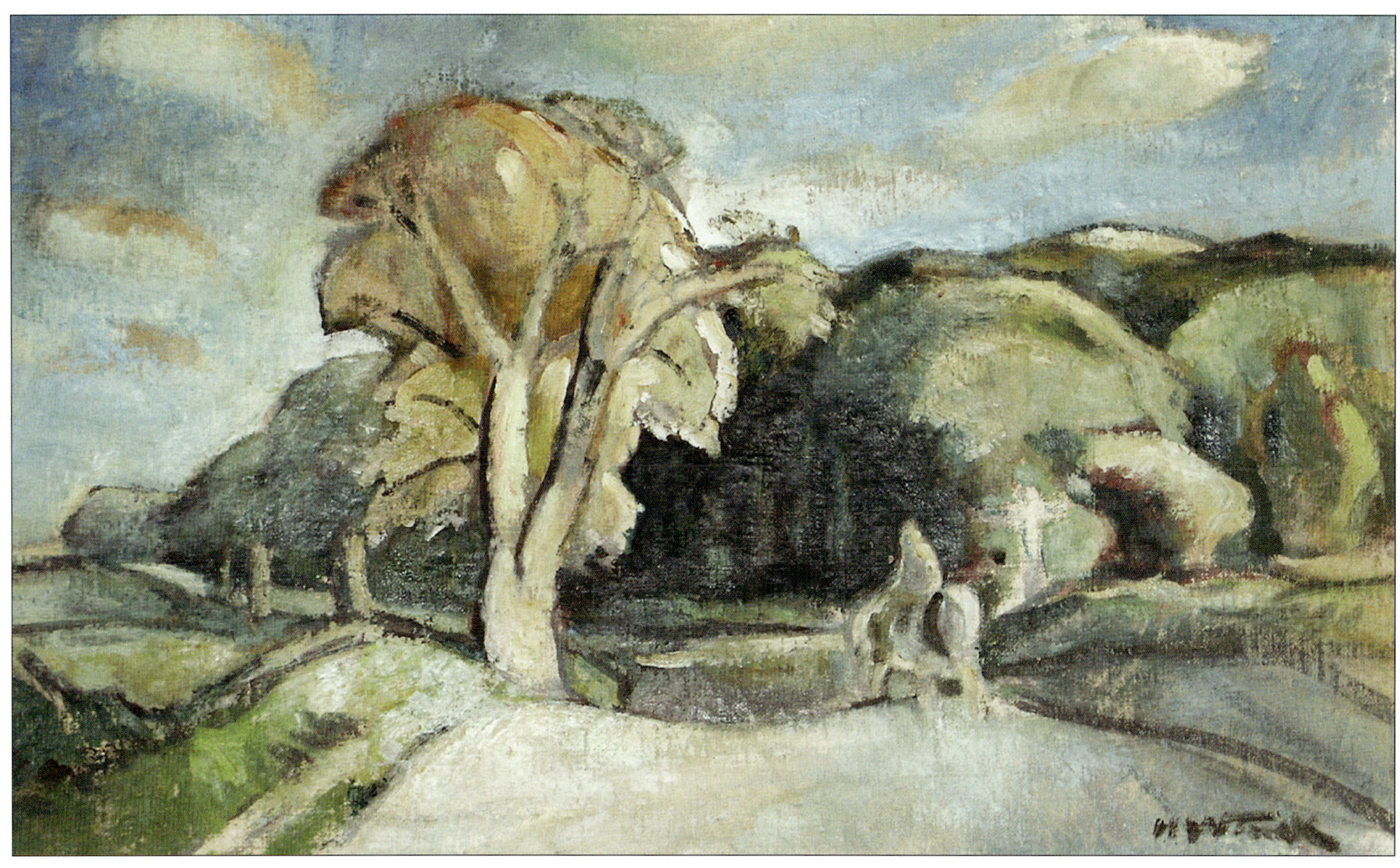

Oakwood.
On the coast road between Sheringham and Cromer.
oil on canvas
18x13.5 inches

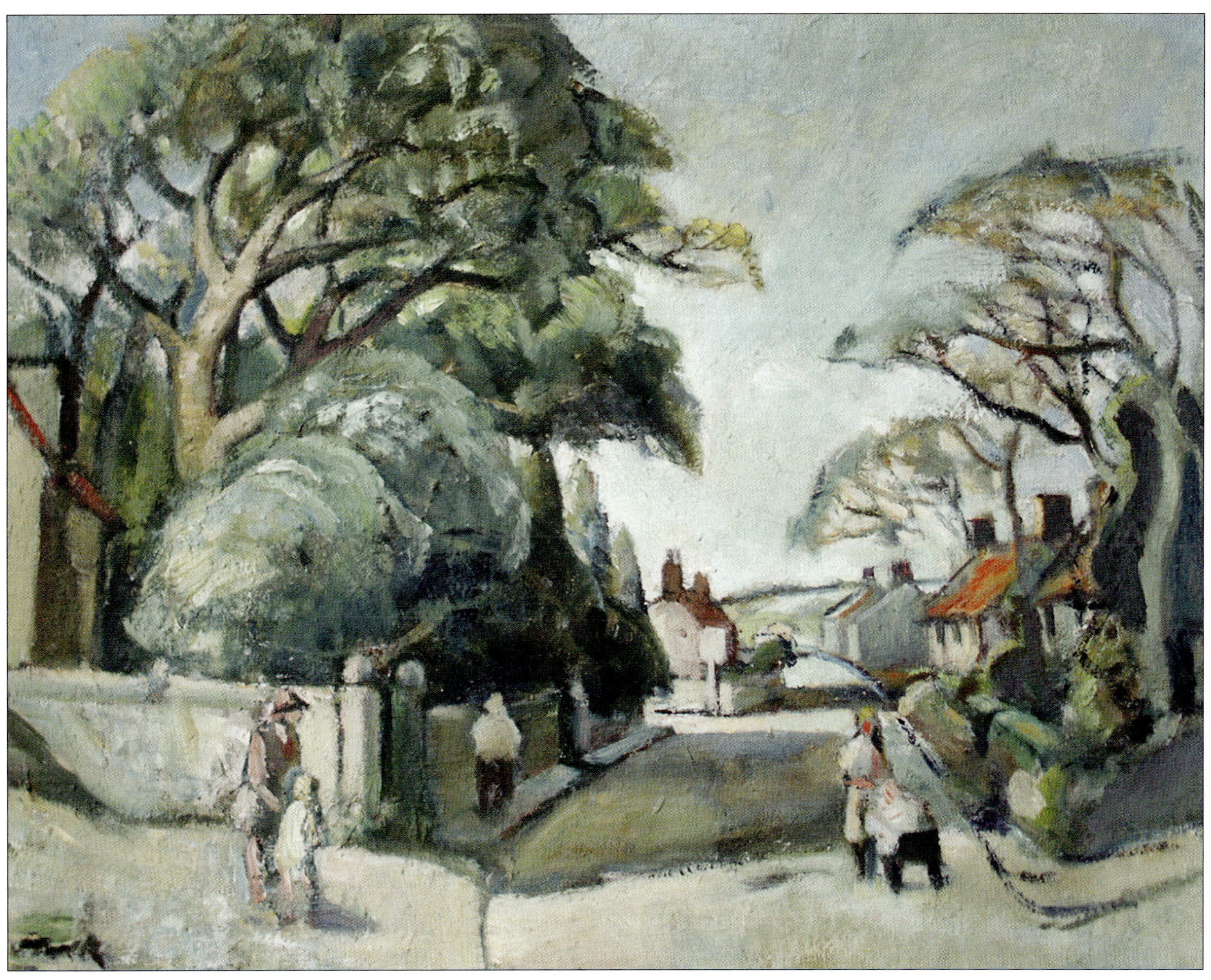

A Sleepy Norfolk Village
oil on canvas
17x13 inches

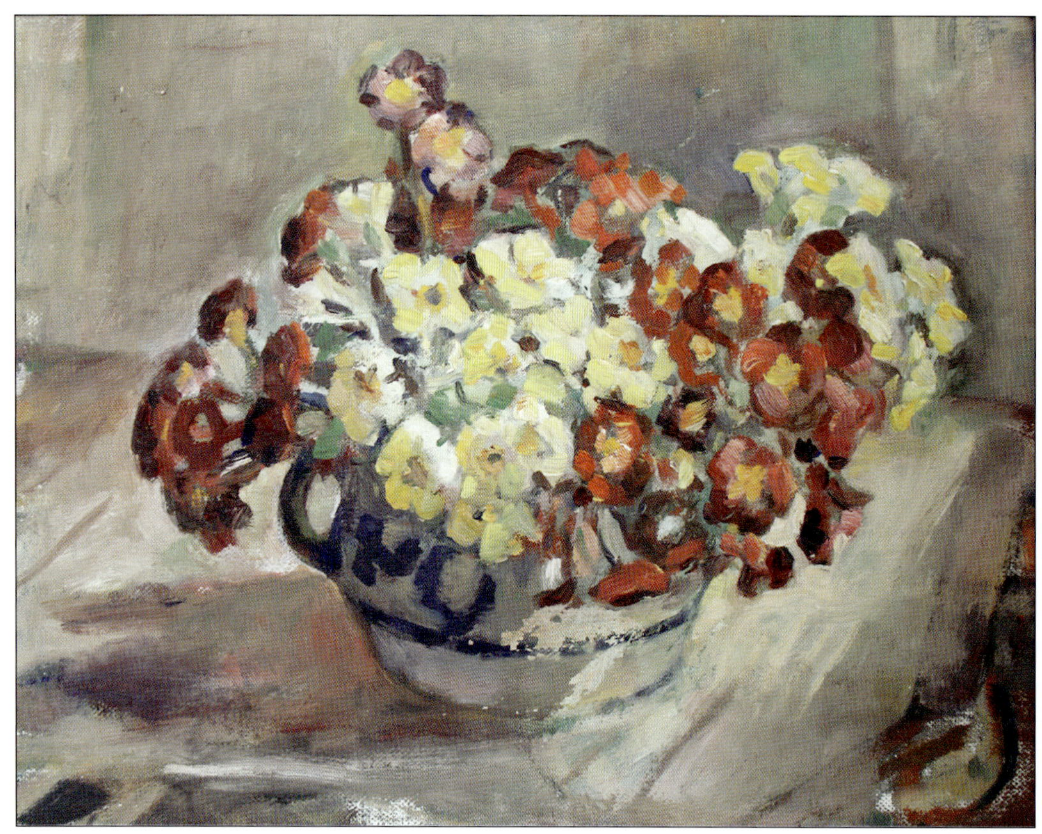

Blue Bowl and Primulas
oil on canvas
8x10 inches

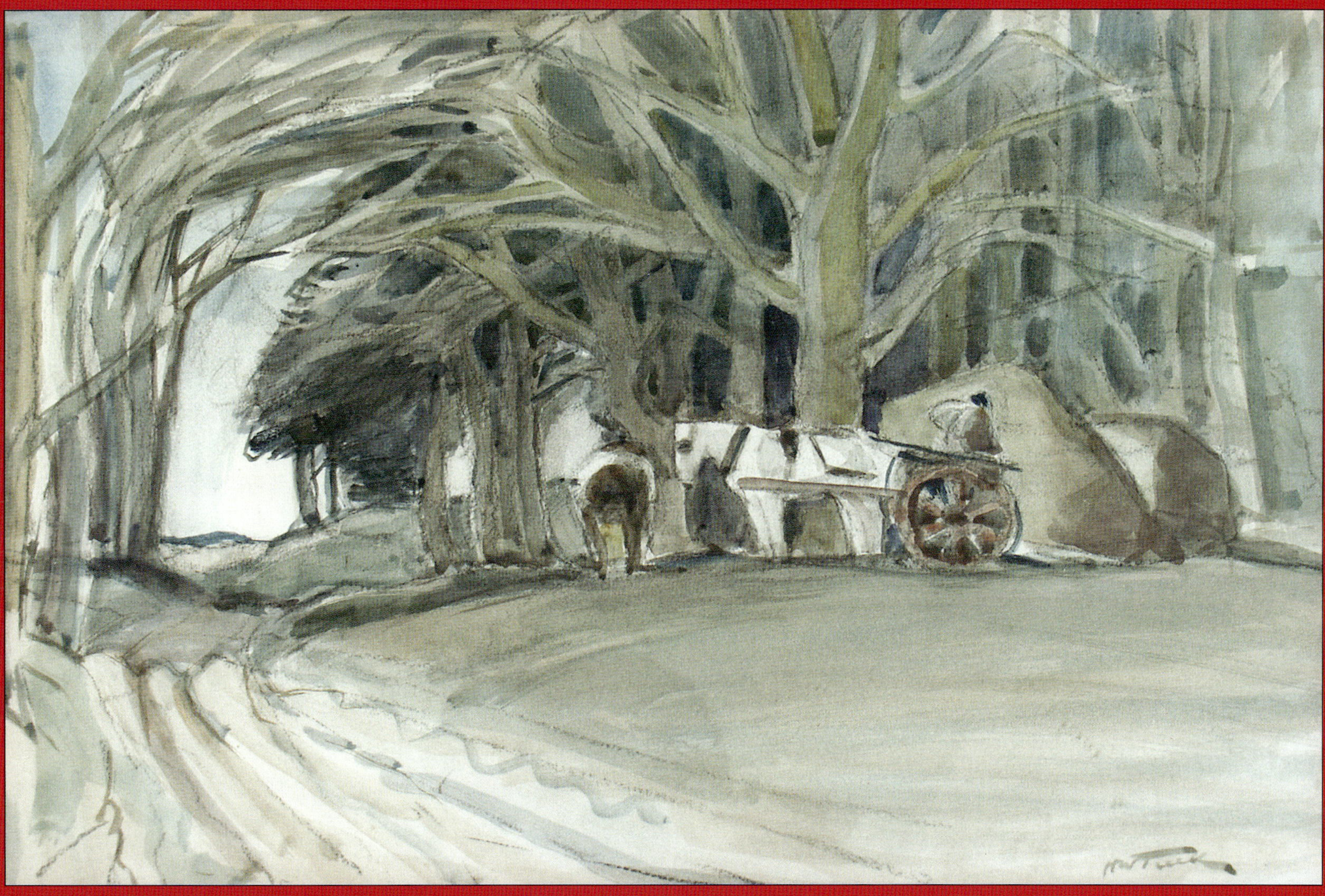

At the Edge of the Wood
watercolour
13.5x9 inches

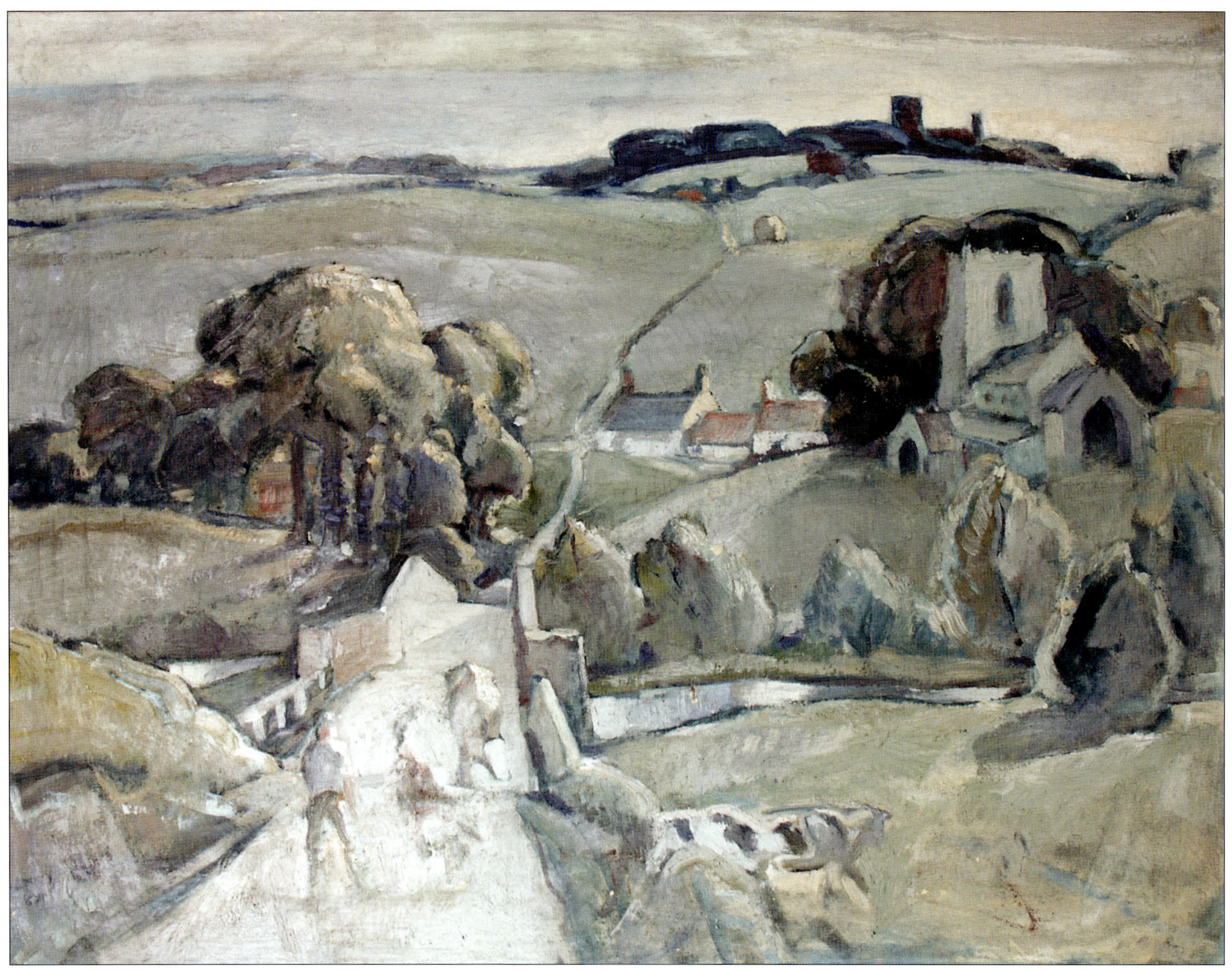

At the End of the Day.
Wiveton Church and Bridge
oil on canvas
23x18 inches

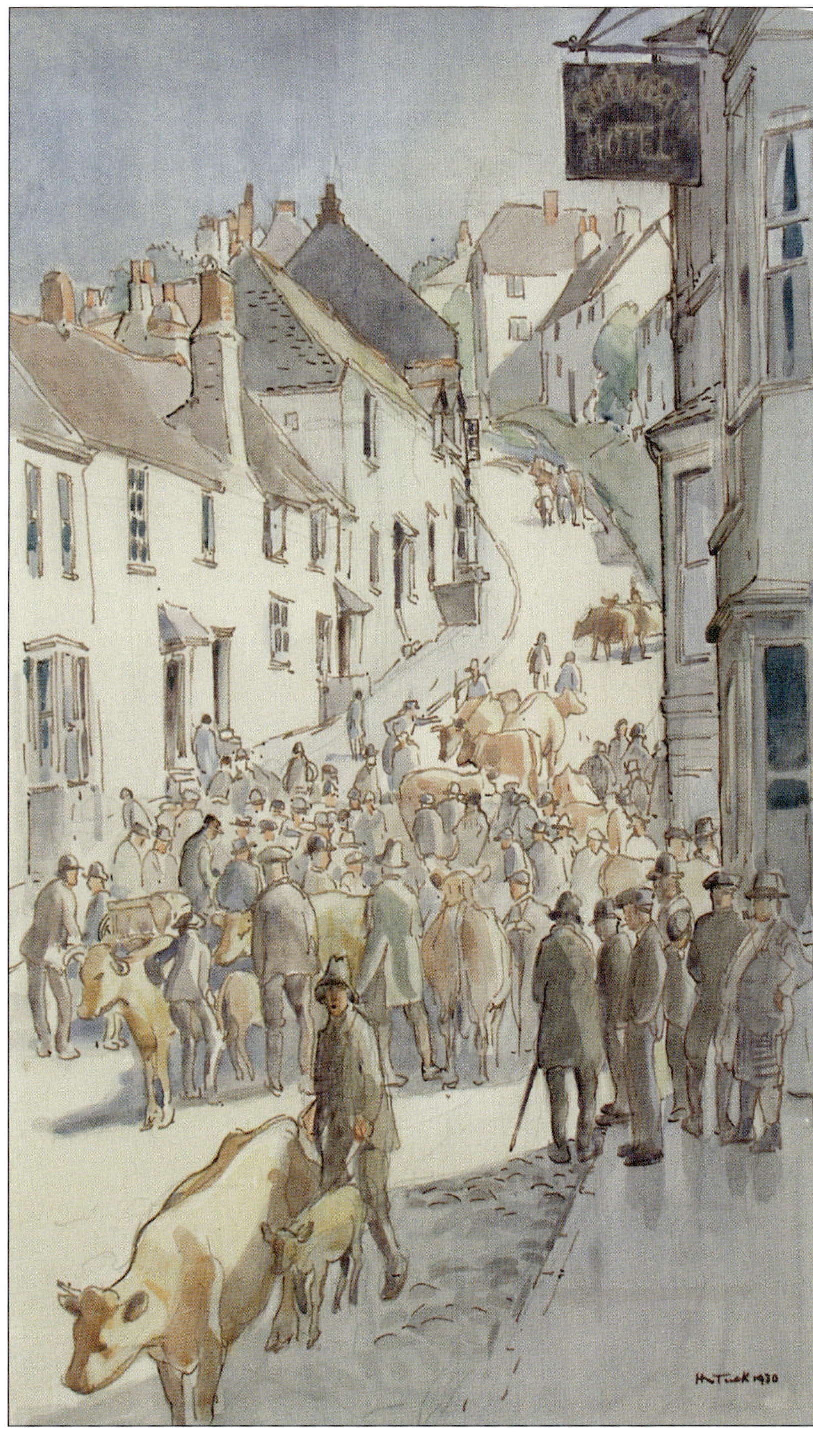

The Cattlemarket
watercolour
15x10 inches

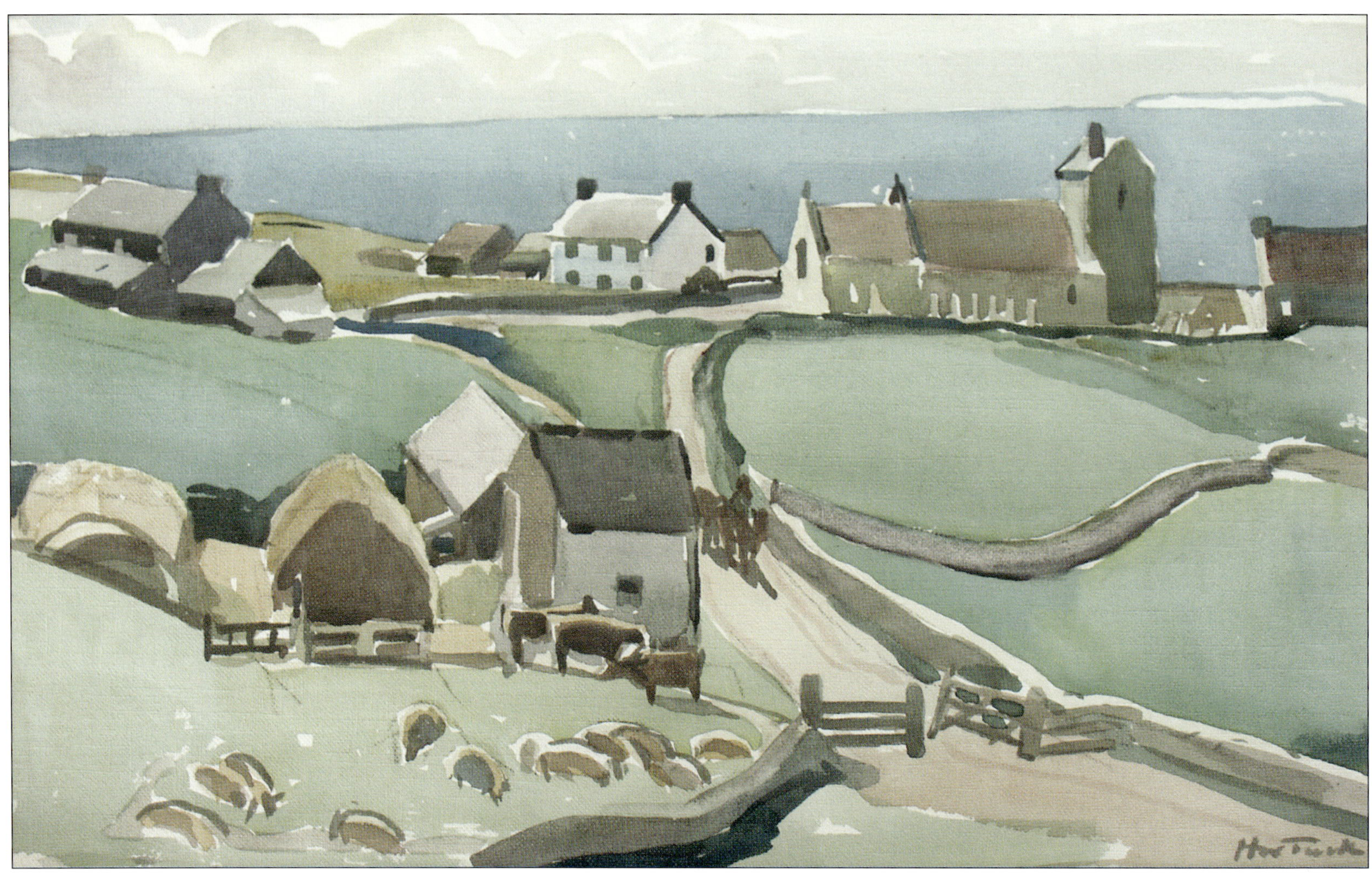

Farmland and View to the Sea
watercolour
14.5x10inches

Opposite:
Down the Deep Lane
oil on canvas
21x18.5inches

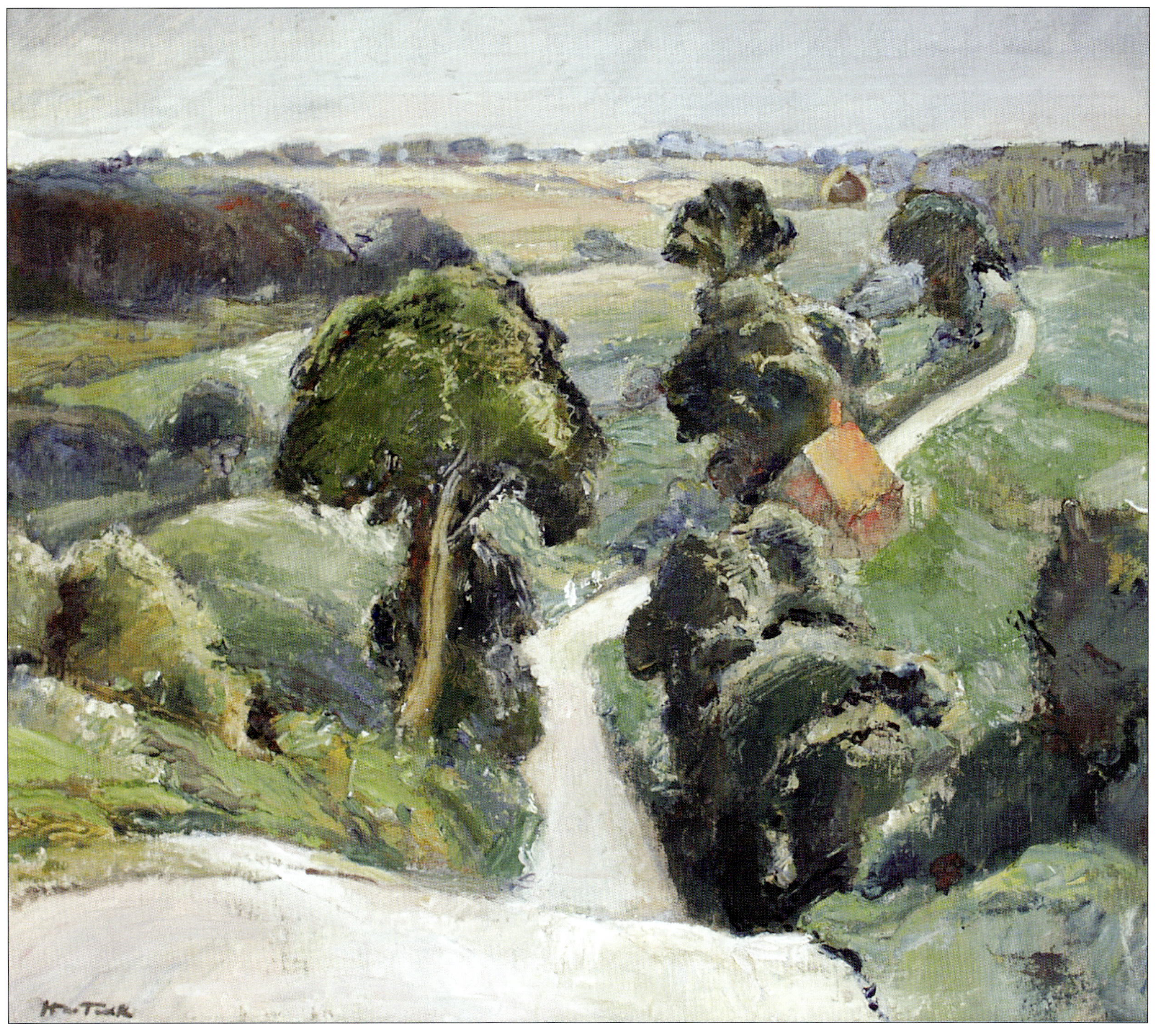

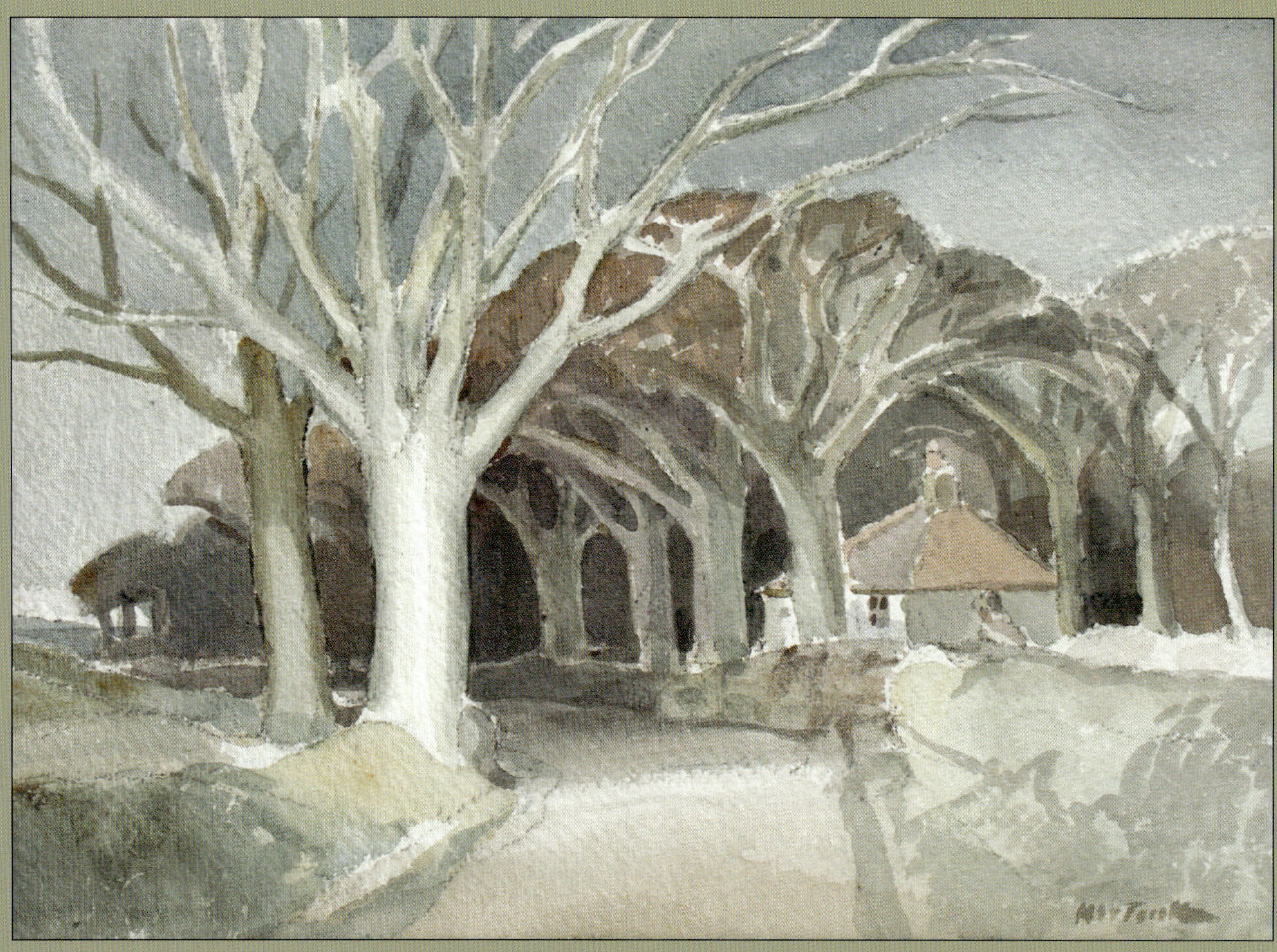

The House in the Trees
watercolour
13.5x9 inches

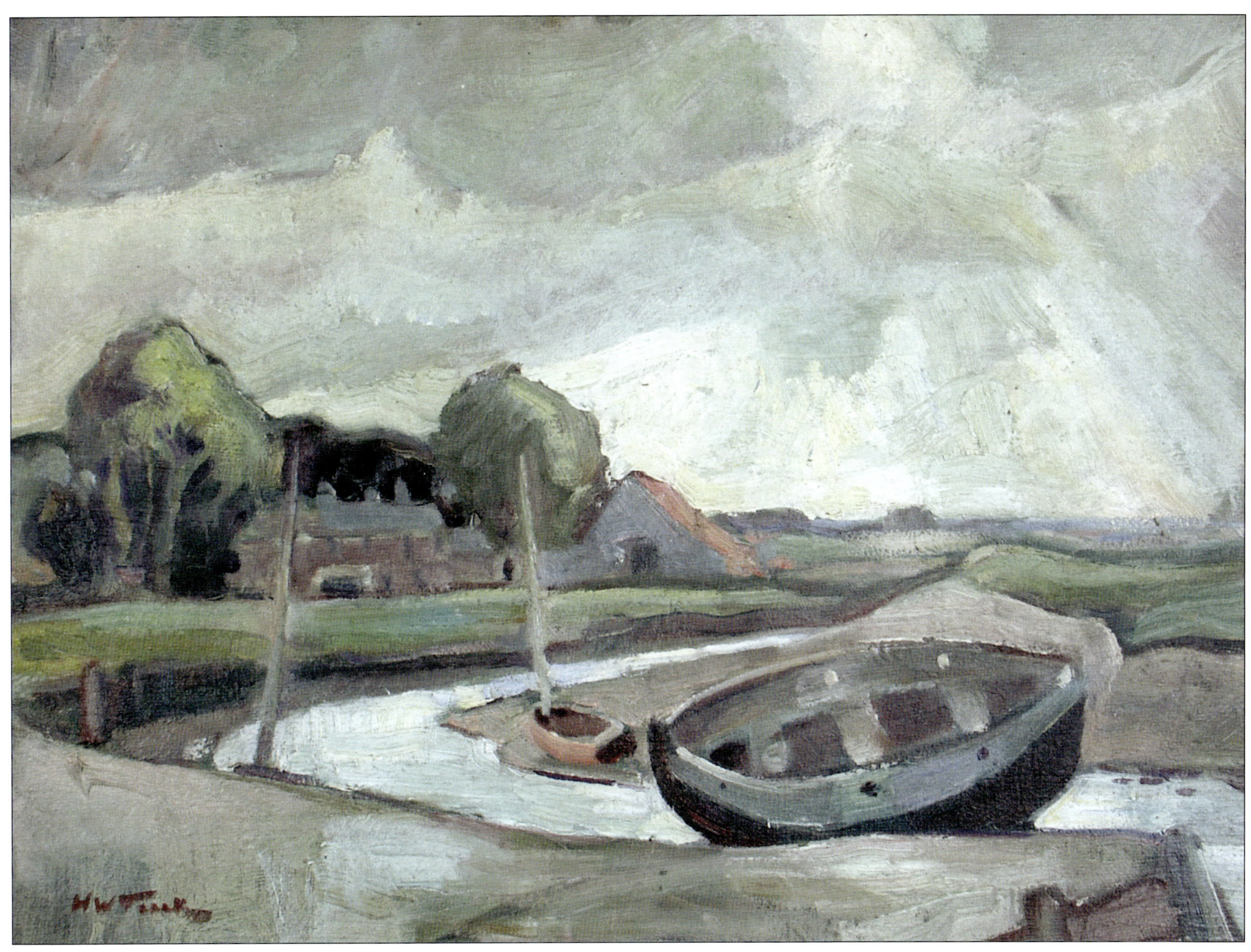

Low Tide, Blakeney
oil on canvas
15x11 inches

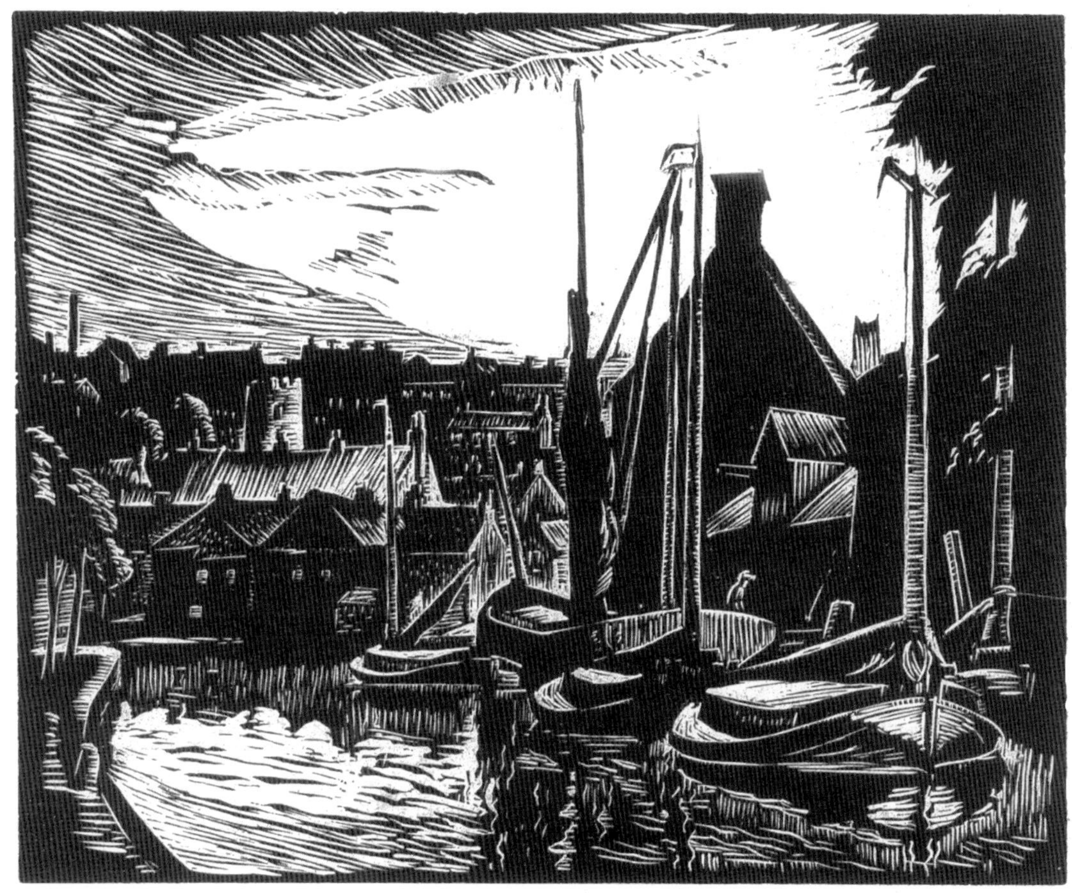

Riverside, Norwich
woodcut

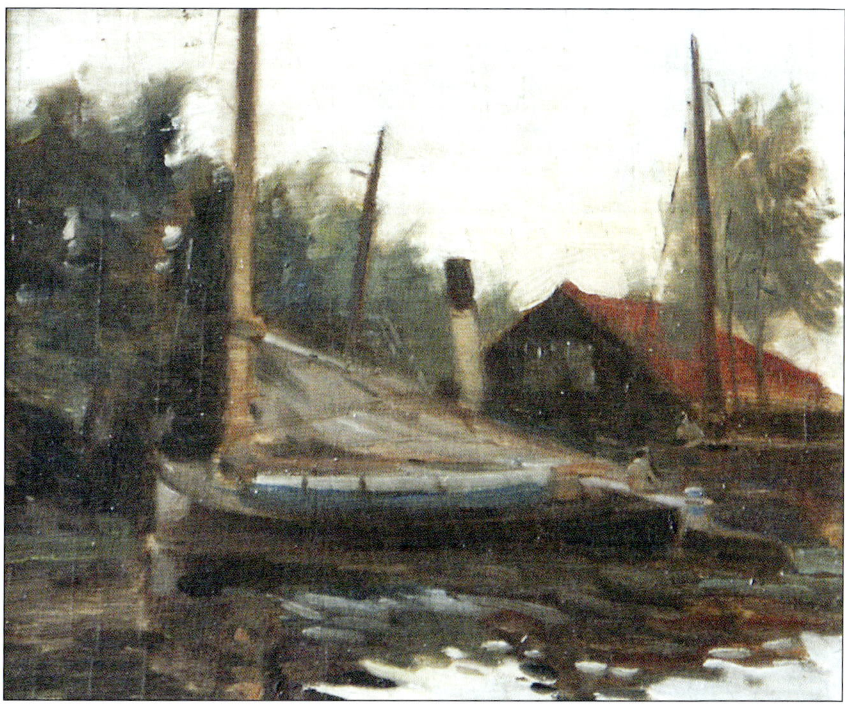

Riverside Boatyard I, Norwich
oil sketch
8.5x6.5 inches

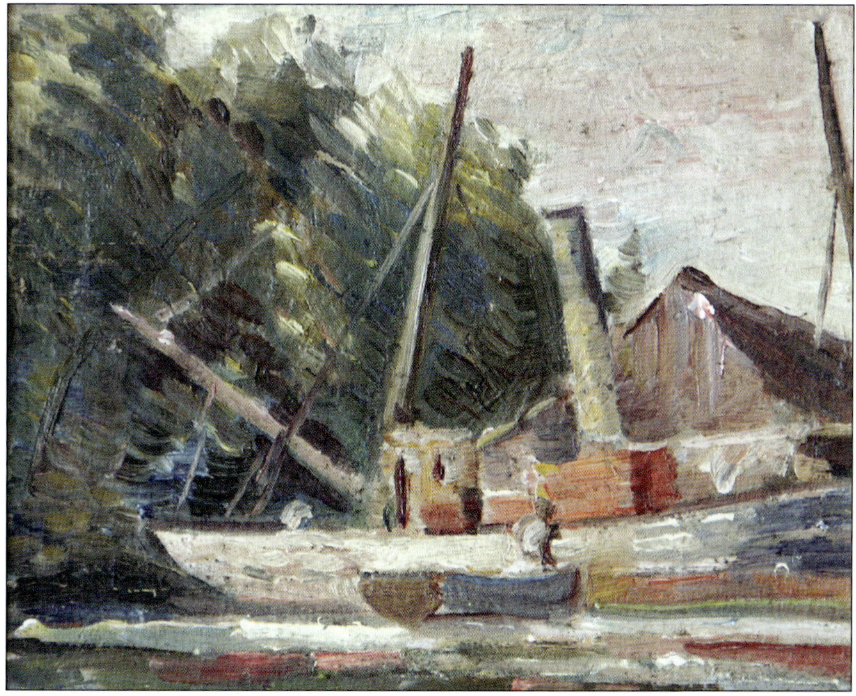

Riverside Boatyard II, Norwich
oil sketch
8.5x6.5 inches

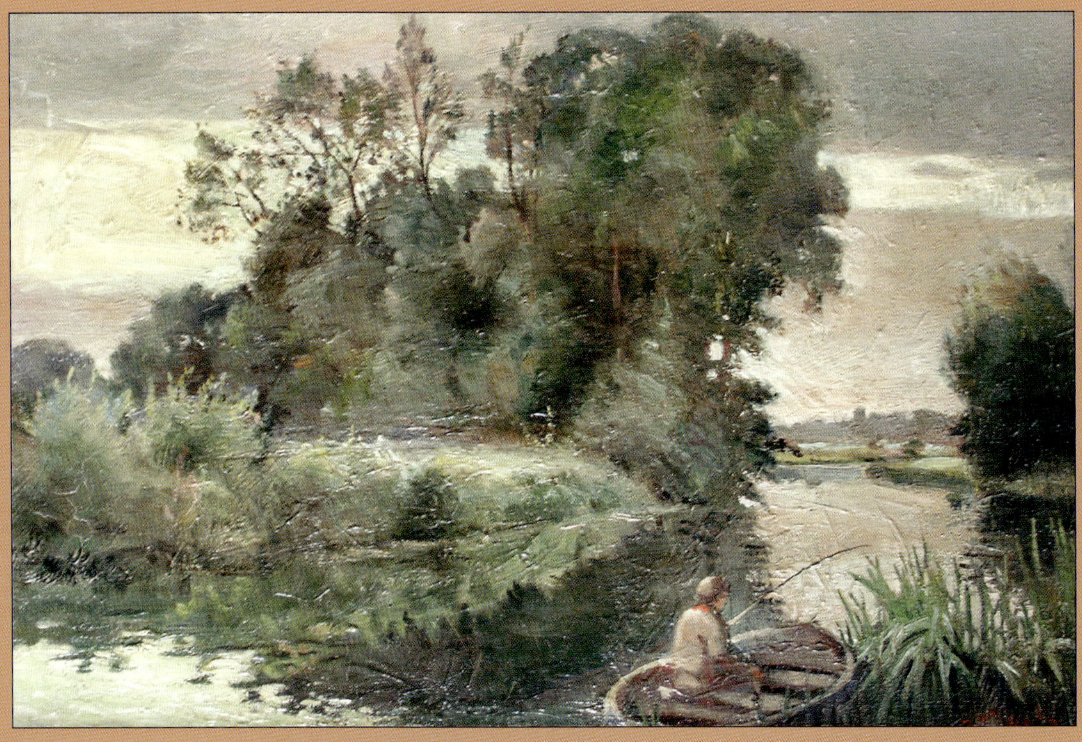

Fishing on the Broads
oil on canvas
8.5x6.5 inches

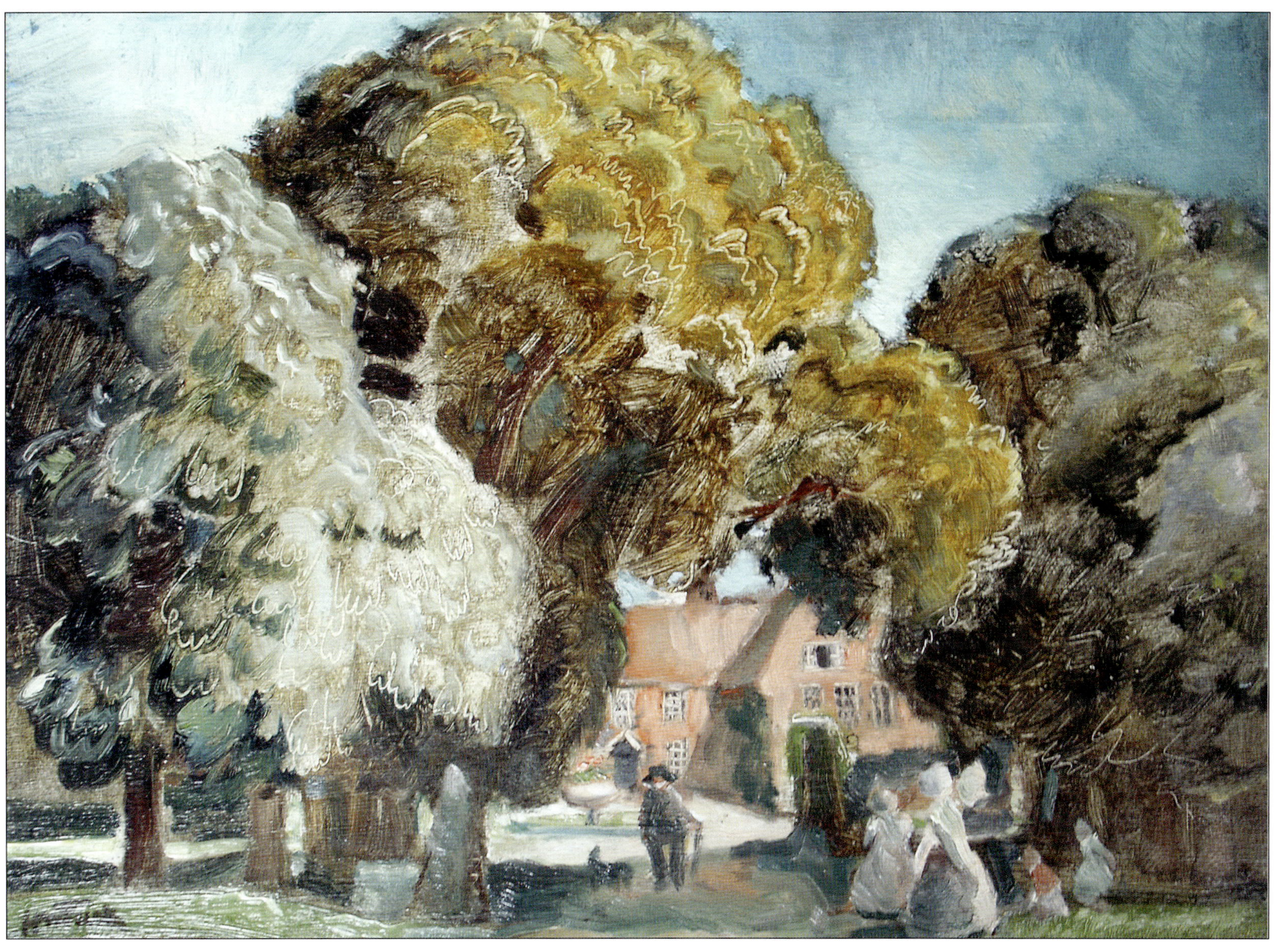

The Family Home
oil on canvas
12x9 inches

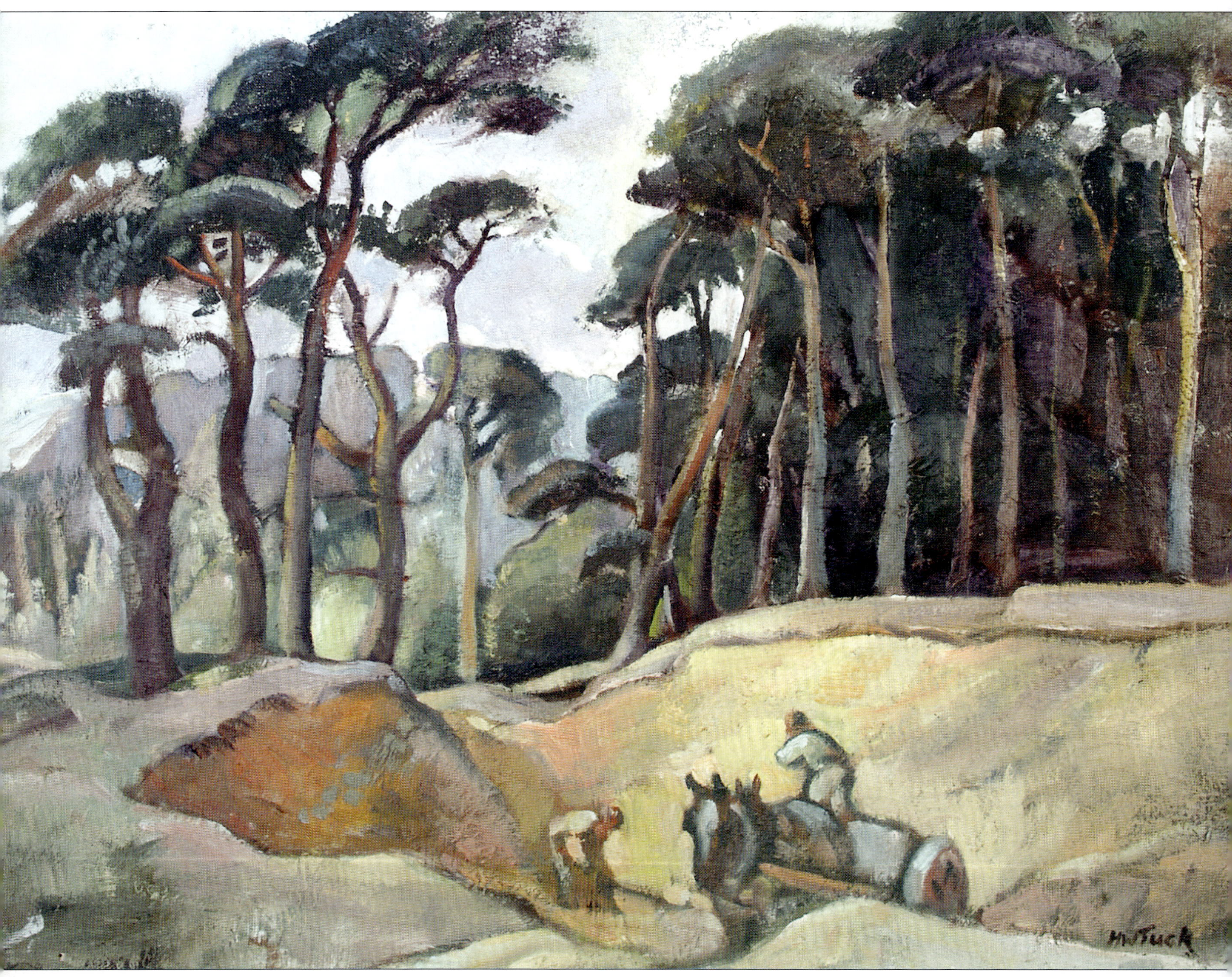

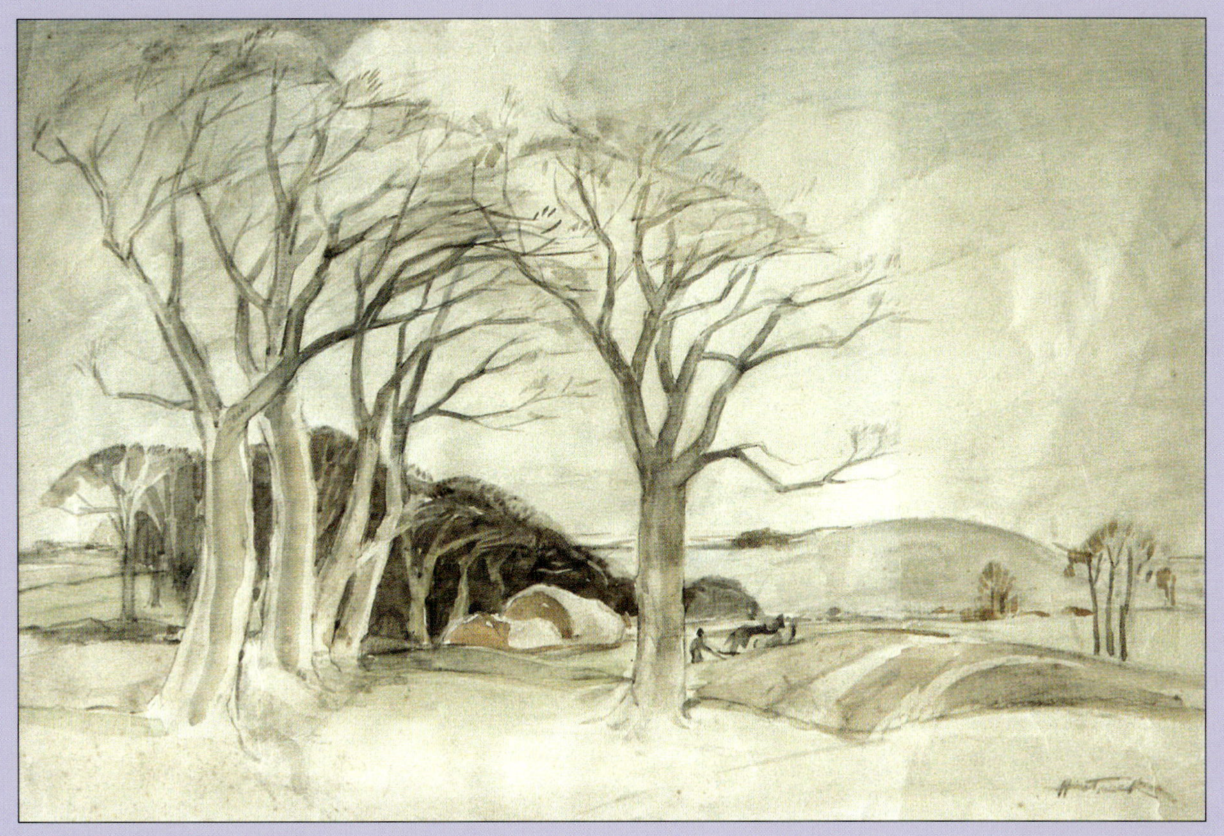

Winter Ploughing
watercolour
14x9.5 inches

Opposite:
The Sandpit, Upper Sheringham, 1930
oil on canvas
24x18 inches

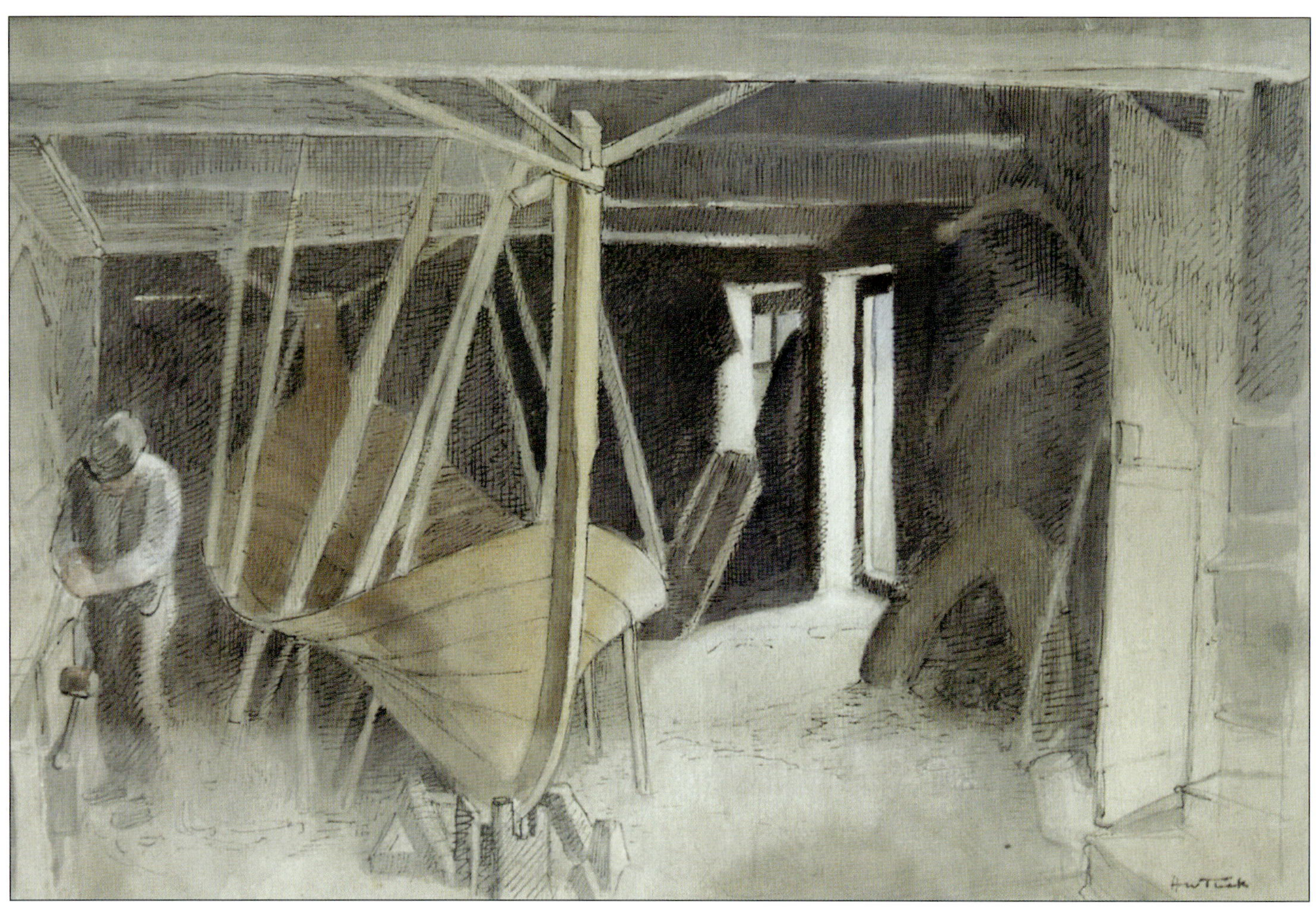

Boatbuilder I. Mr Emery, Sheringham
watercolour
14.5x10 inches

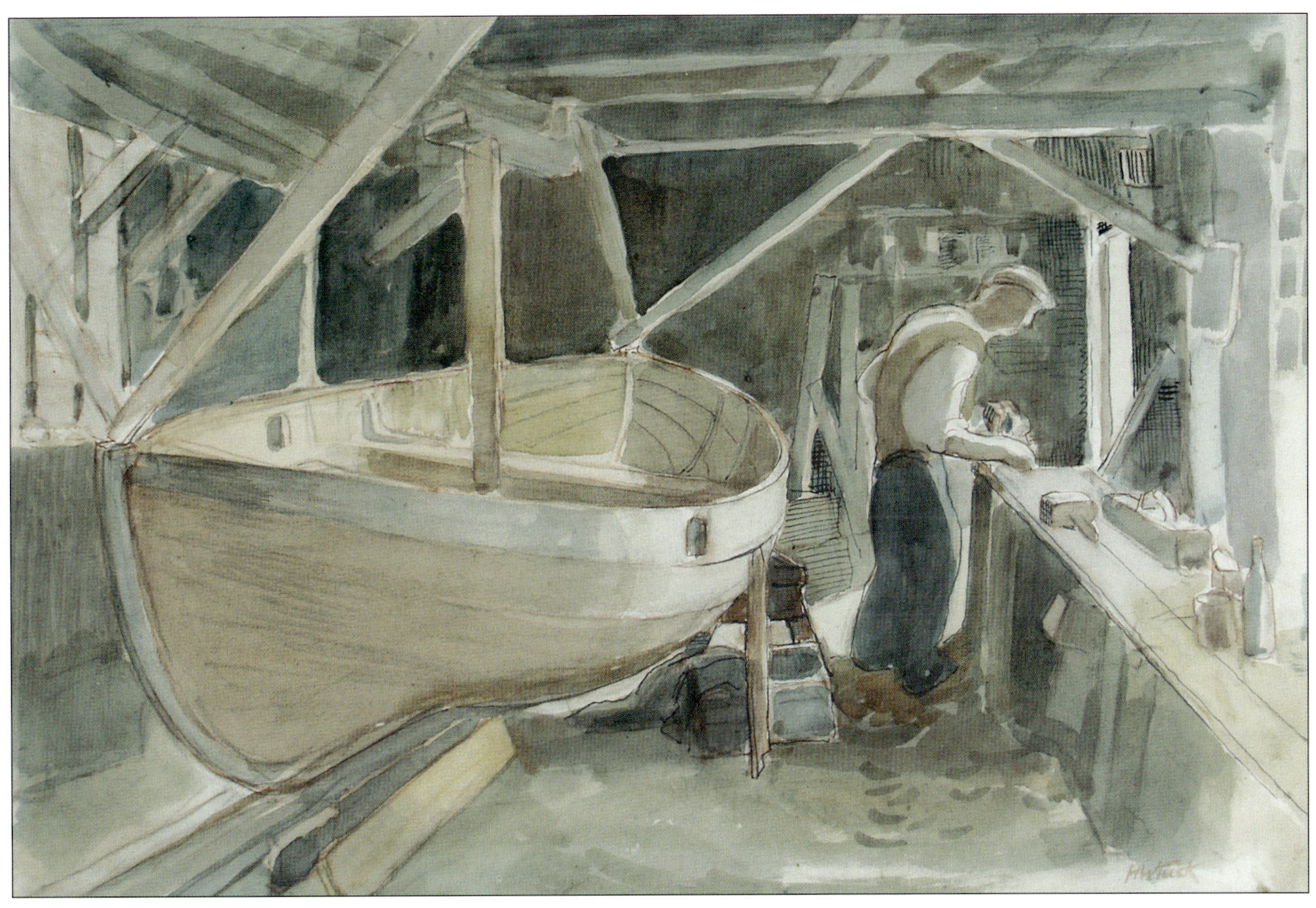

Boatbuilder II. Mr Emery, Sheringham
watercolour
14.5x10 inches

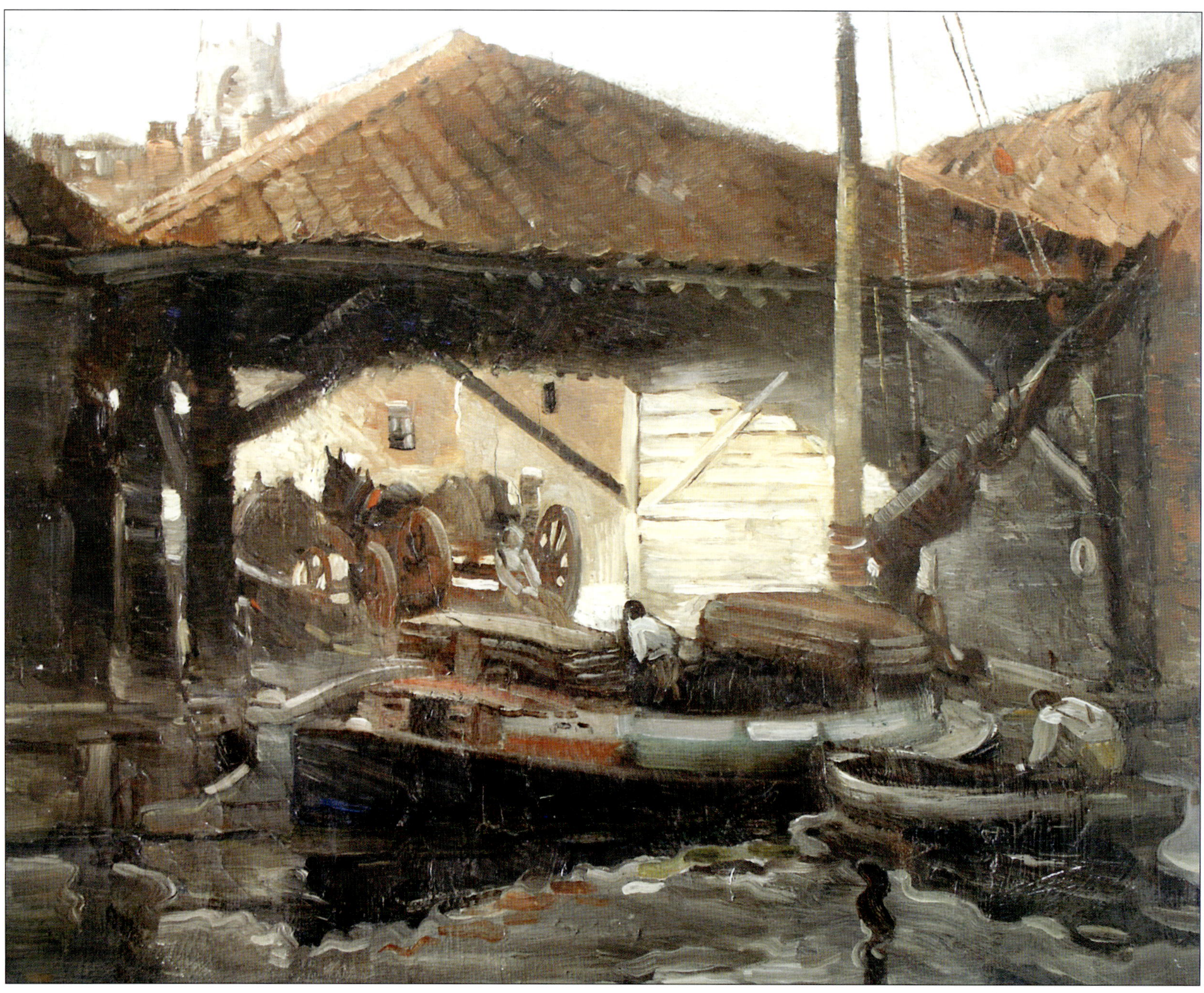

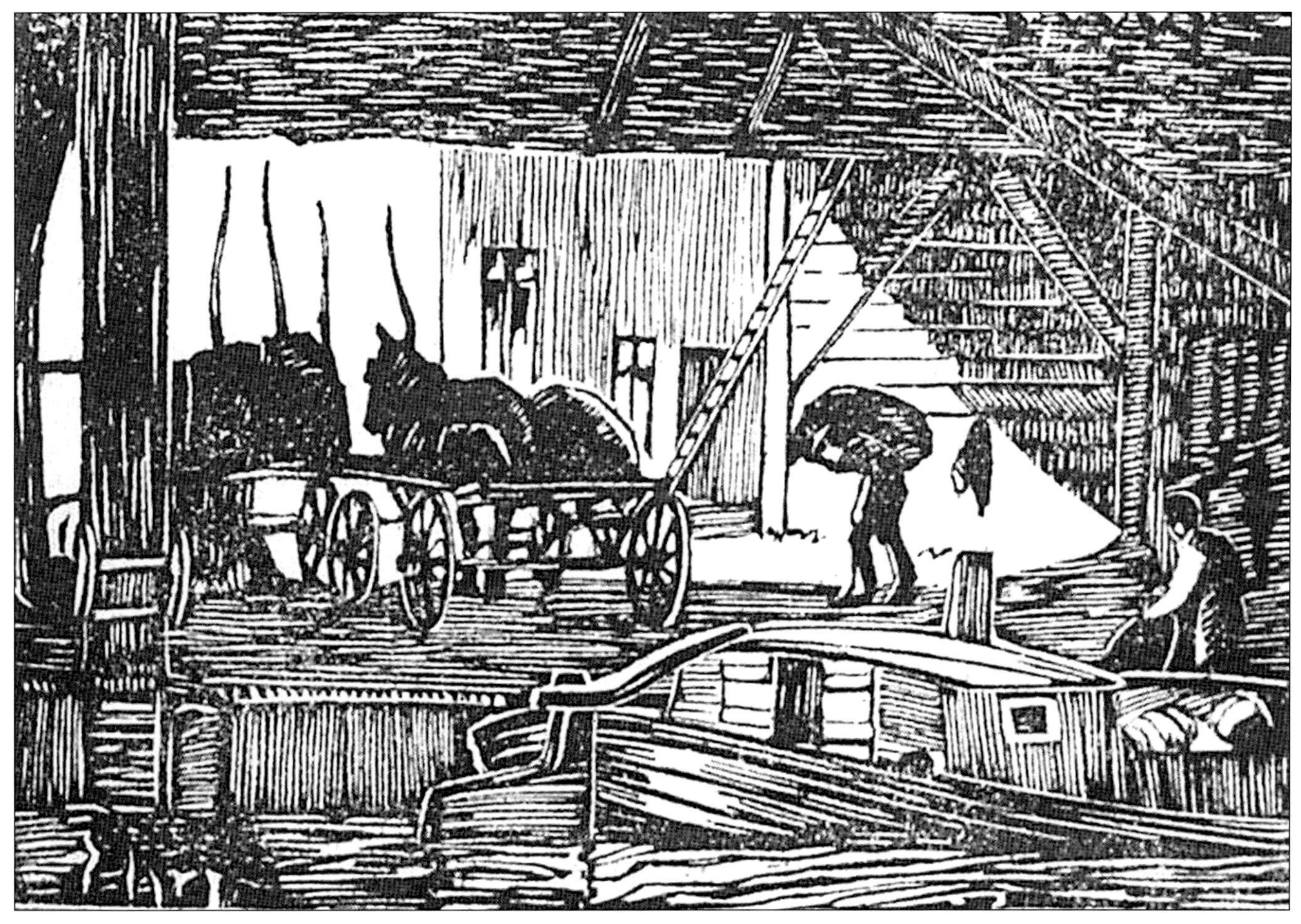

Unloading a Wherry, Norwich
linocut

Opposite:
Unloading a Wherry, Norwich
oil on canvas
14.5x10 inches

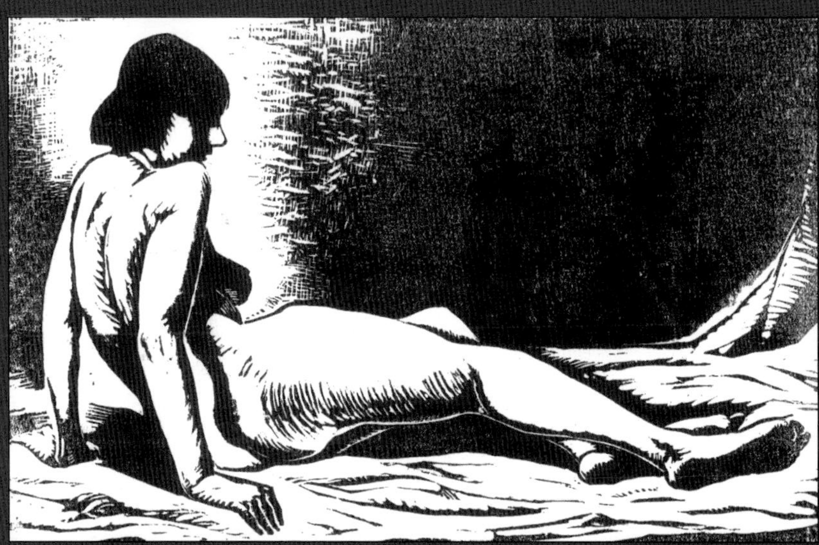

Nude
linocut

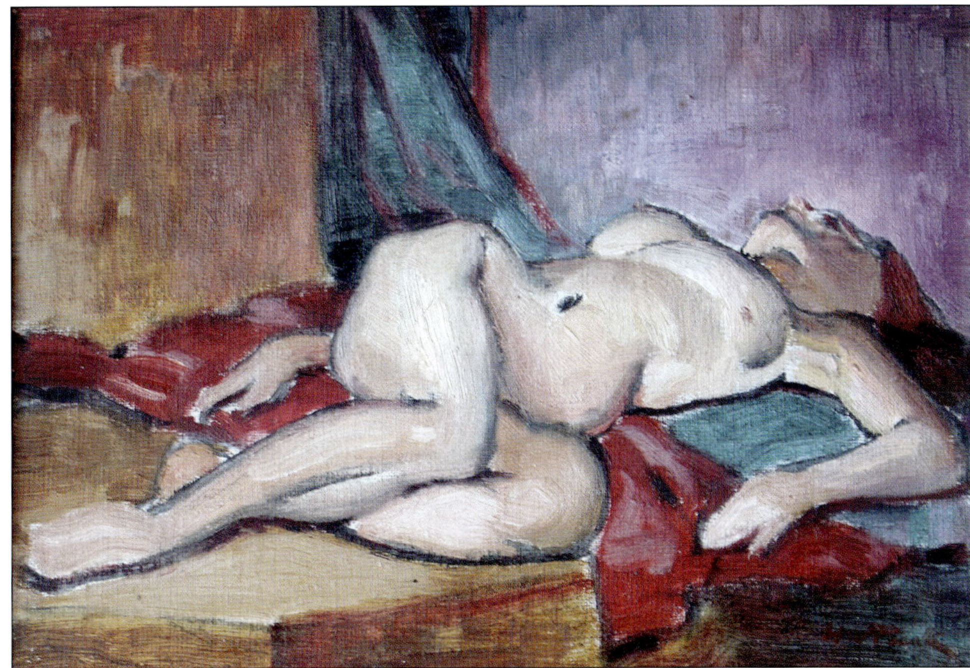

Red Nude
oil on canvas
9.5x6.5 inches

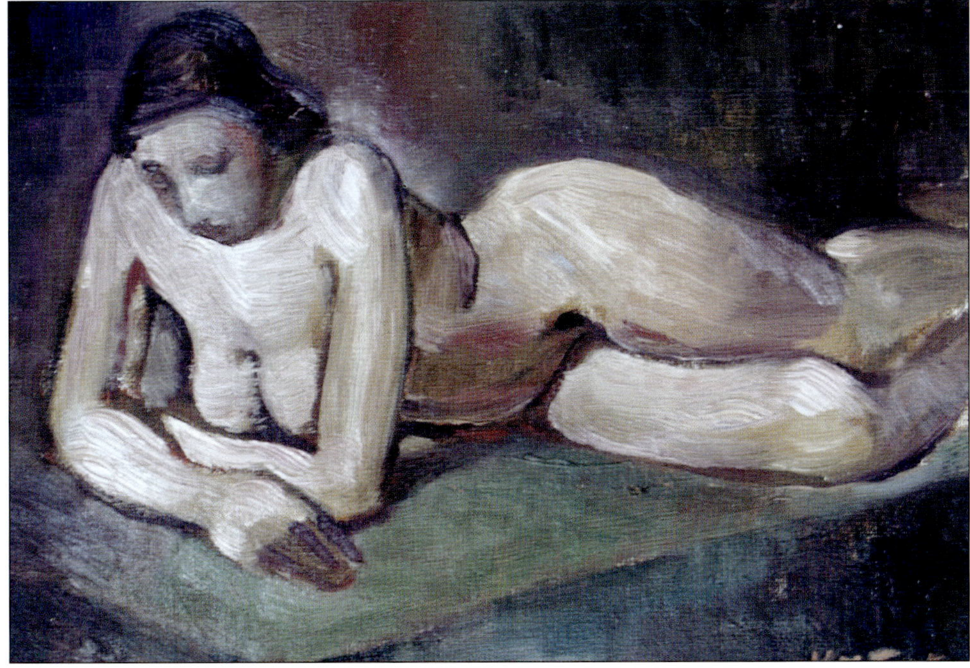

Blue Nude
oil on canvas
9.5x6.5 inches

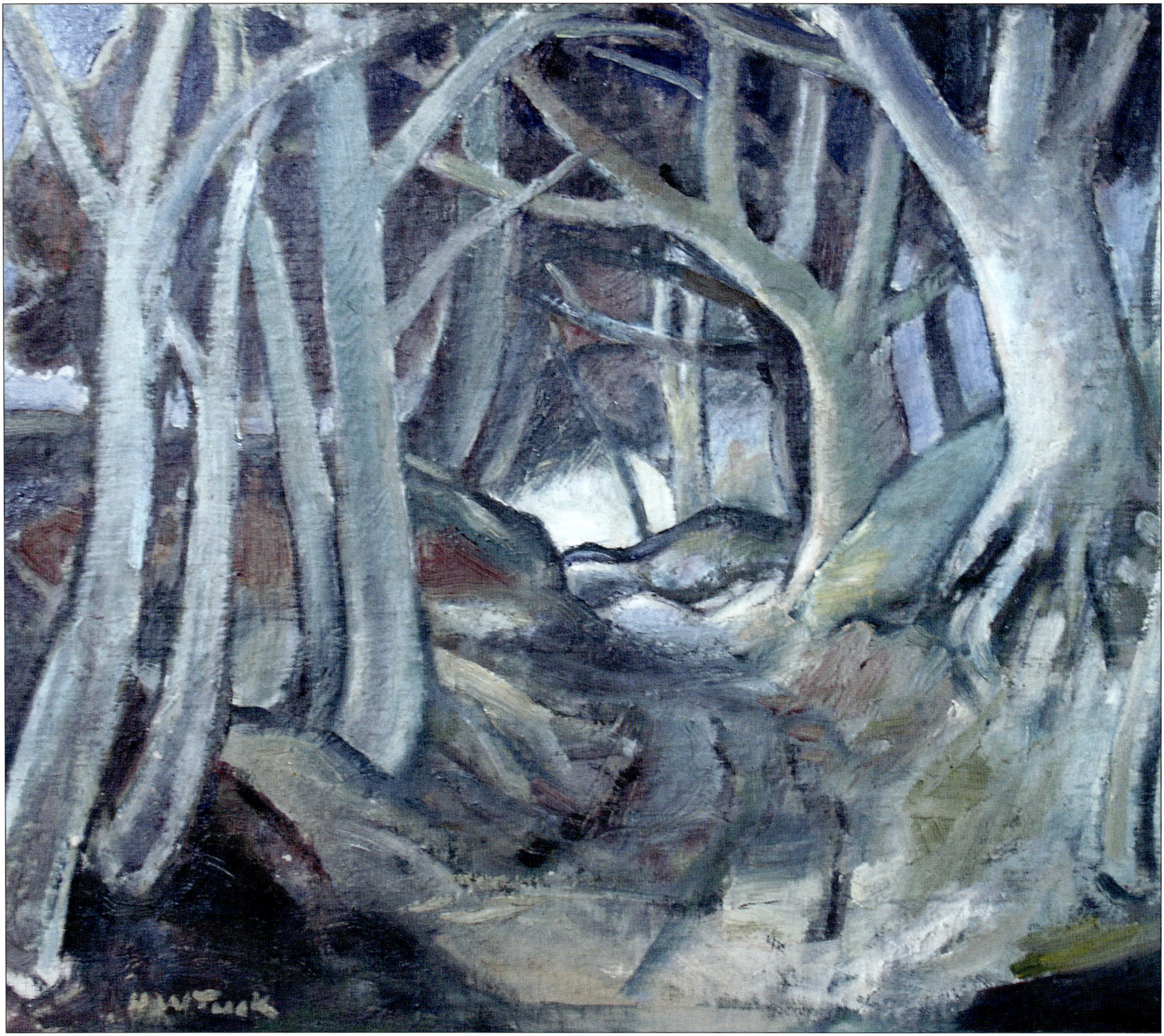

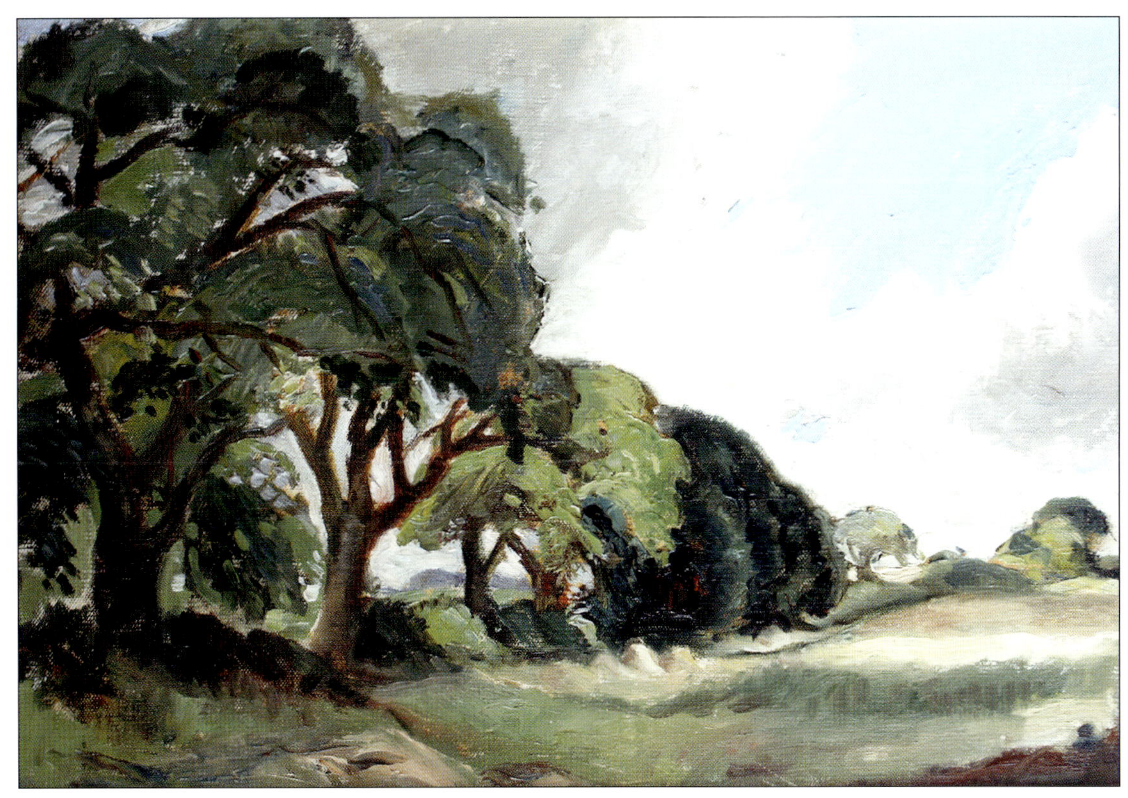

Hedgerow
oil on canvas
18x15 inches

Opposite:
Blue Lane
oil on canvas
18x15 inches

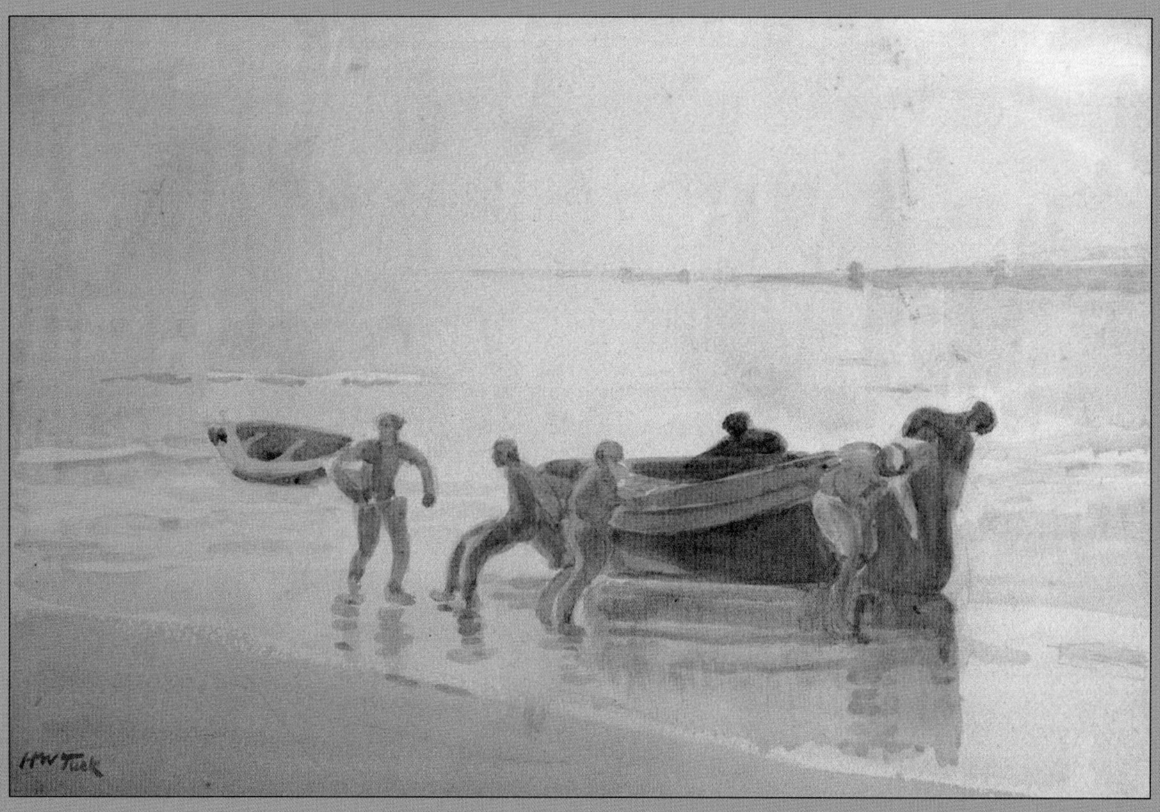

Landing the Shrimp Boat, Sheringham
watercolour
15x10 inches

Opposite:
Drifters off the Norfolk Coast
oil on canvas
12x10inches

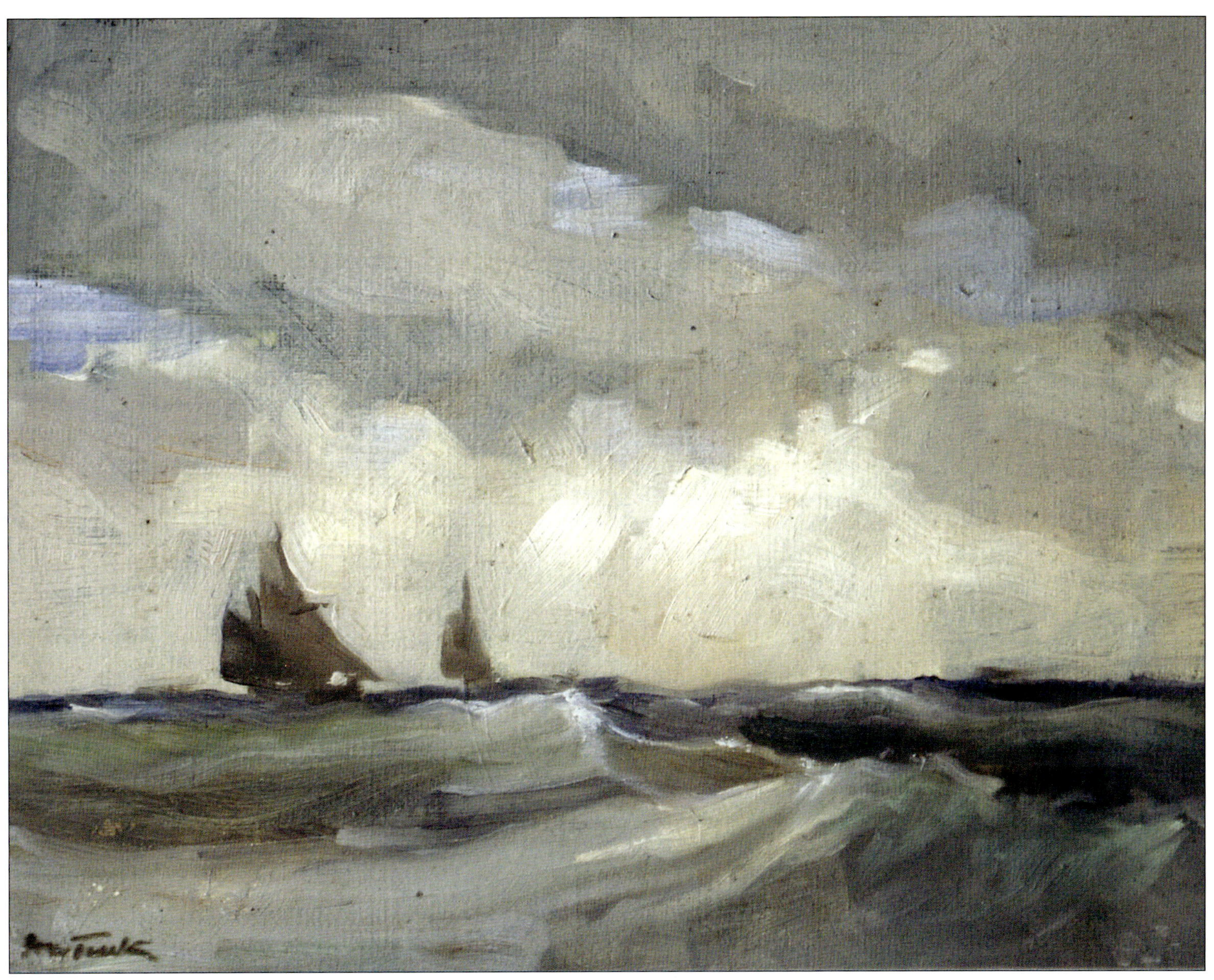

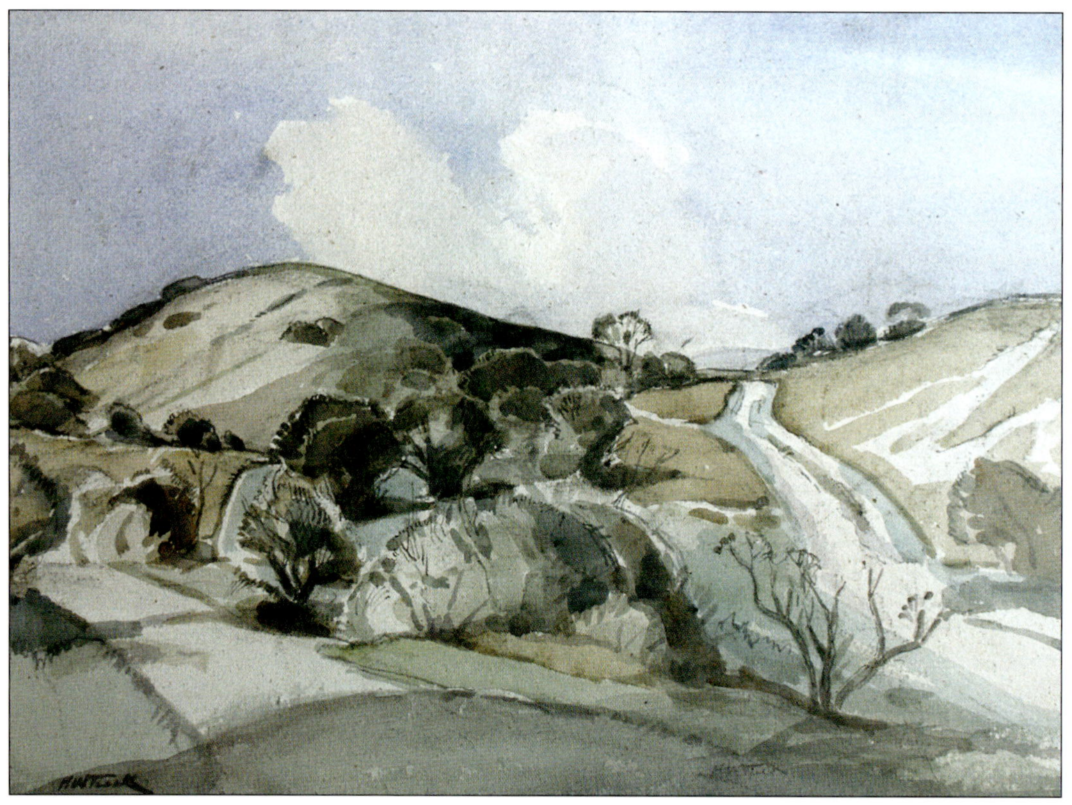

The Little Valley
watercolour
14x10 inches

Opposite:
A North Norfolk Farm
oil on canvas
22x16 inches

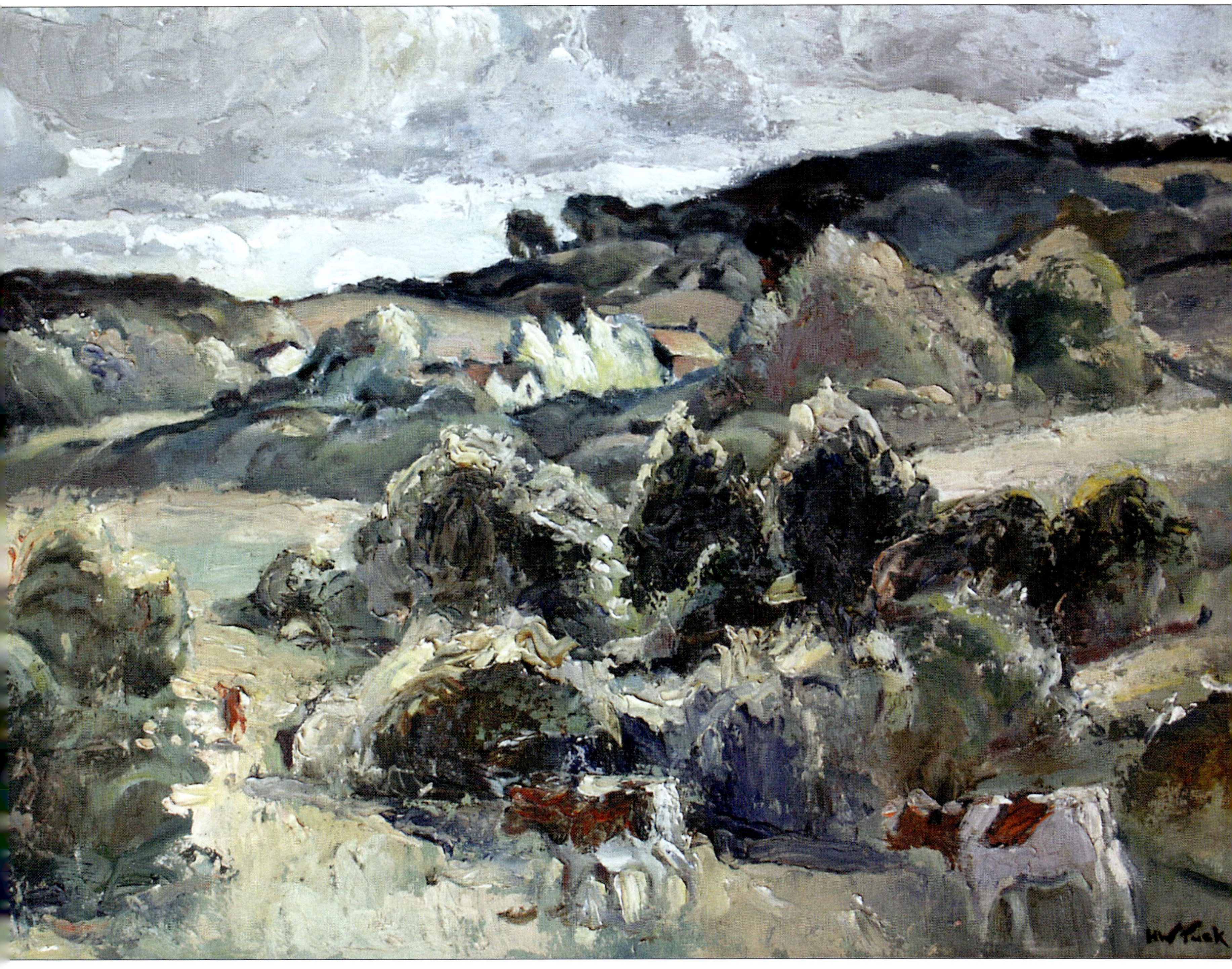

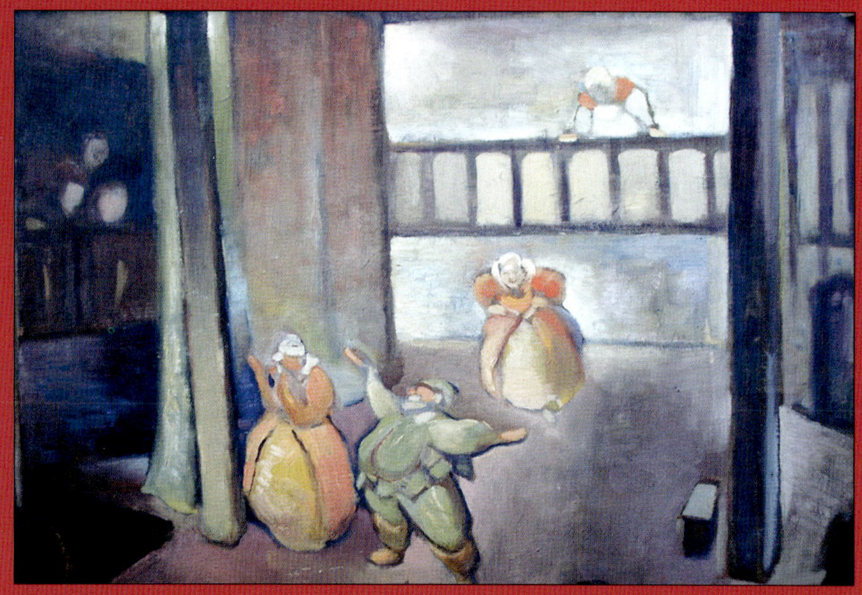

At the Maddermarket Theatre, Norwich
painted on verso of oil on canvas
14x10 inches

Opposite:
The Maddermarket Theatre, Norwich
oil on canvas
23x22 inches

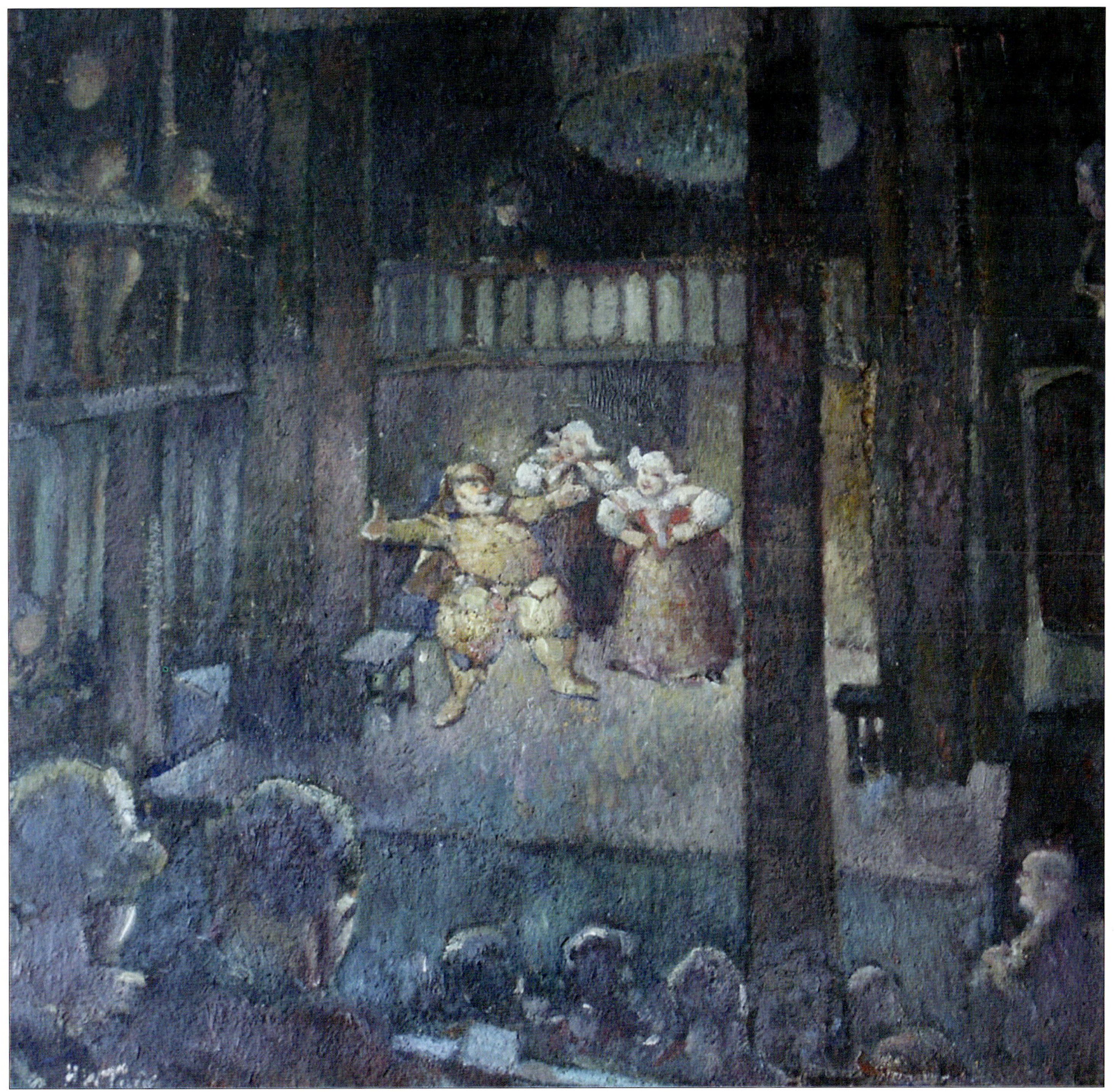

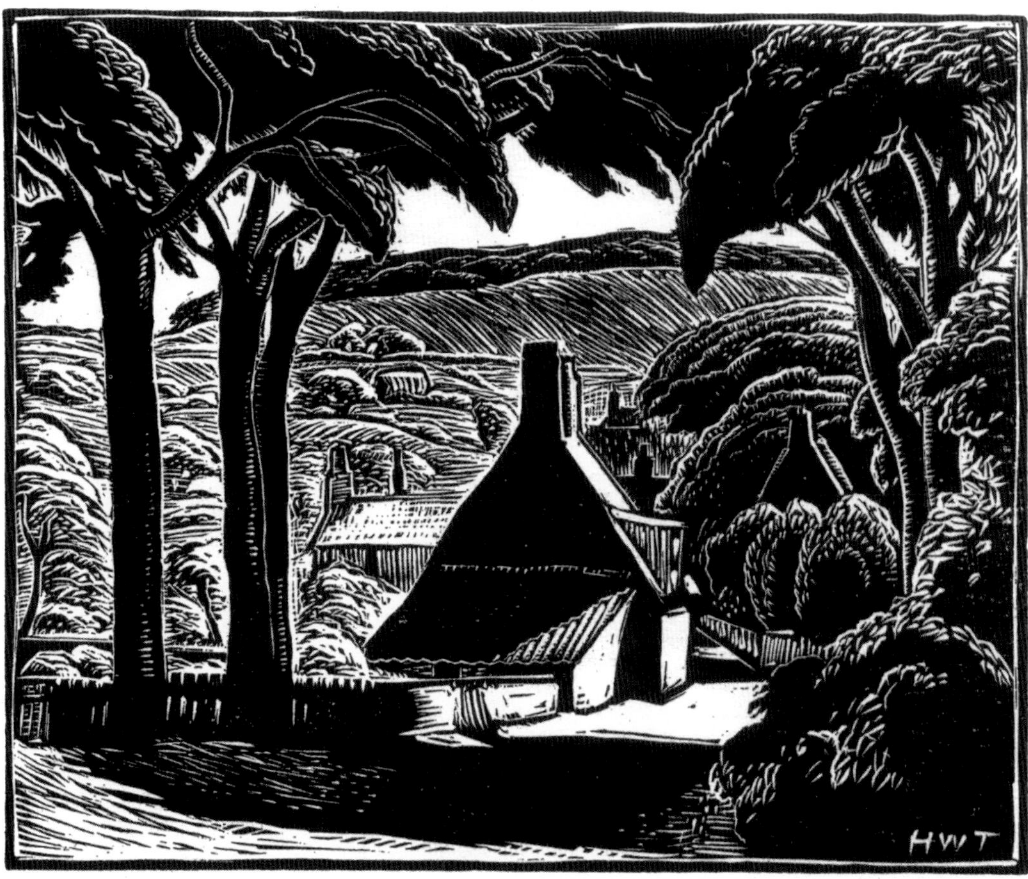

The Farm
woodcut

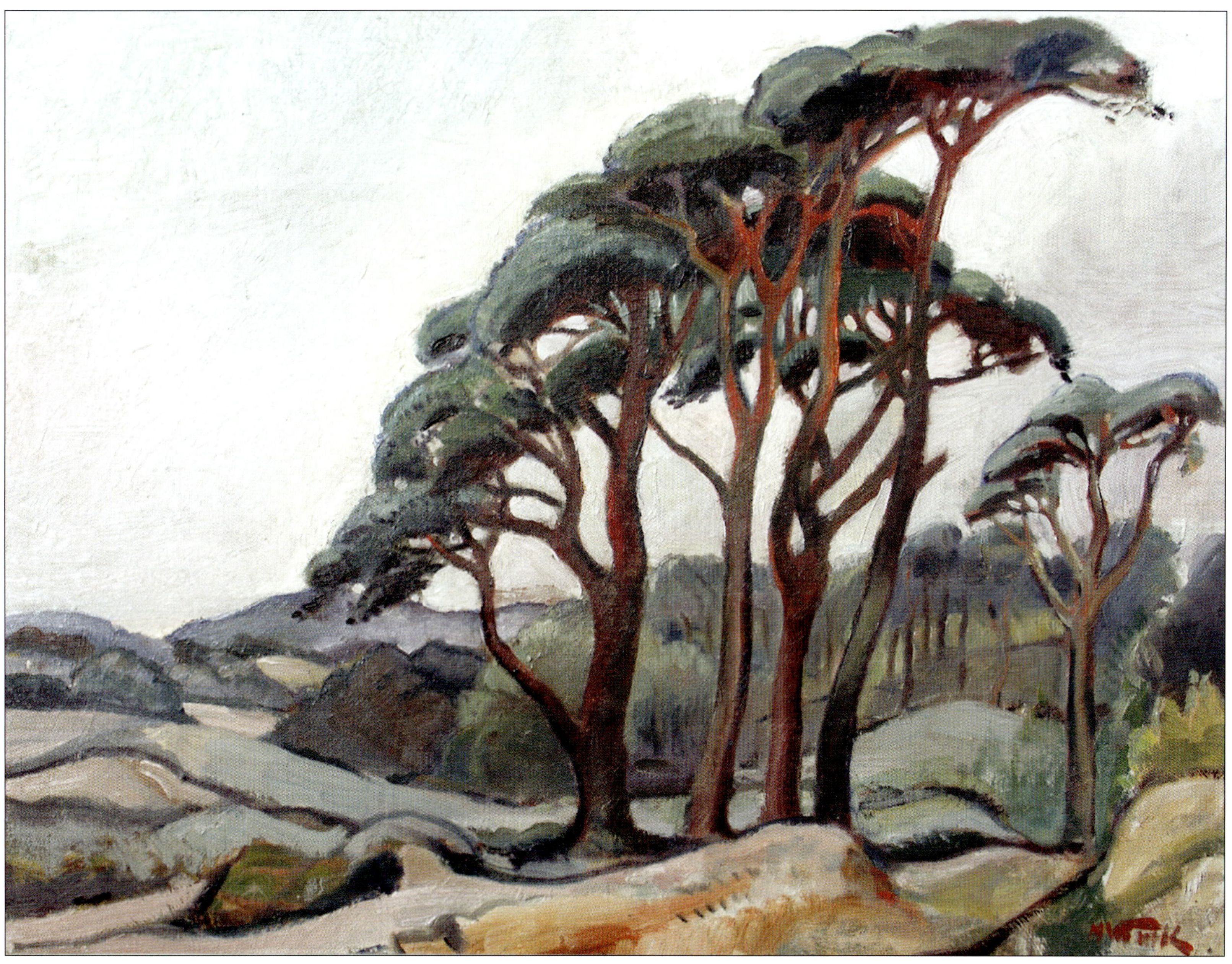

Five Pines, near Holt
oil on canvas
14x10 inches

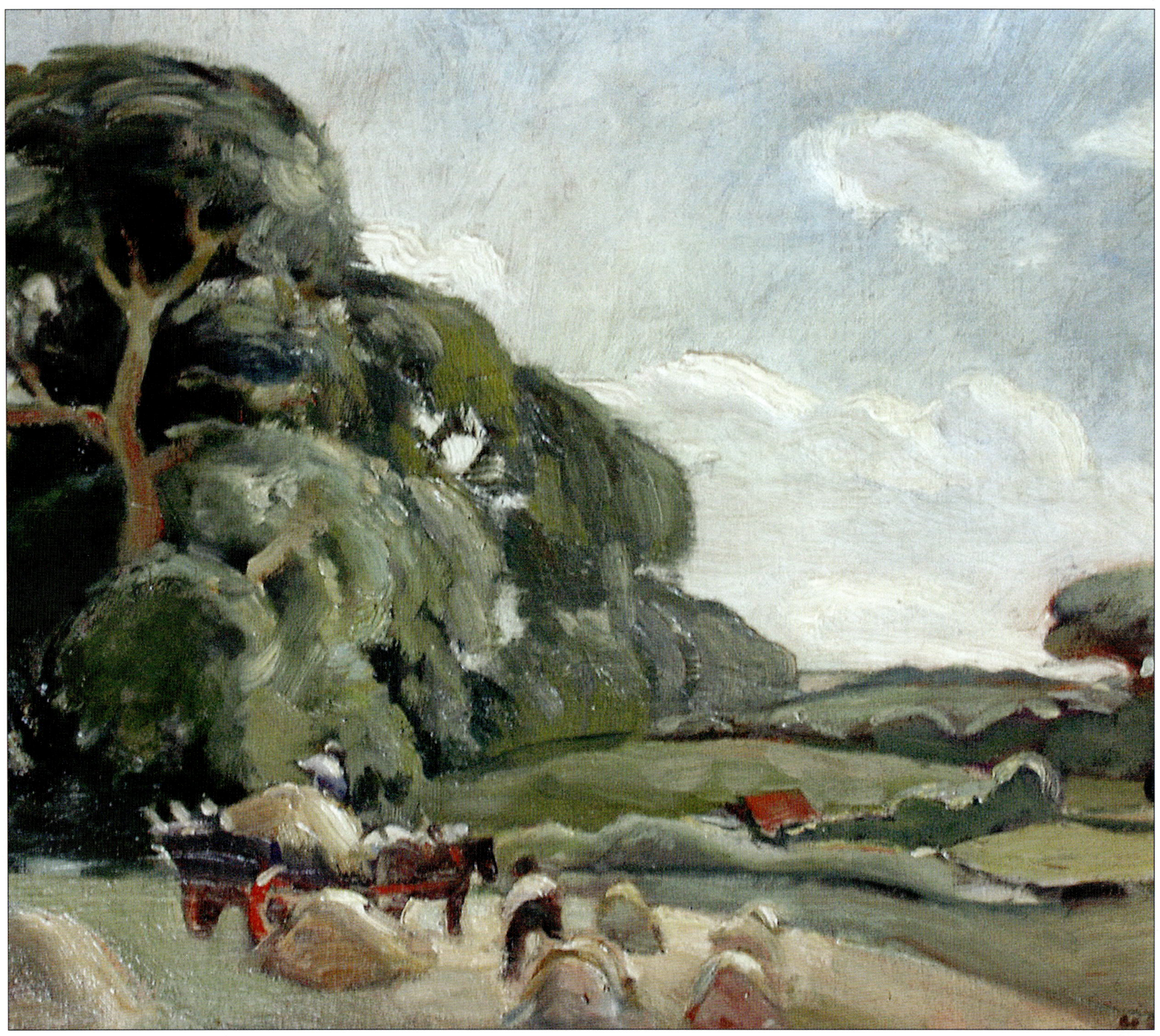

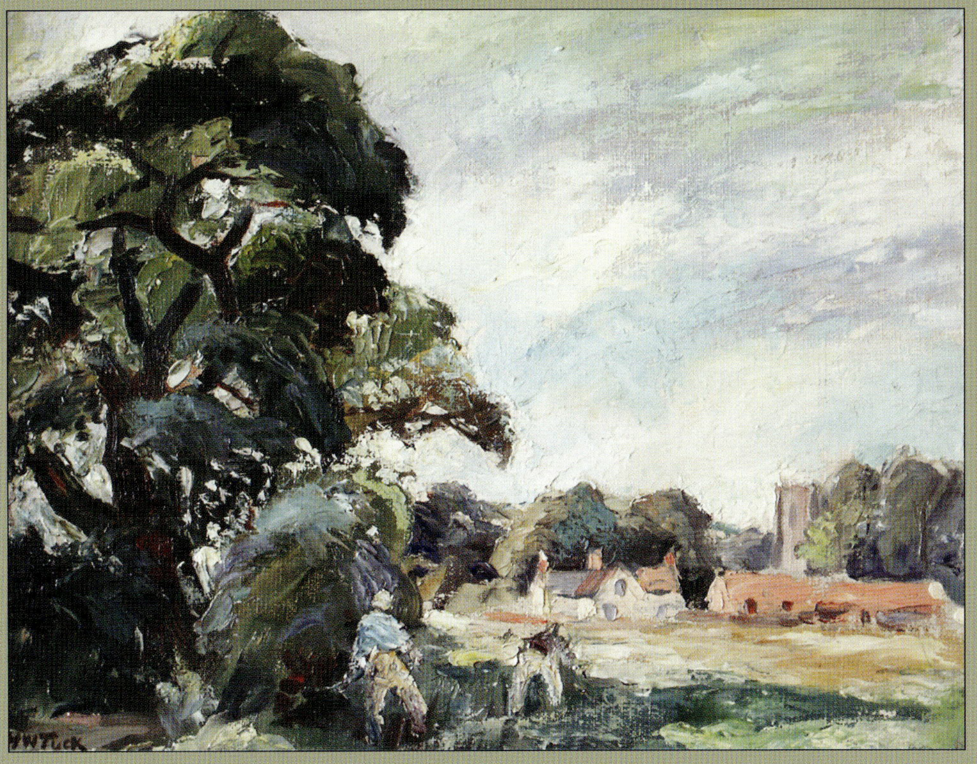

The Haymakers
oil on canvas
18x15 inches

Opposite:
Haymaking on a Norfolk Farm
oil on canvas
13.5x9.5 inches

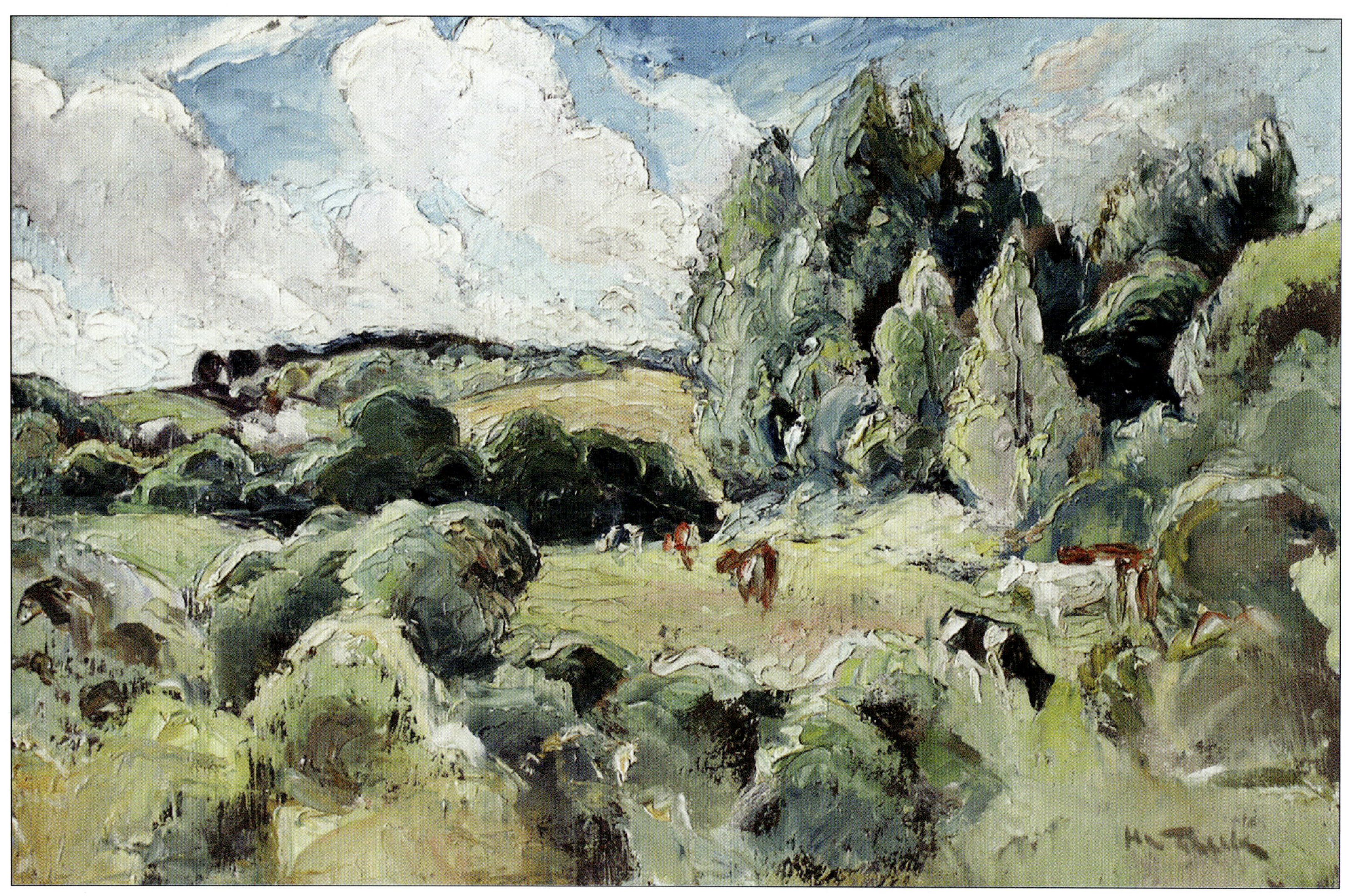

Milking Time on a Norfolk Farm
oil on canvas
22.5x14.5 inches

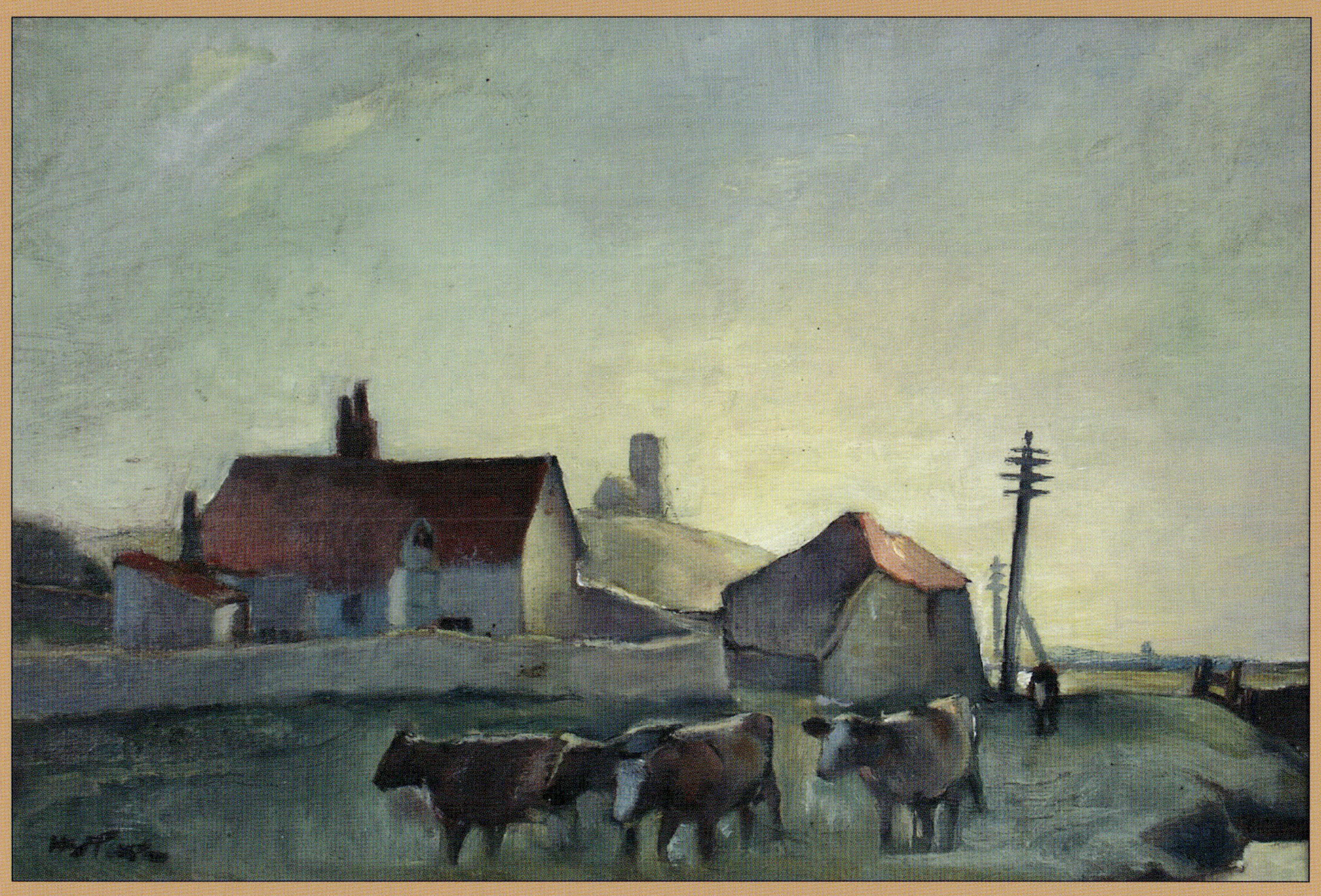

Eventide at Salthouse, Norfolk
oil on canvas
15.5x9.5 inches

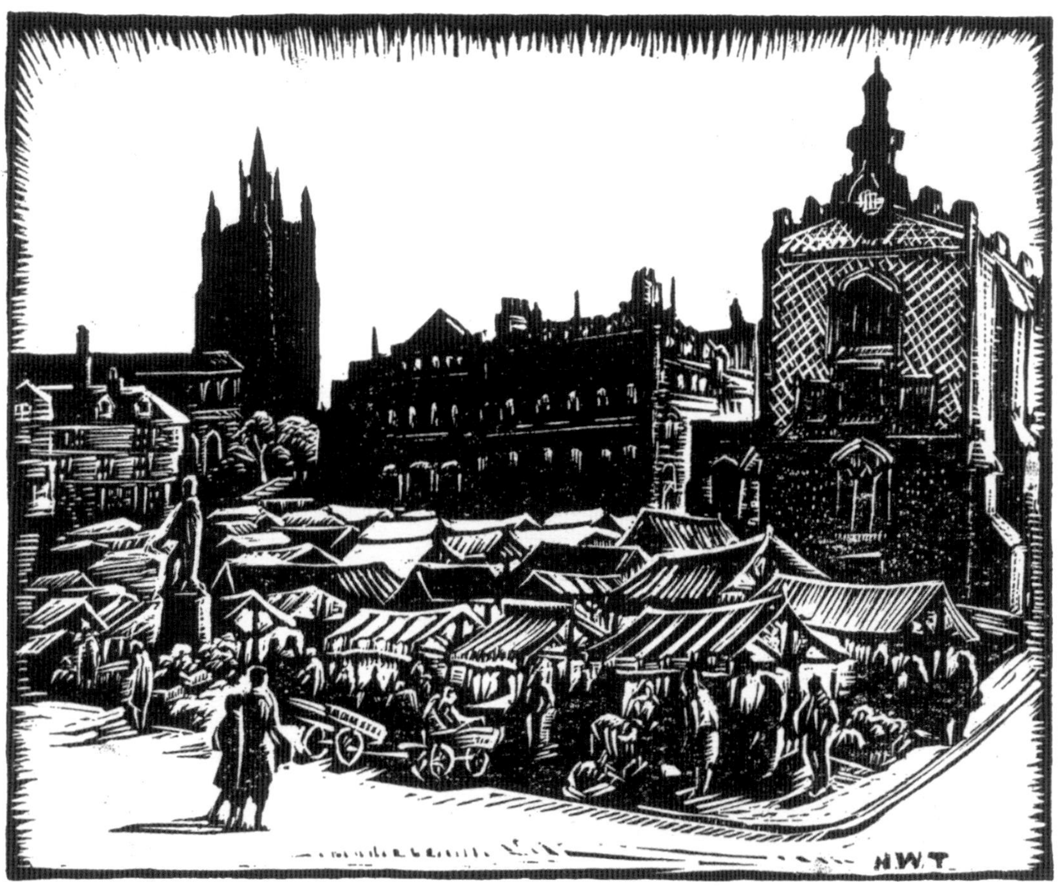

The Market, Norwich
woodcut

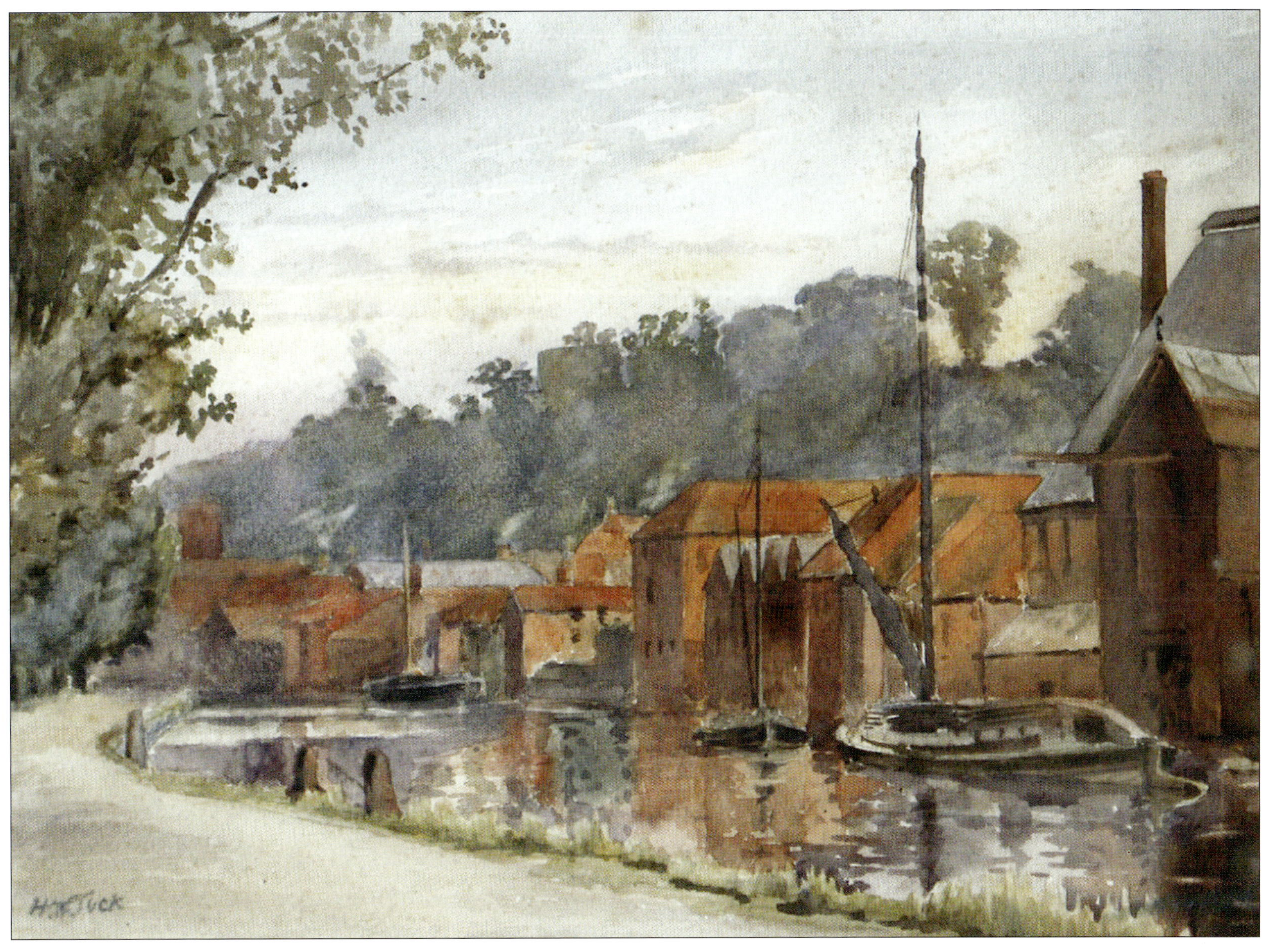

On the Wensum, Norwich
(looking towards the Colman's Mustard factory)
watercolour
11.5x10 inches

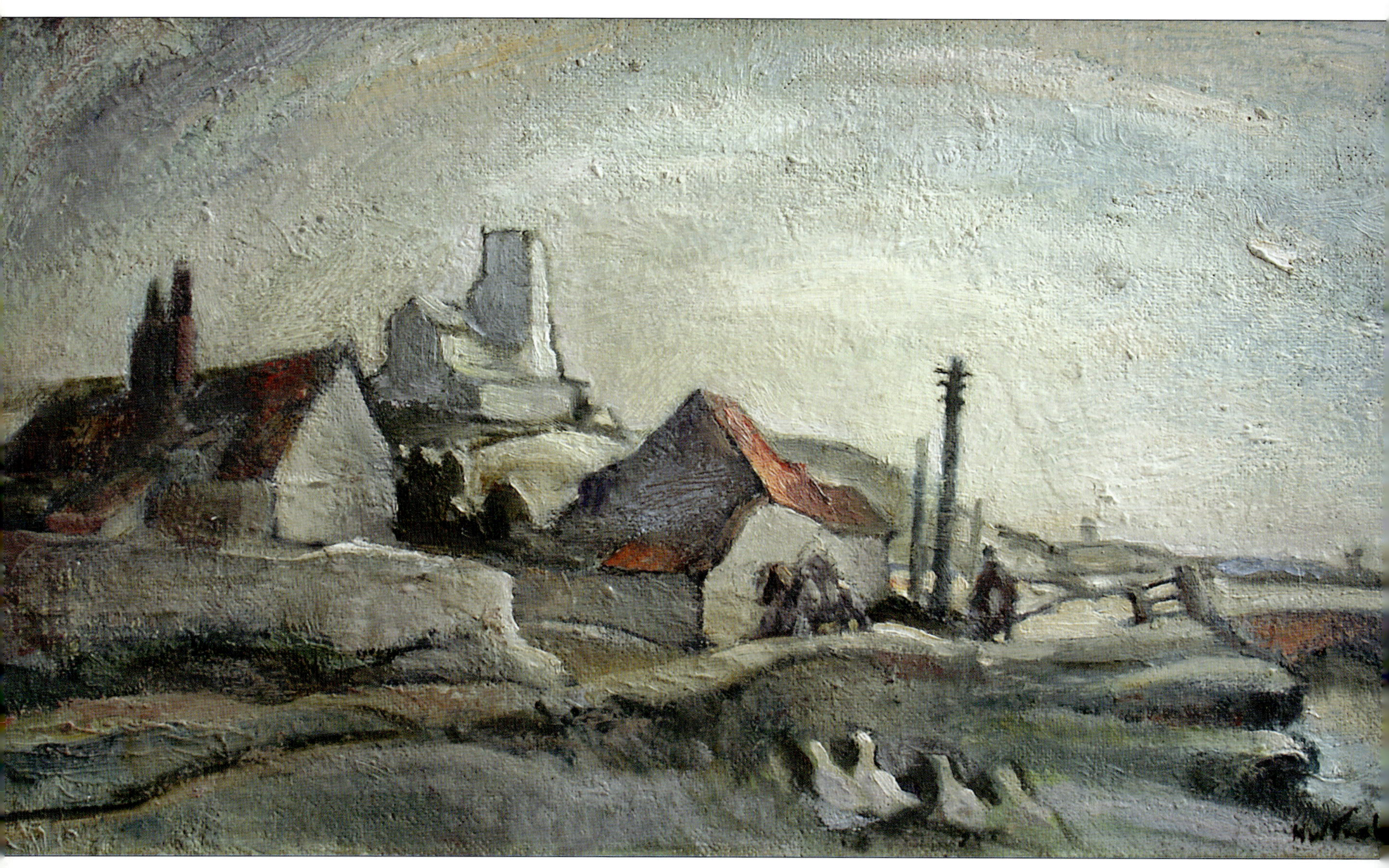

Salthouse Duckpond (detail)
oil on canvas
19.5x11 inches

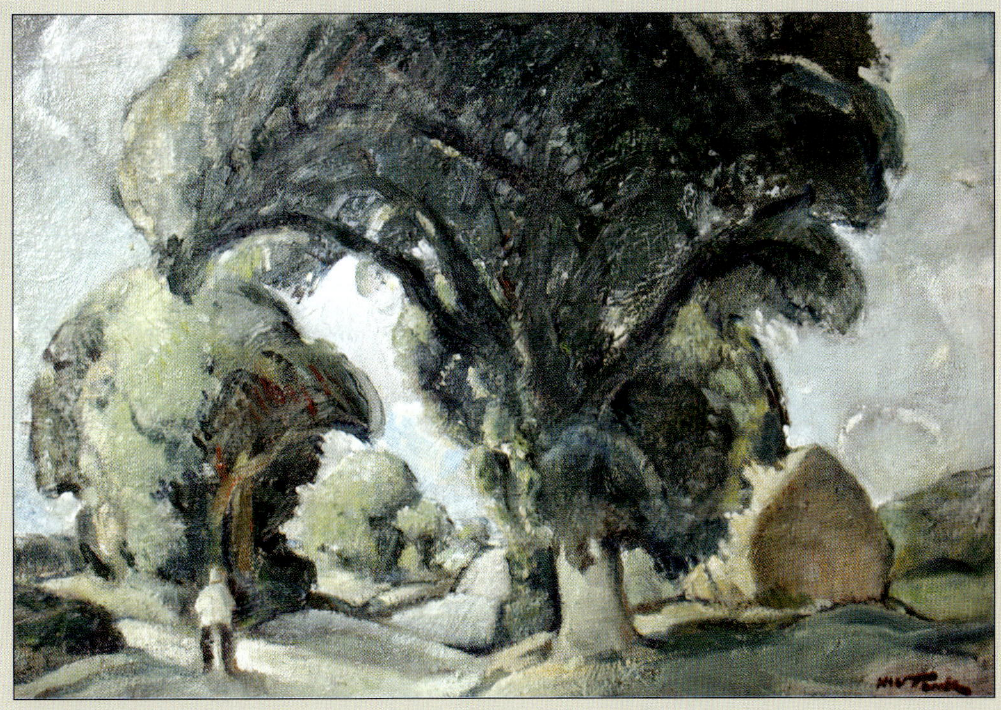

Country Road
oil on canvas
15x11 inches

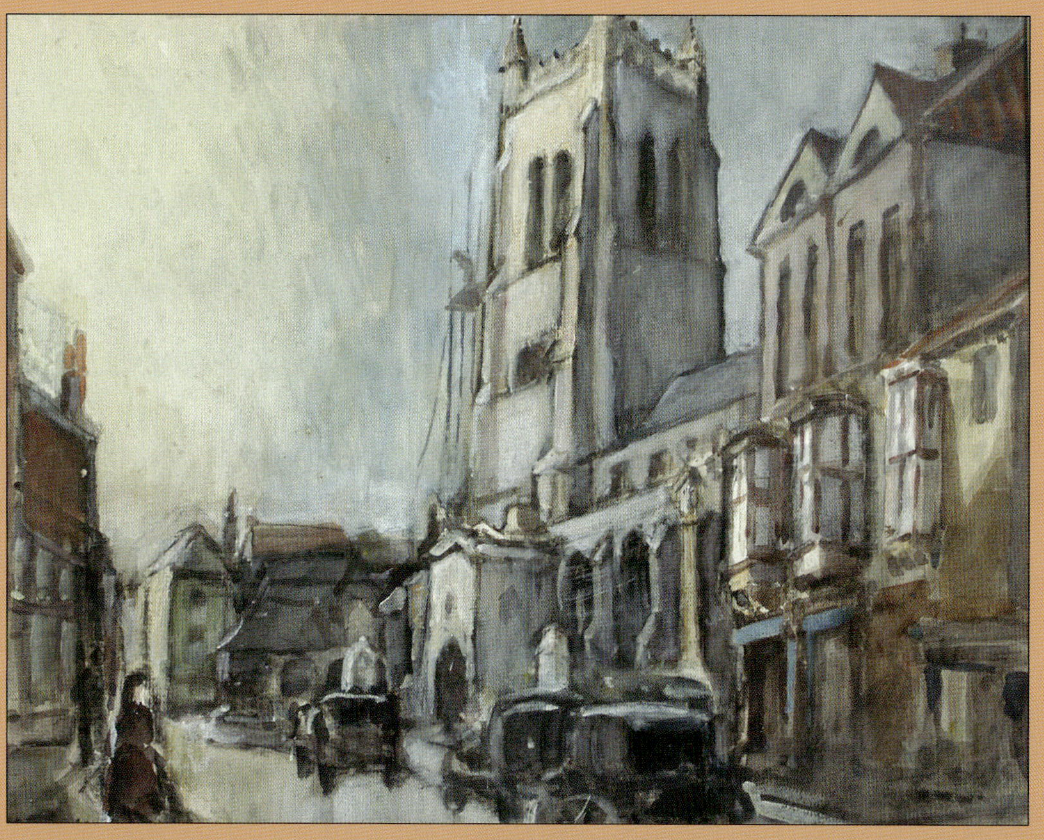

A Rainy Day
watercolour
14.5x11.5 inches

Opposite:
The Roadsweepers
ink wash
12x10 inches

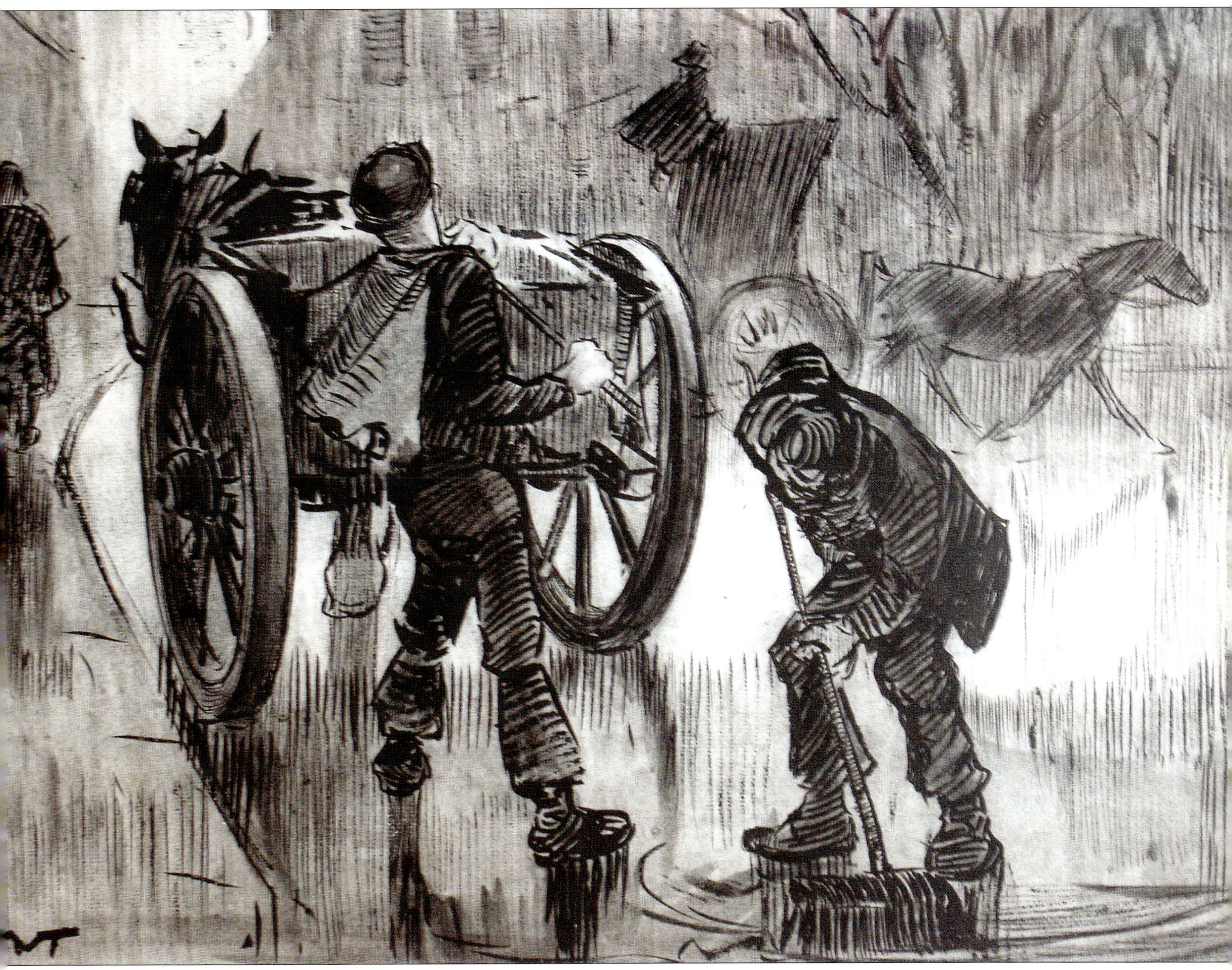

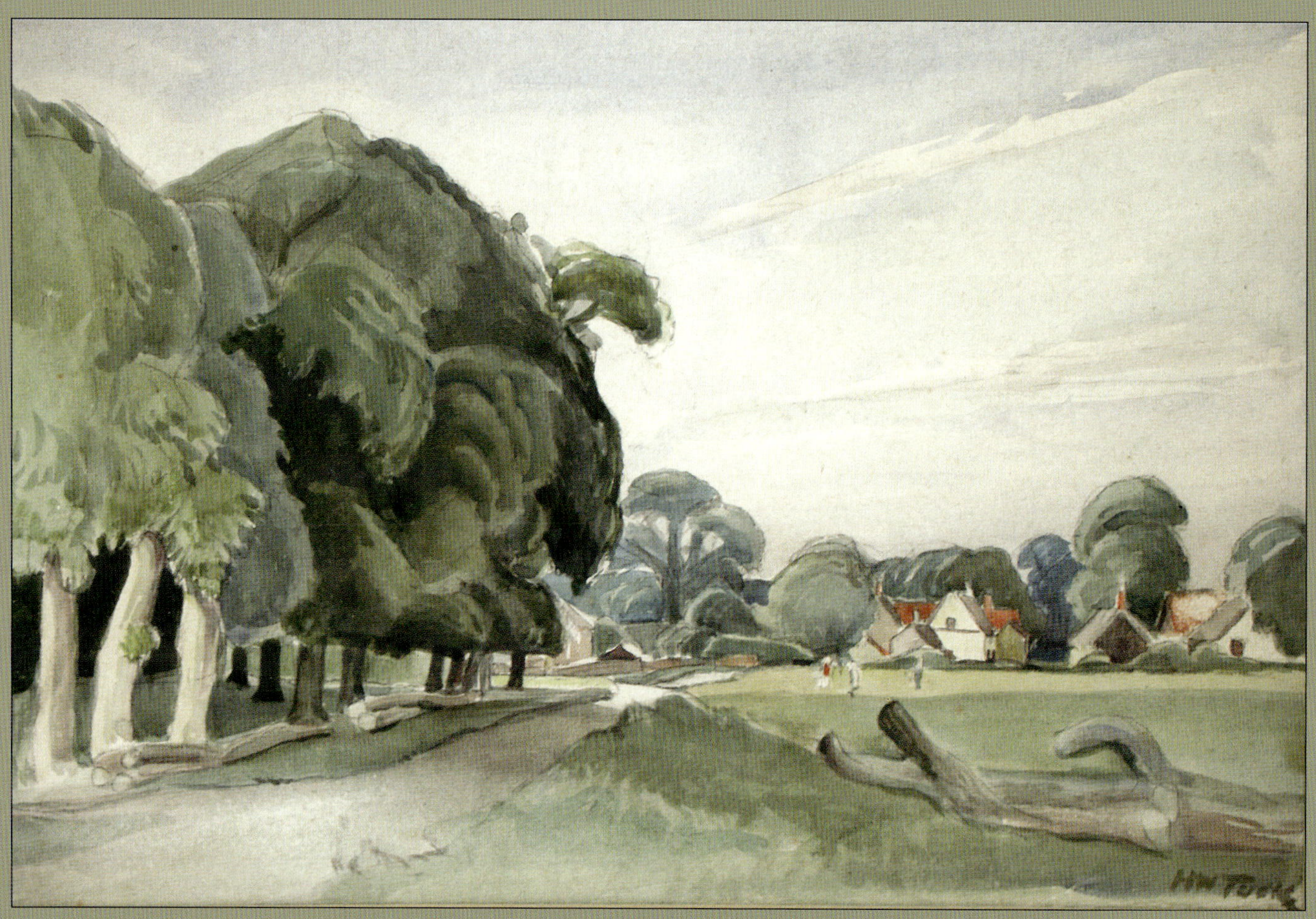

The Village Green
watercolour
14.5x11.5 inches

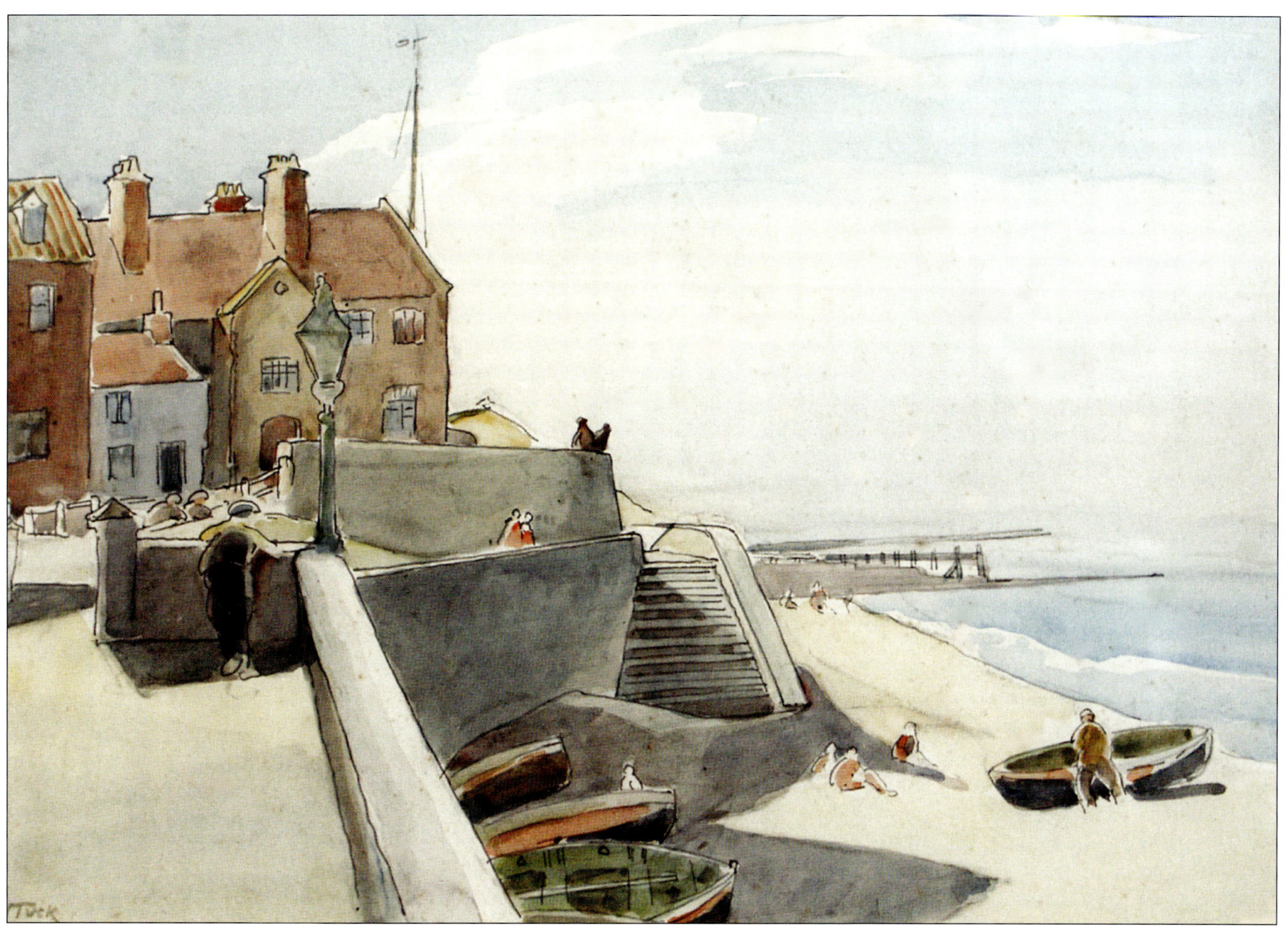

Beach Scene II.
The western end of the Gangway, Sheringham
watercolour
10x13.5 inches

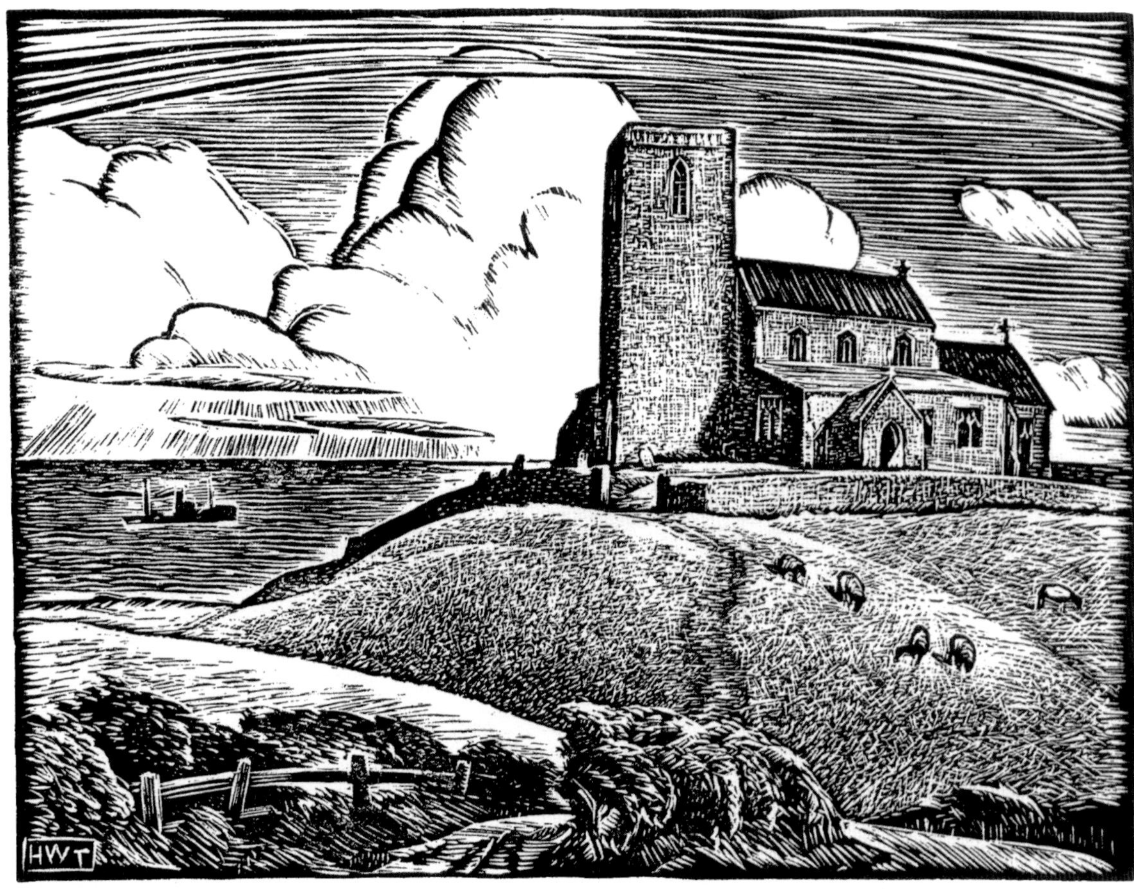

Beeston Church, Norfolk
woodcut

Opposite:
Rain At Sea
The view towards Beeston Bump
oil on canvas
13.5x10 inches

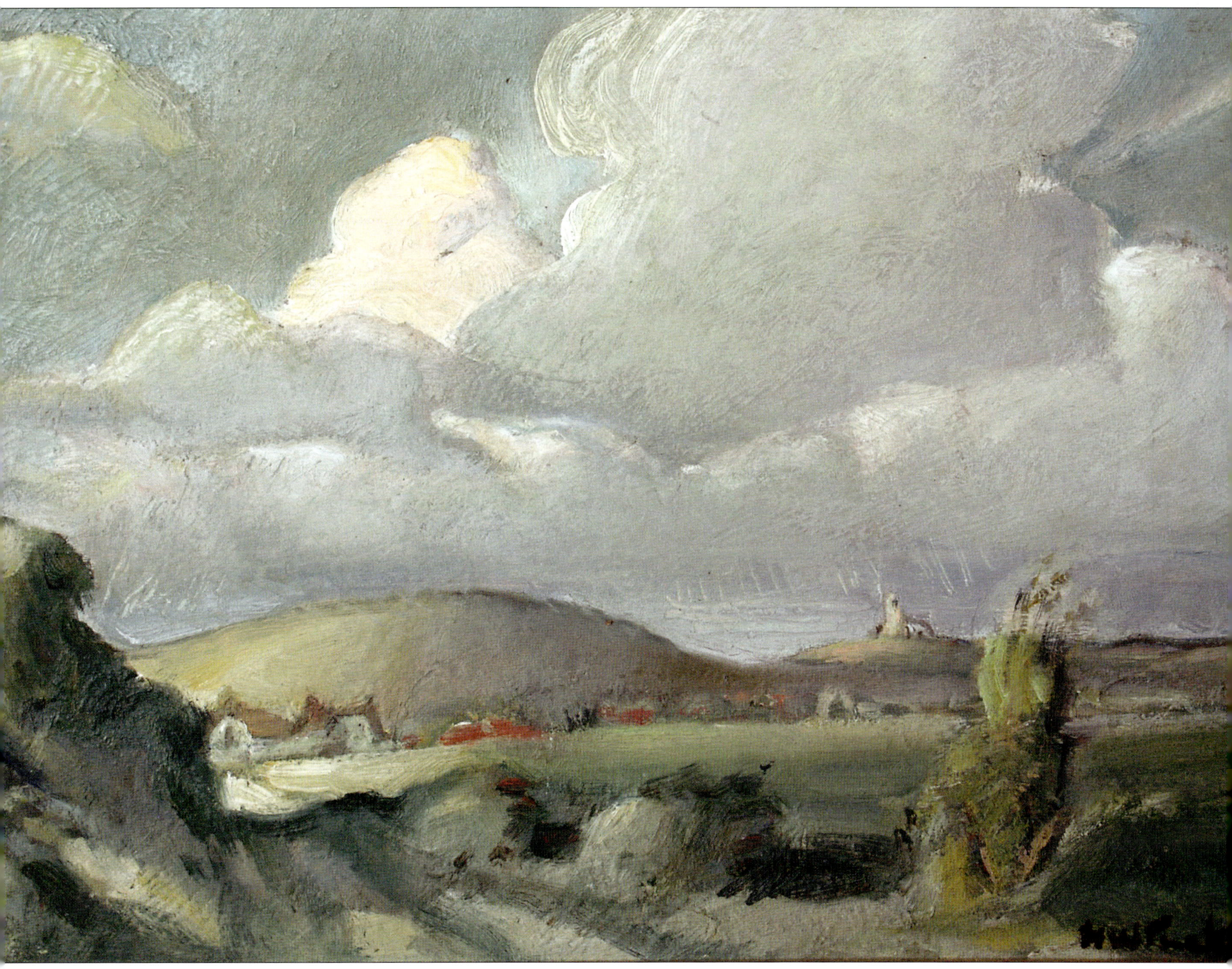

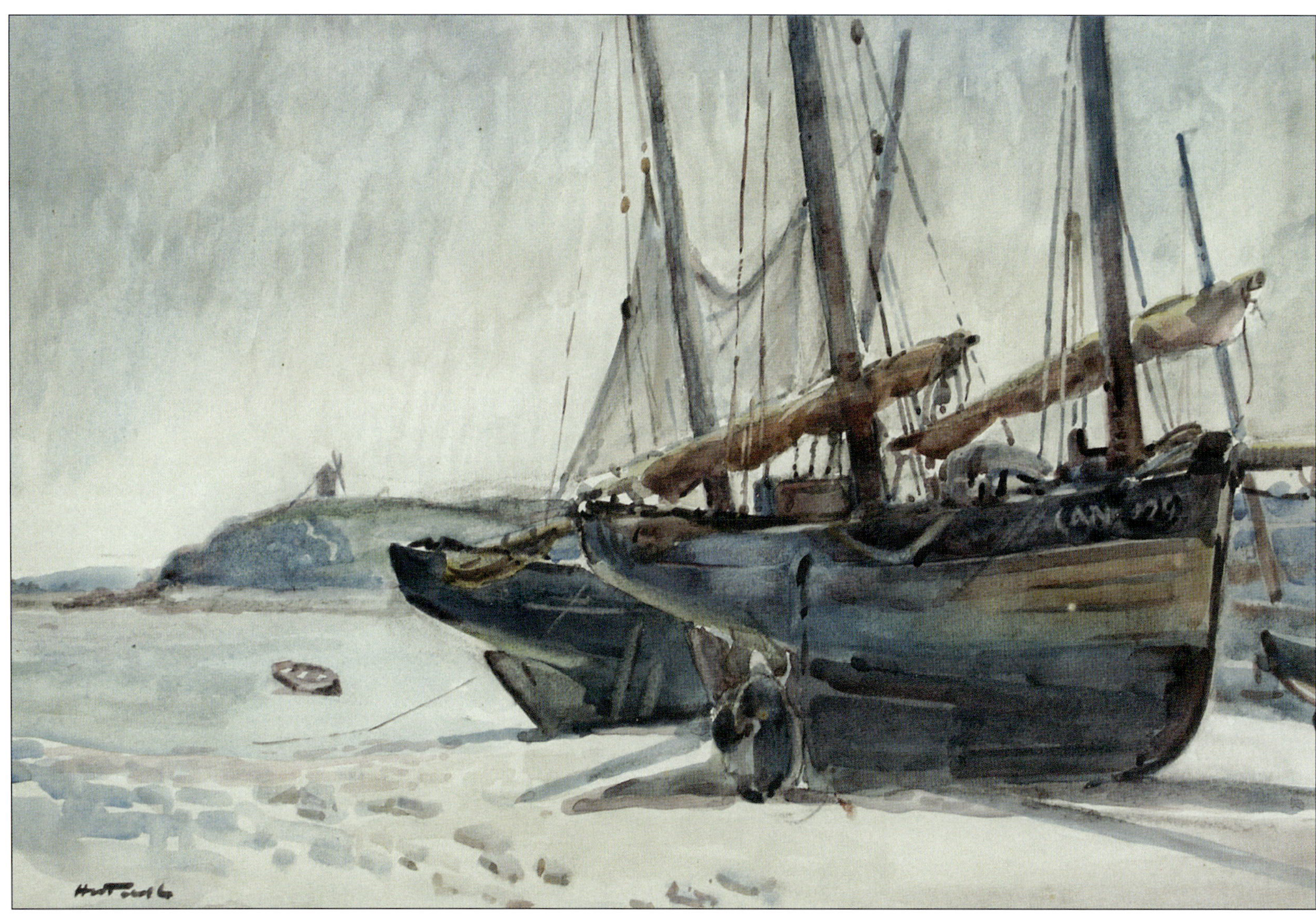

Hauled Ashore.
Drifters on a Norfolk Beach
watercolour
15x10 inches

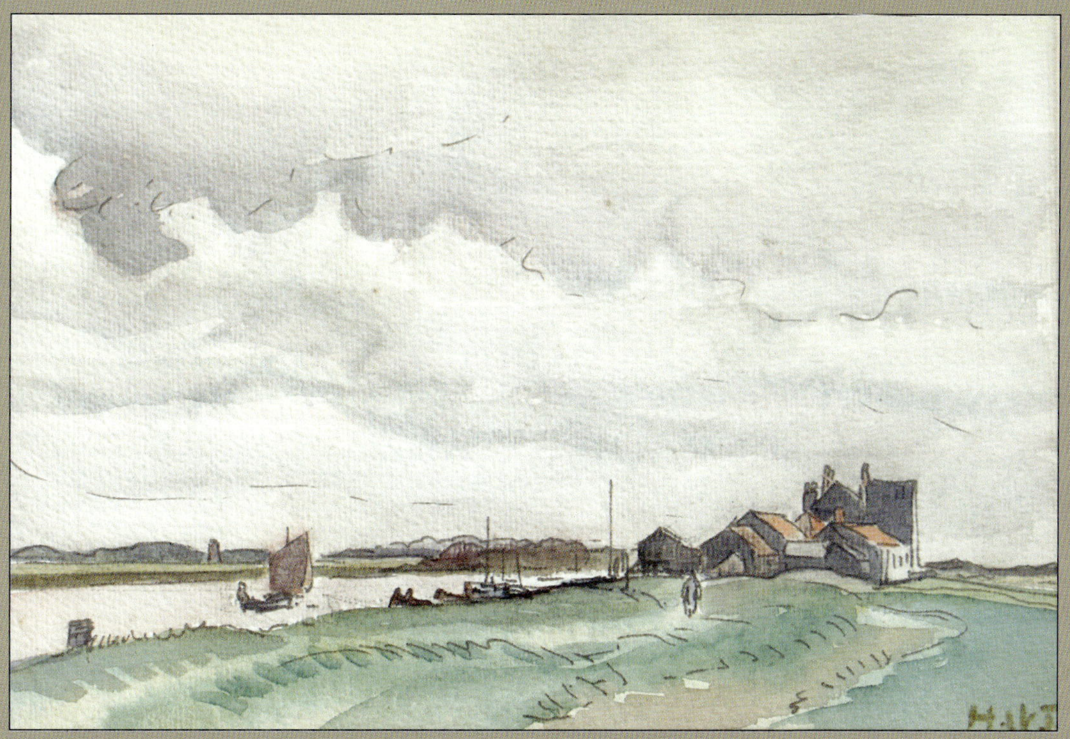

Broadland
watercolour
7.5x10.5 inches

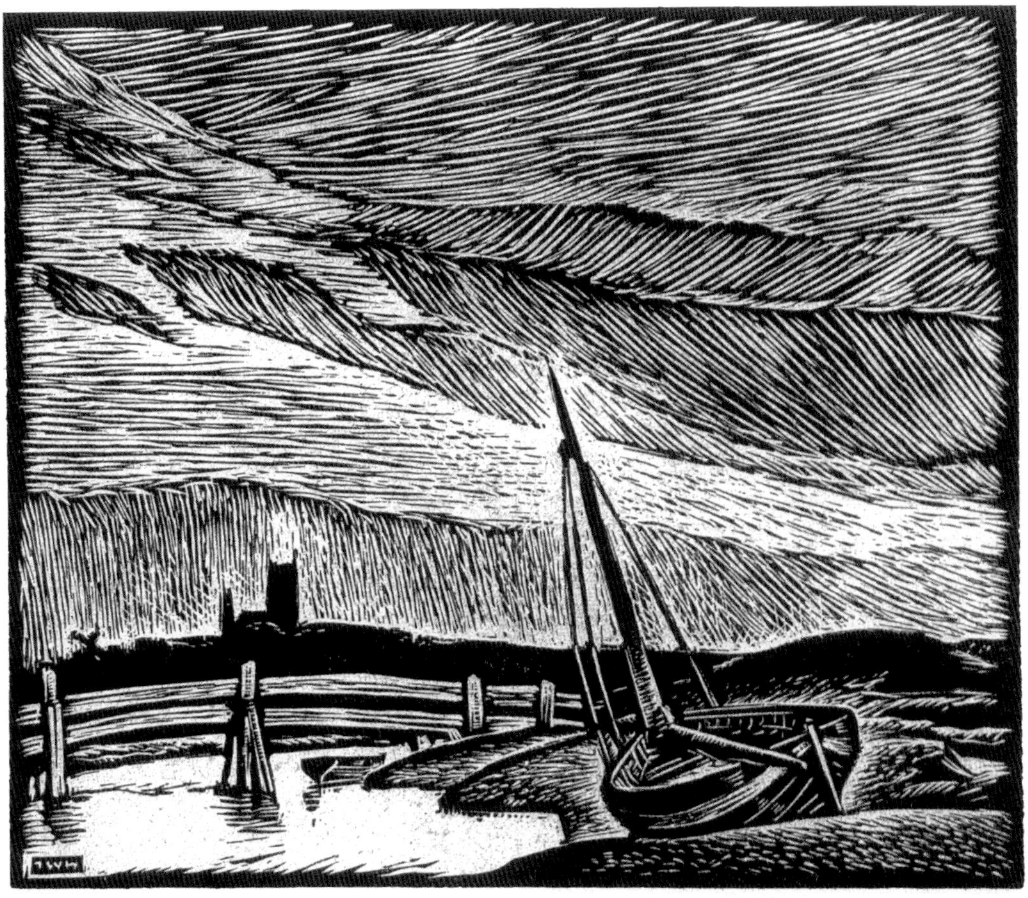

Morston
woodcut

Opposite:
Morston, towards Blakeney
watercolour
14x10 inches

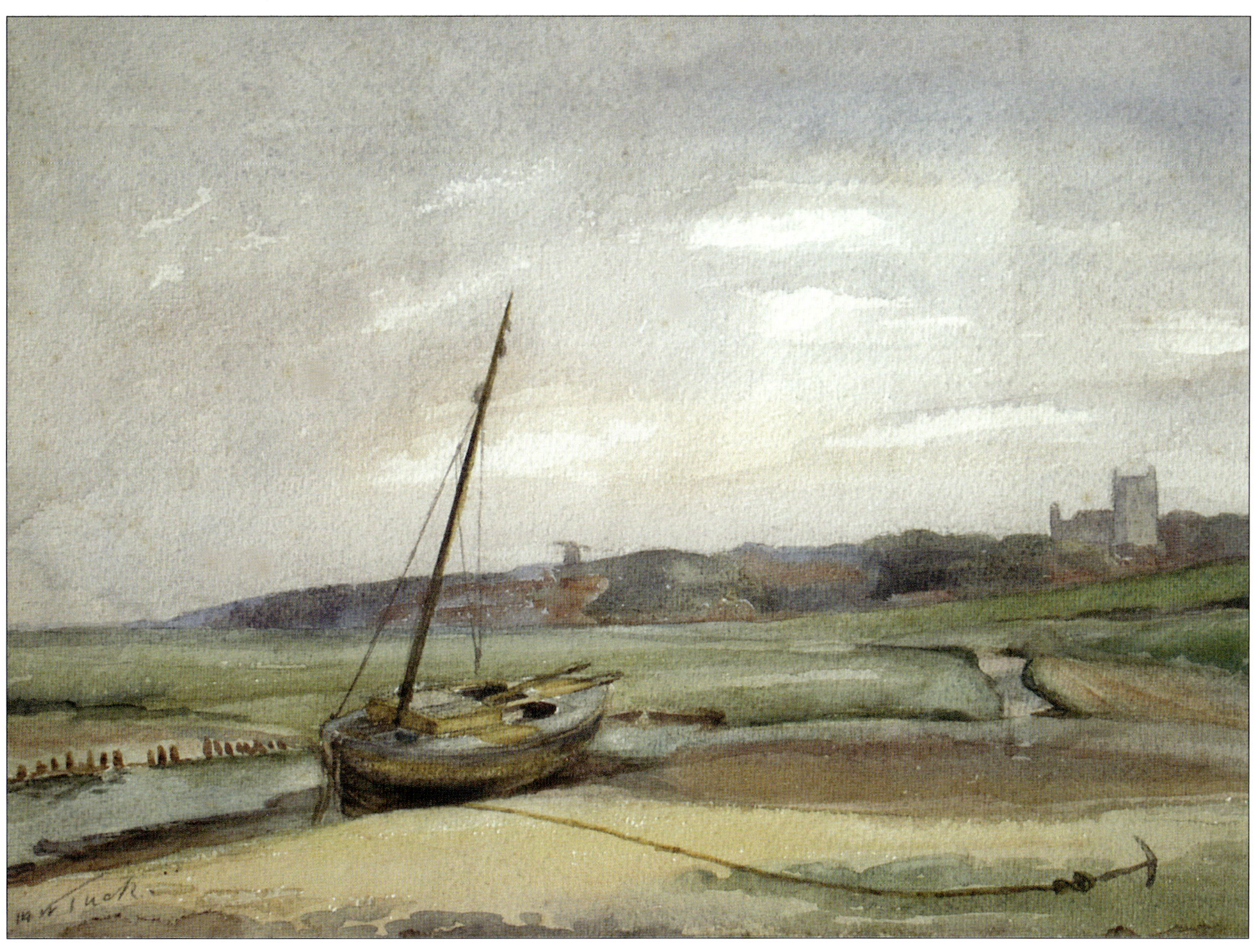

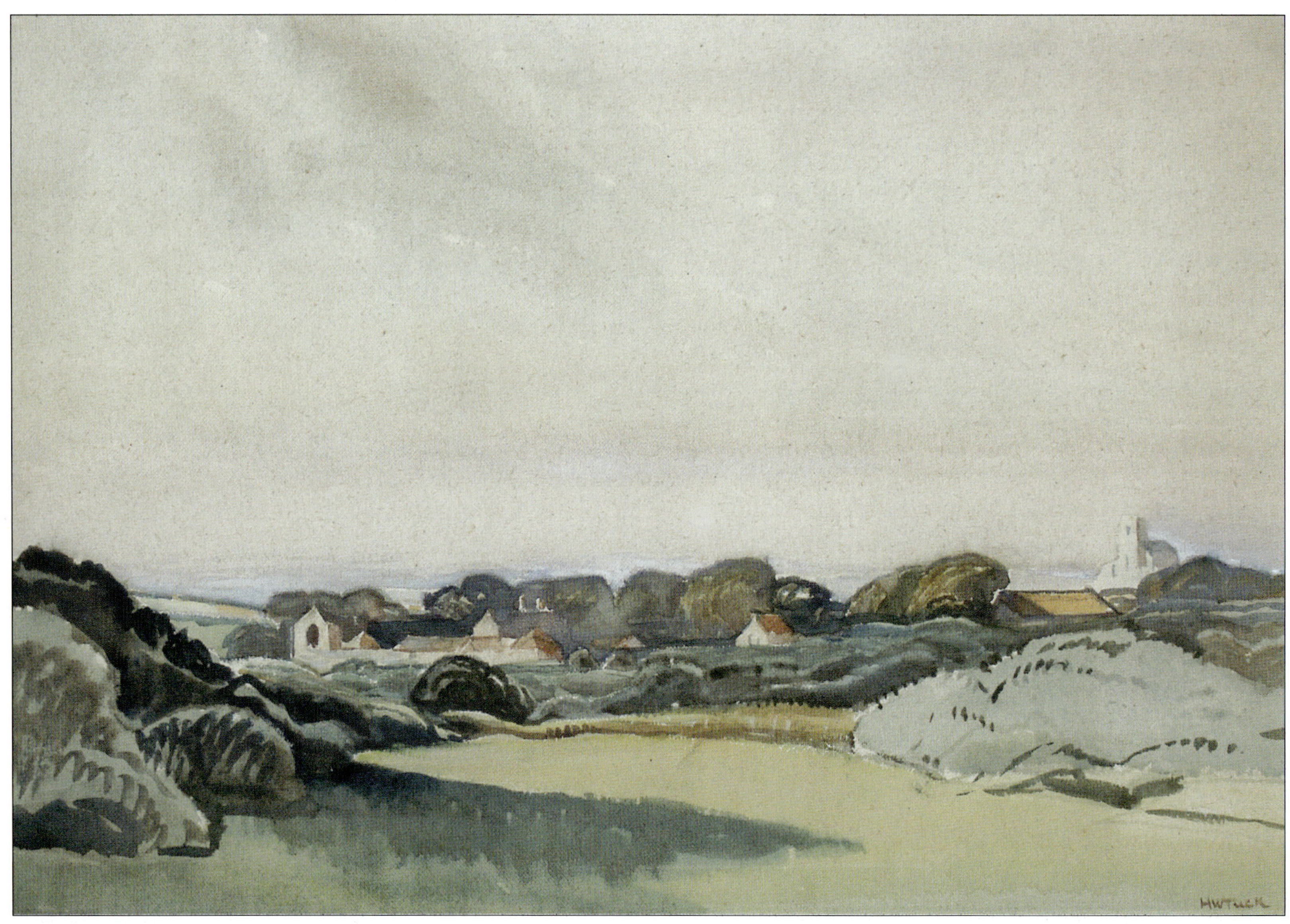

To the Distant Sea
watercolour
19x13.5 inches

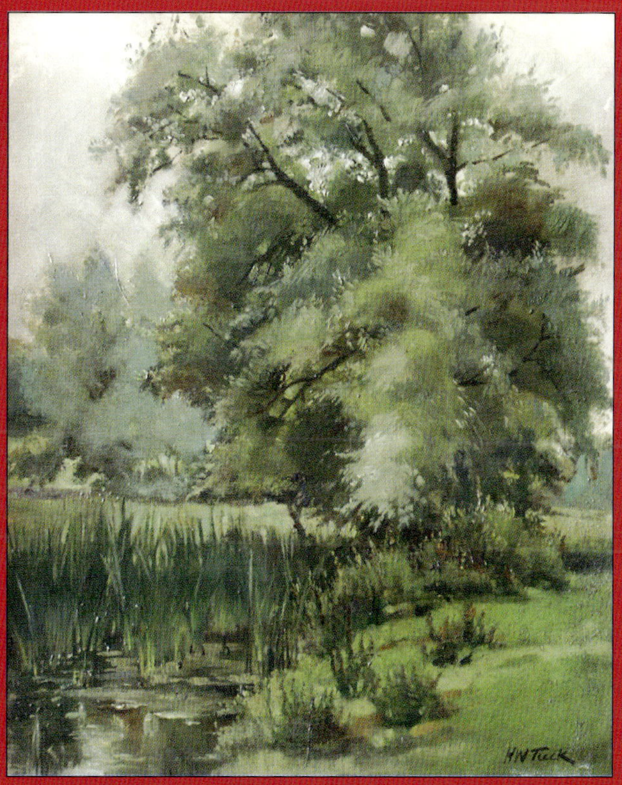

The Iris Pond
oil on canvas
14x11 inches

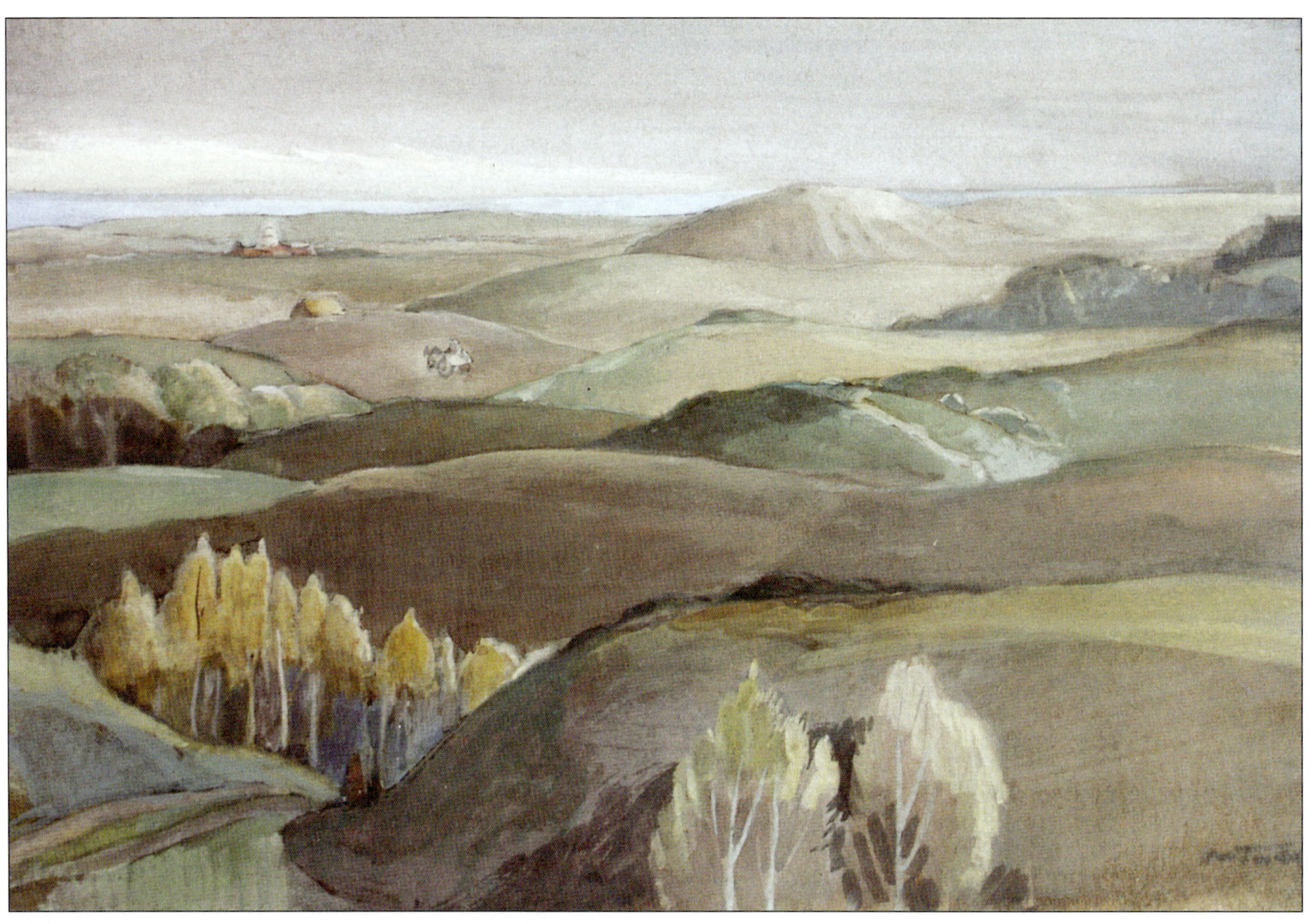

Above the Farmland
watercolour
15x10.5 inches

Opposite:
Rabbit Wood
watercolour
14x9.5 inches

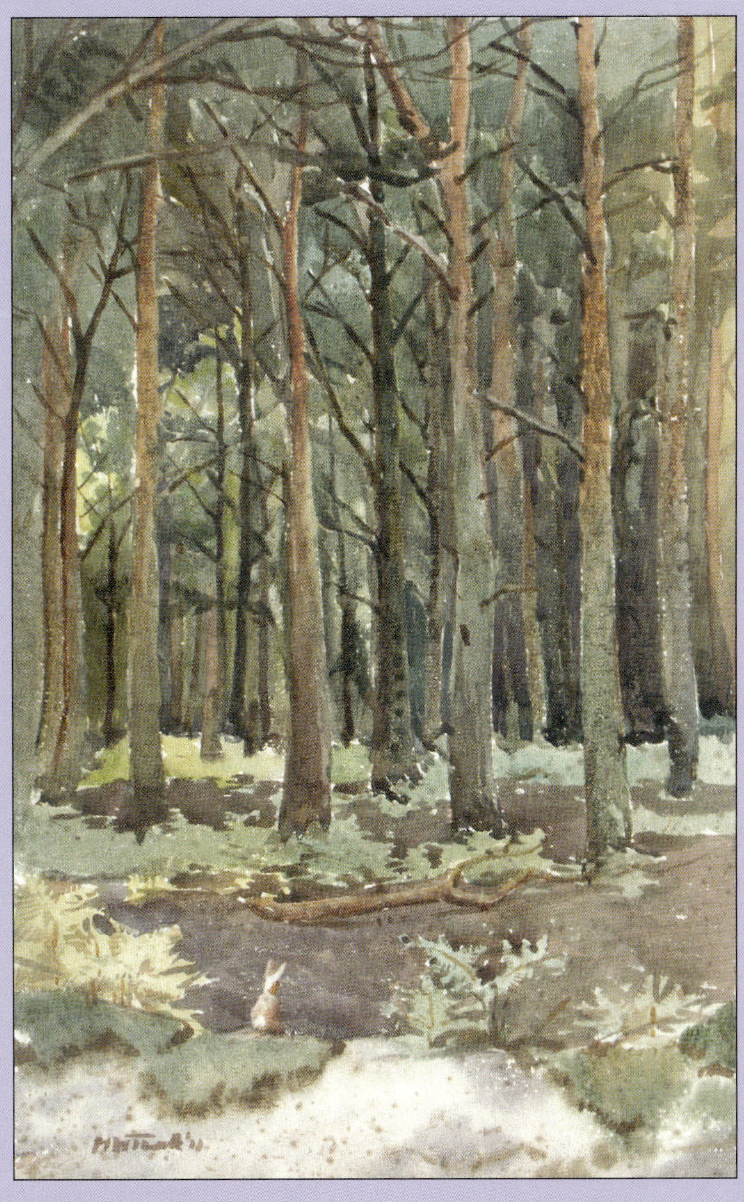

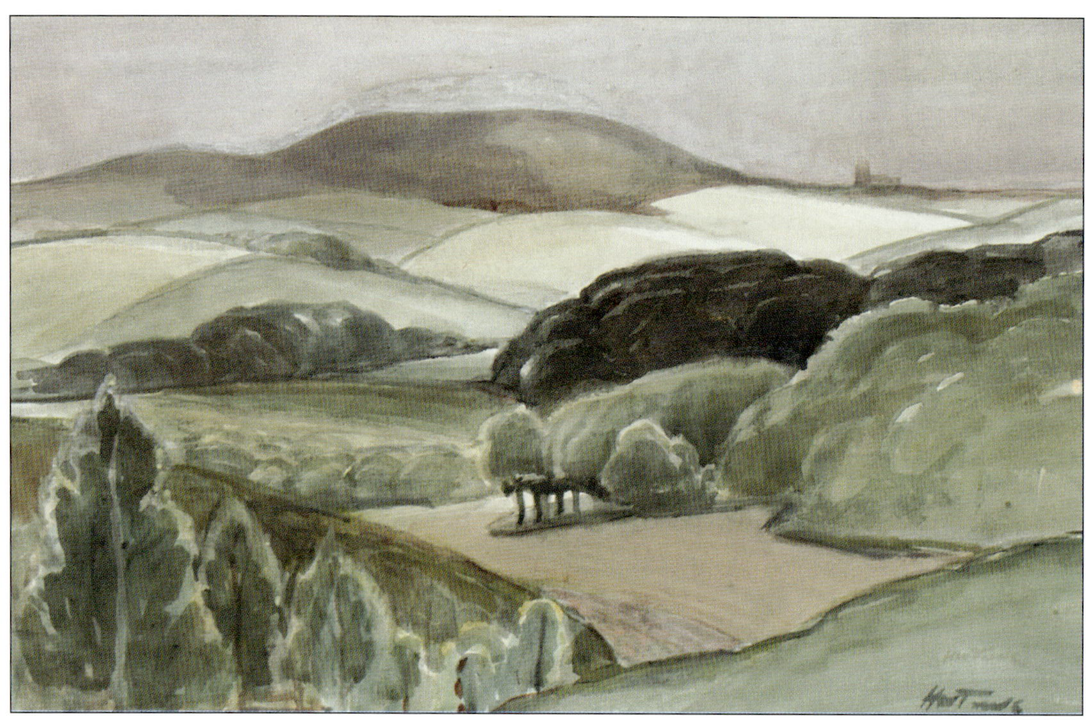

Distant Beeston
watercolour
13.5x10 inches

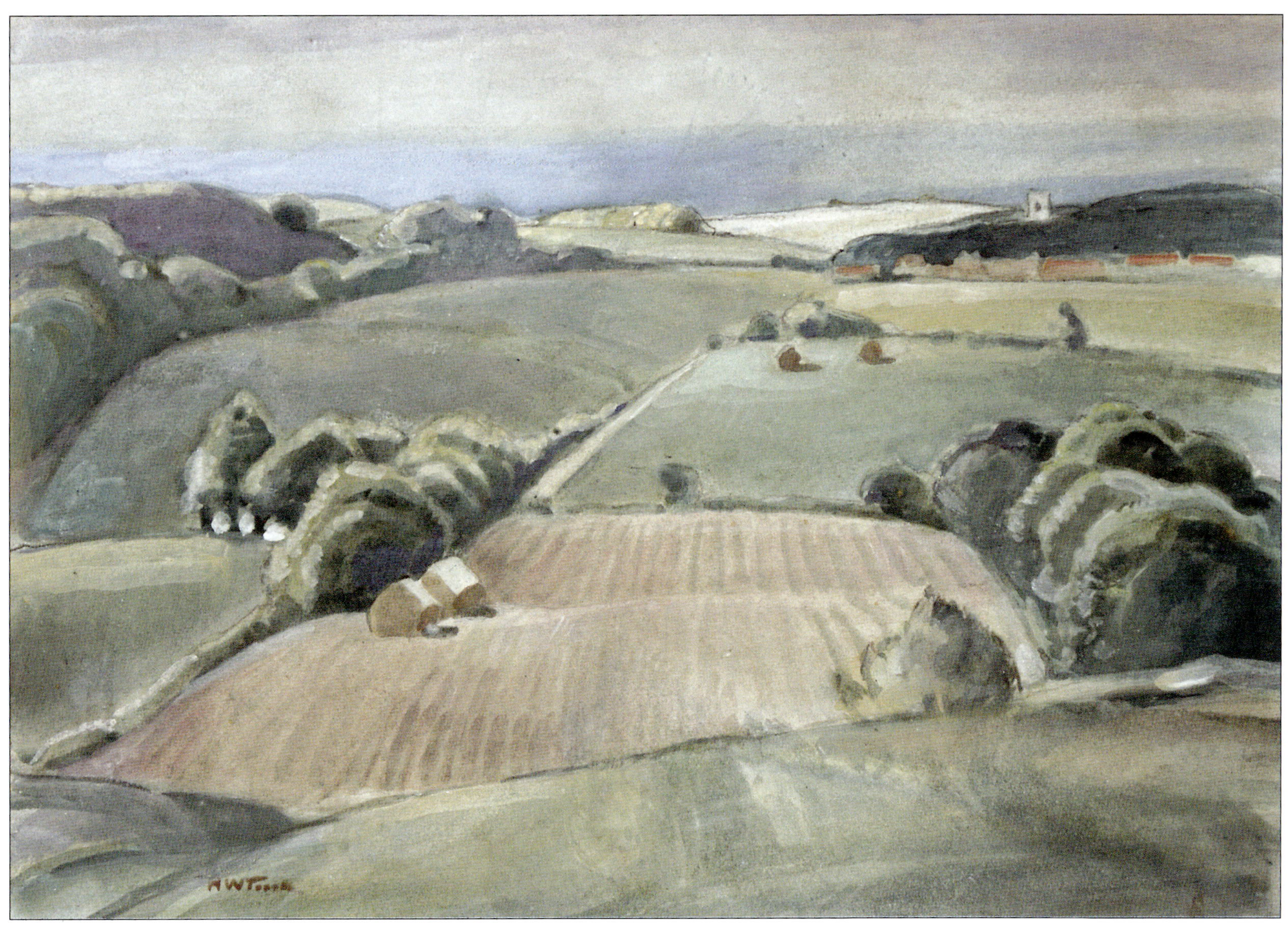

Evening Fields
watercolour
13.5x10 inches

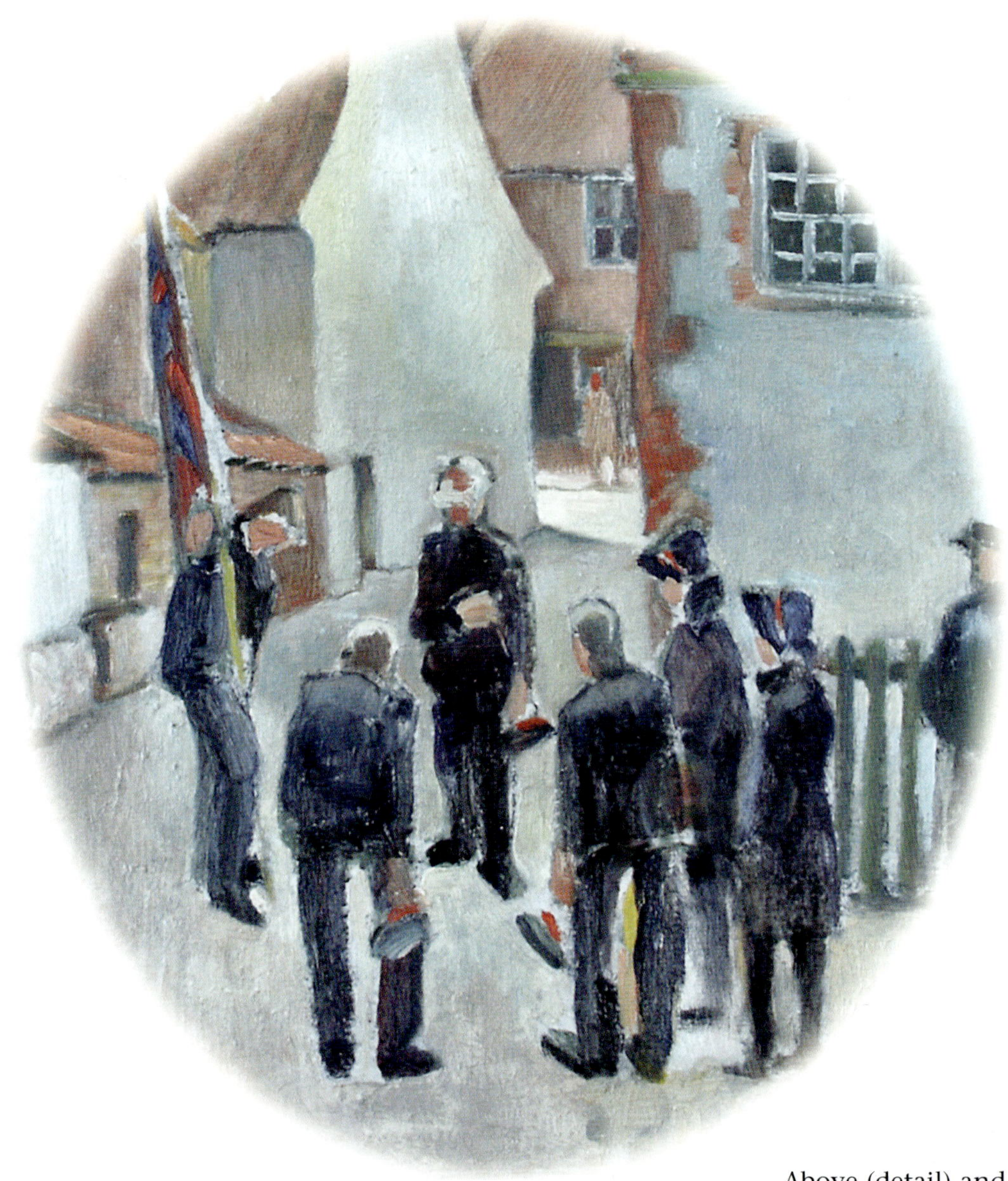

Above (detail) and opposite:
Salvation Army Sunday
oil on canvas
23x18 inches

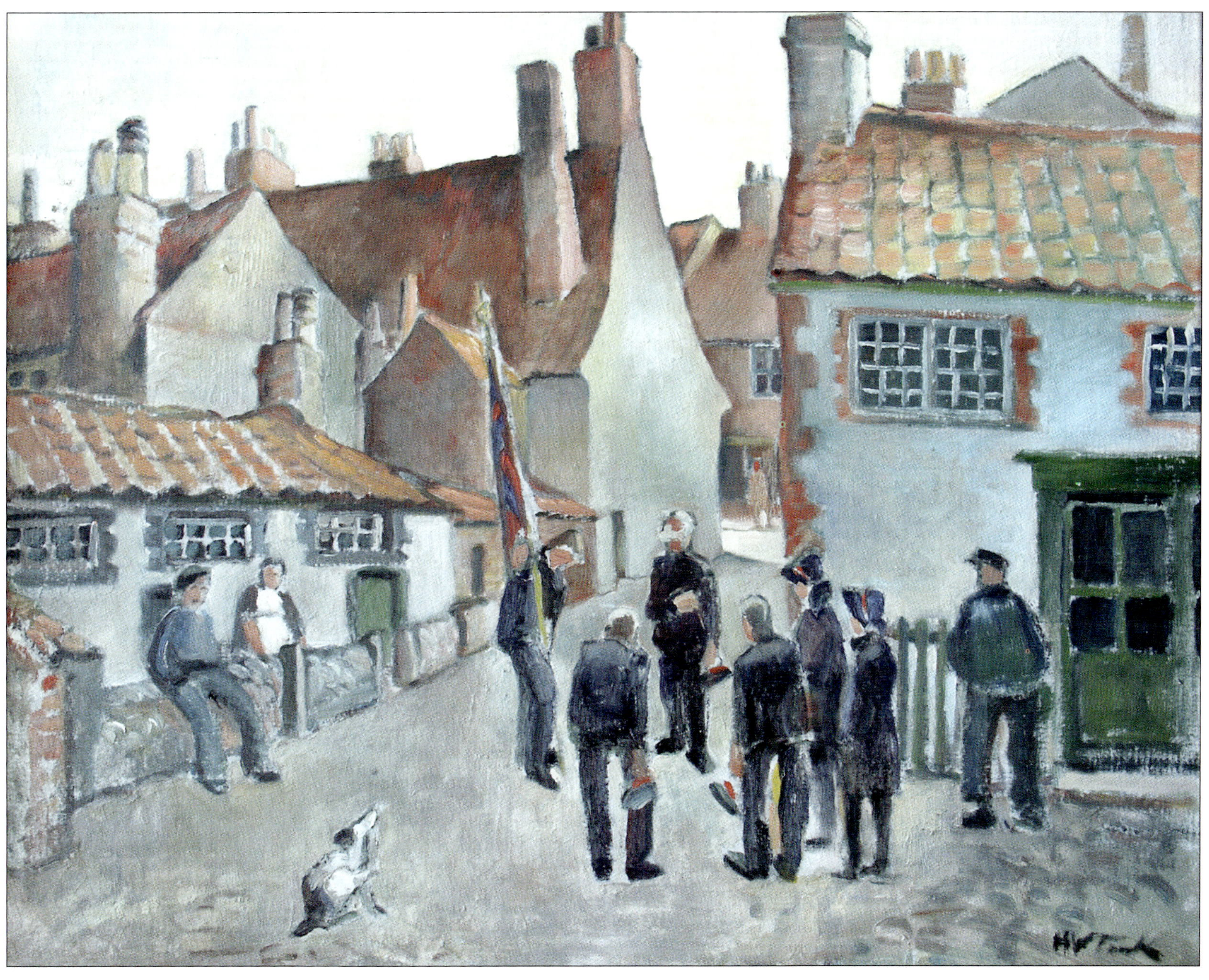

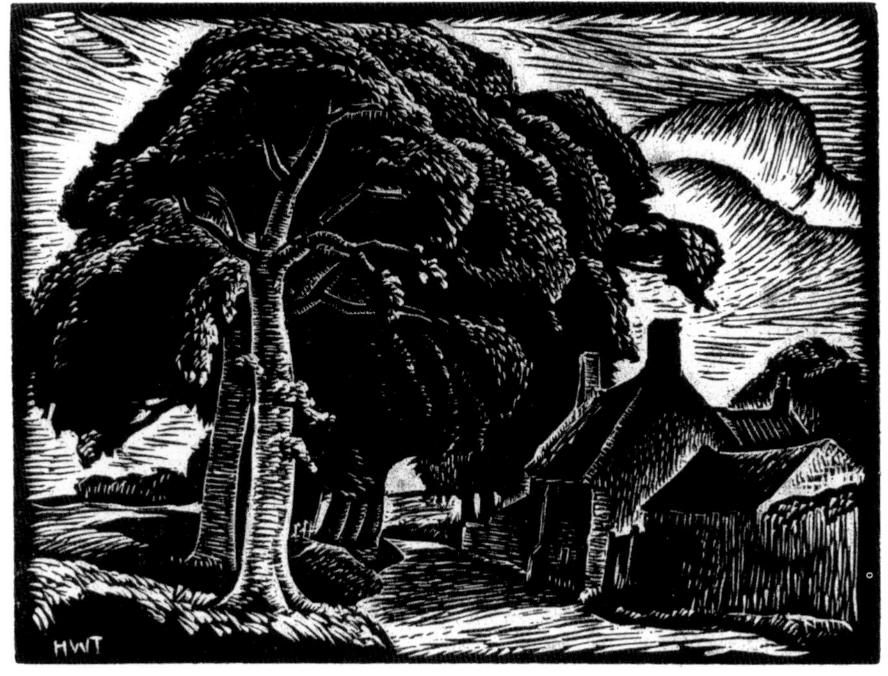

Norfolk Lane
woodcut

Opposite:
The Road to Holt
oil on canvas
24x20 inches

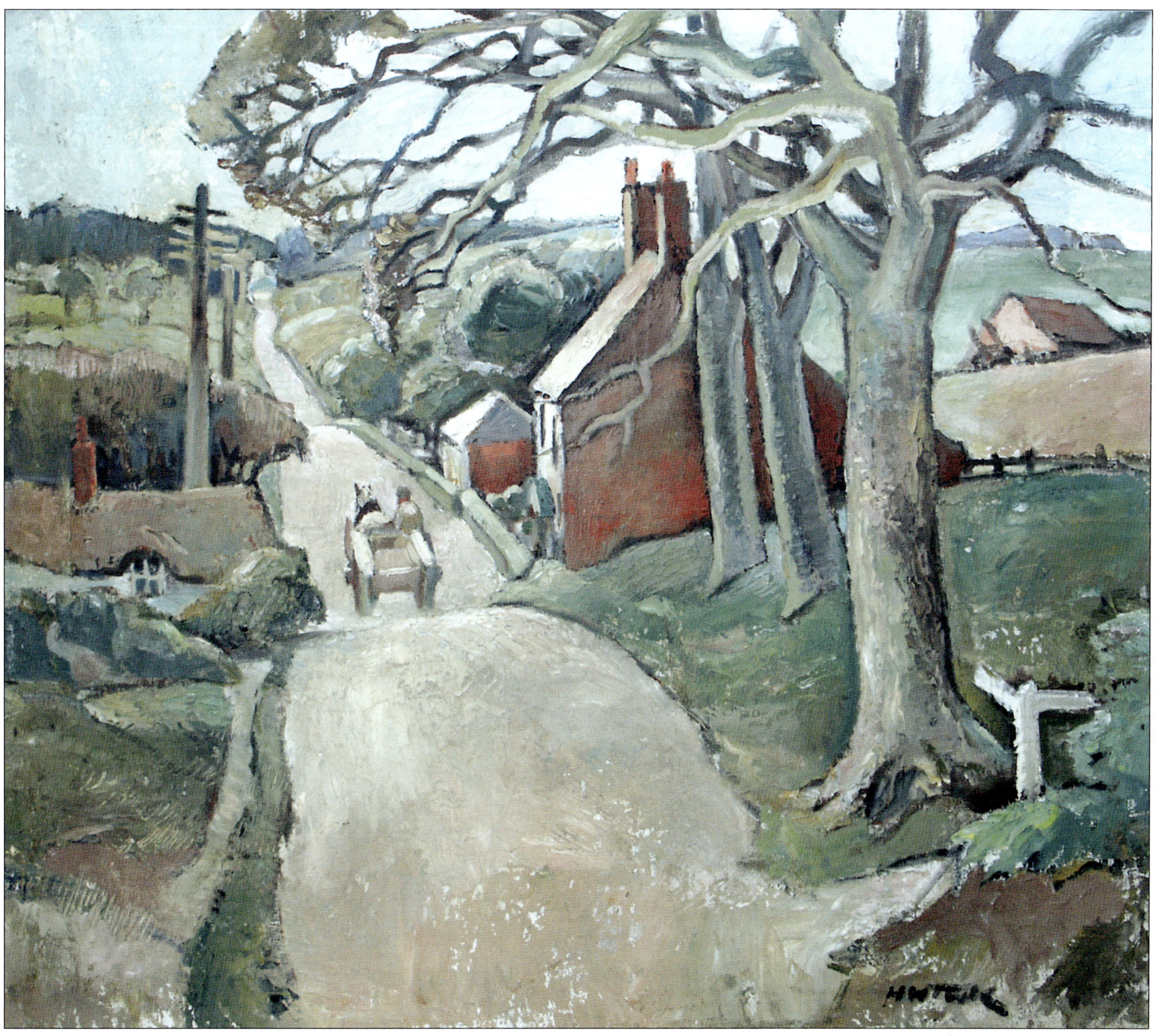

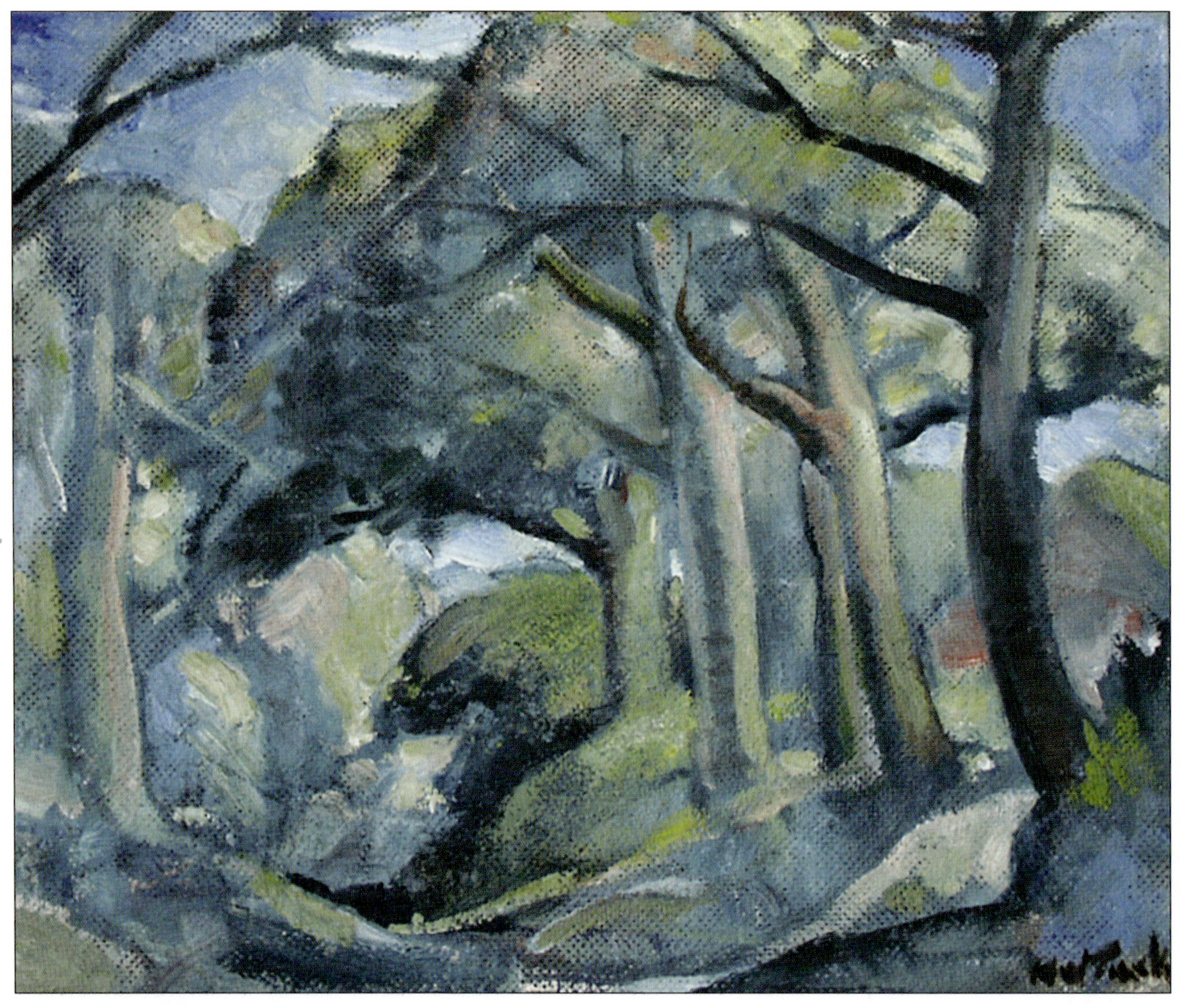

A Leafy Norfolk Lane
oil on board
13x11 inches

Opposite:
Pretty Corner, Sheringham
oil on canvas
23.5x18 inches

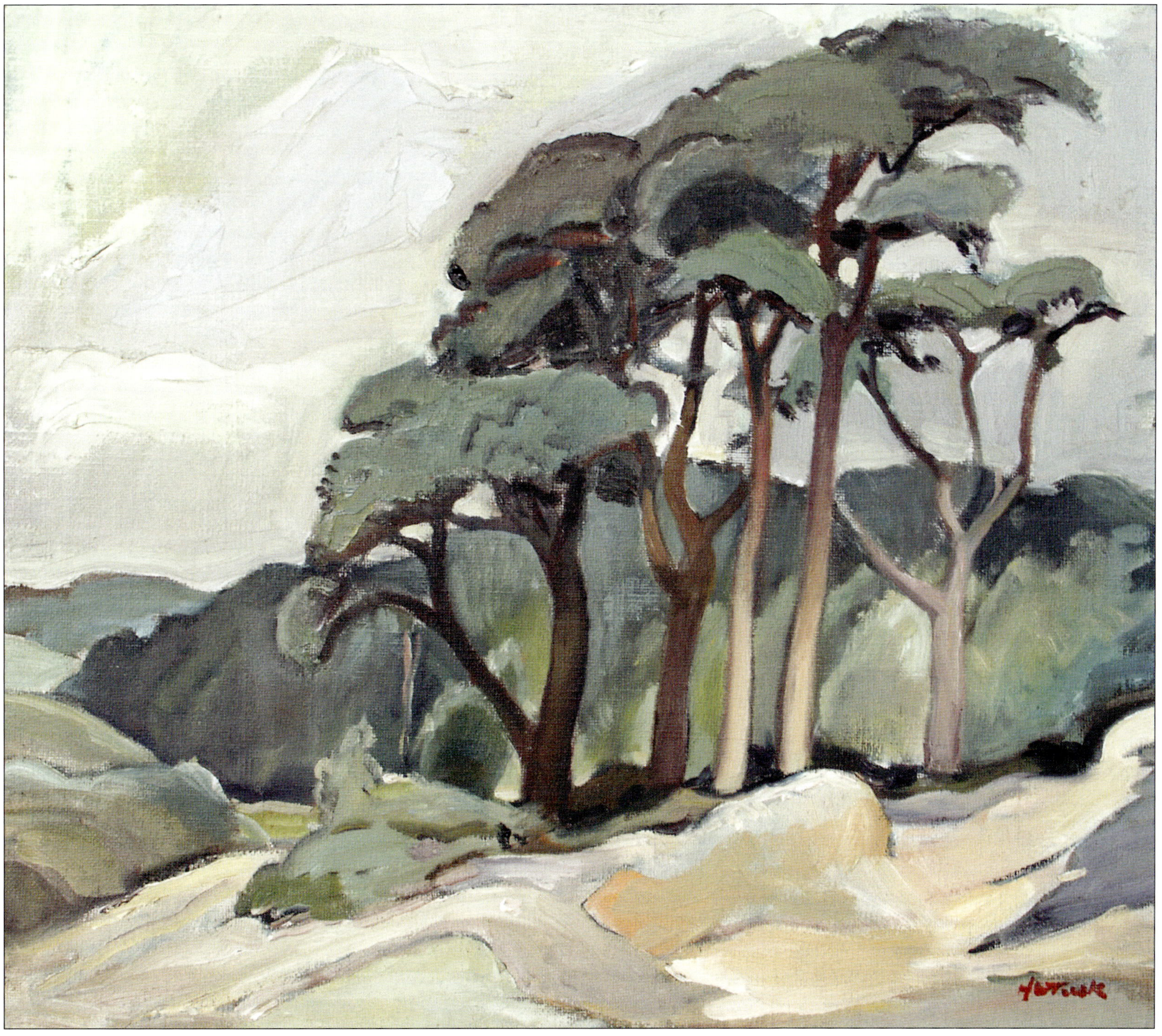

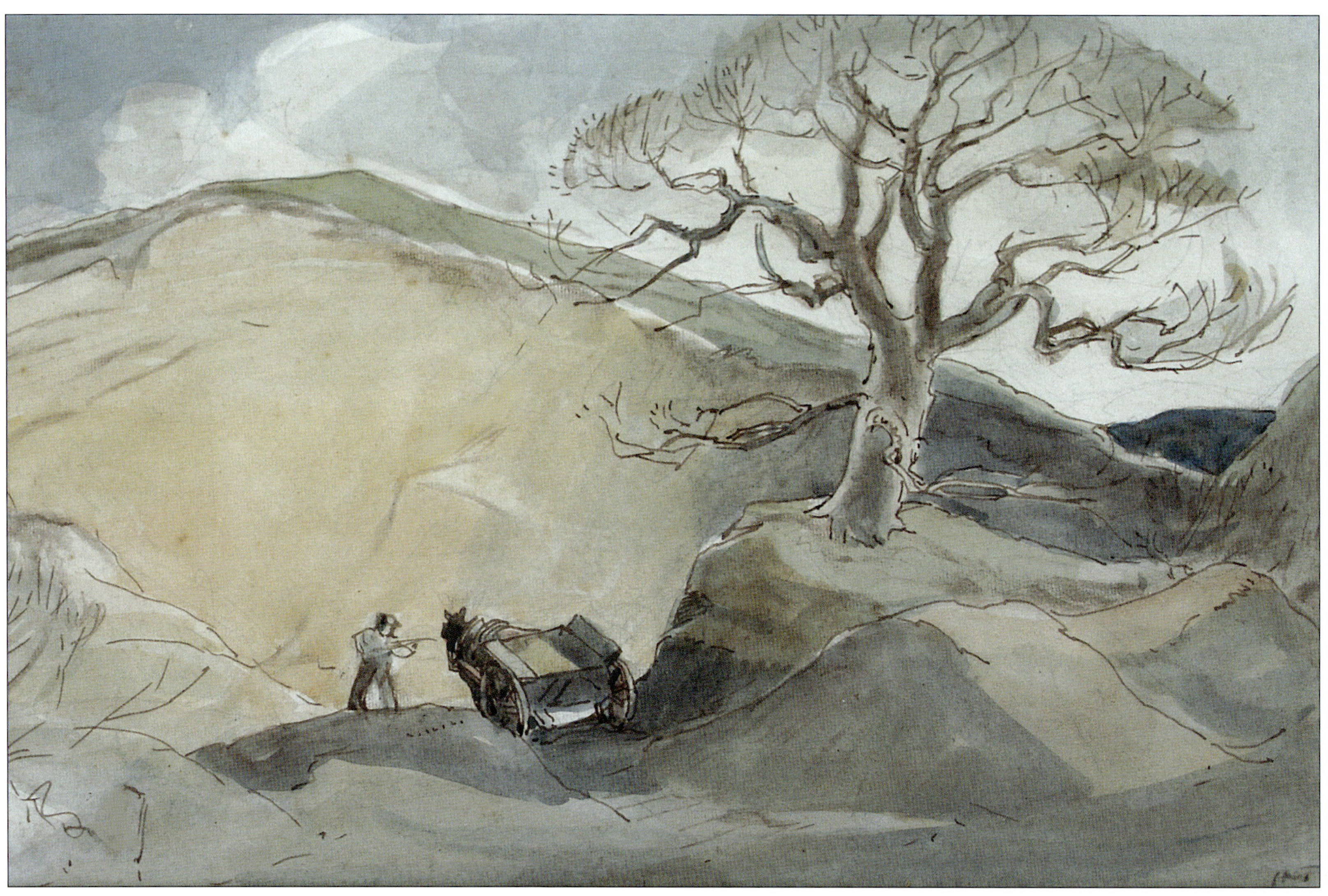

The Edge of the Sandpit, Sheringham
watercolour
12x8 inches

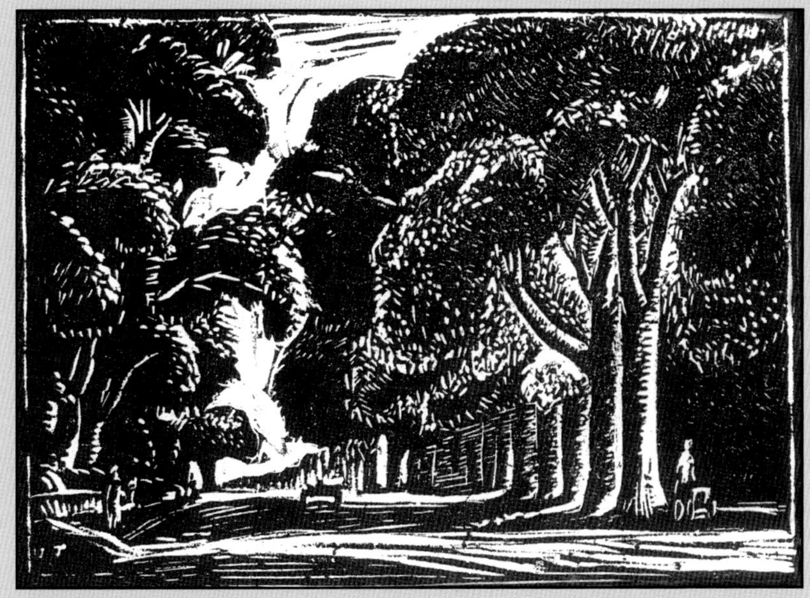

The Road into Norwich
linocut

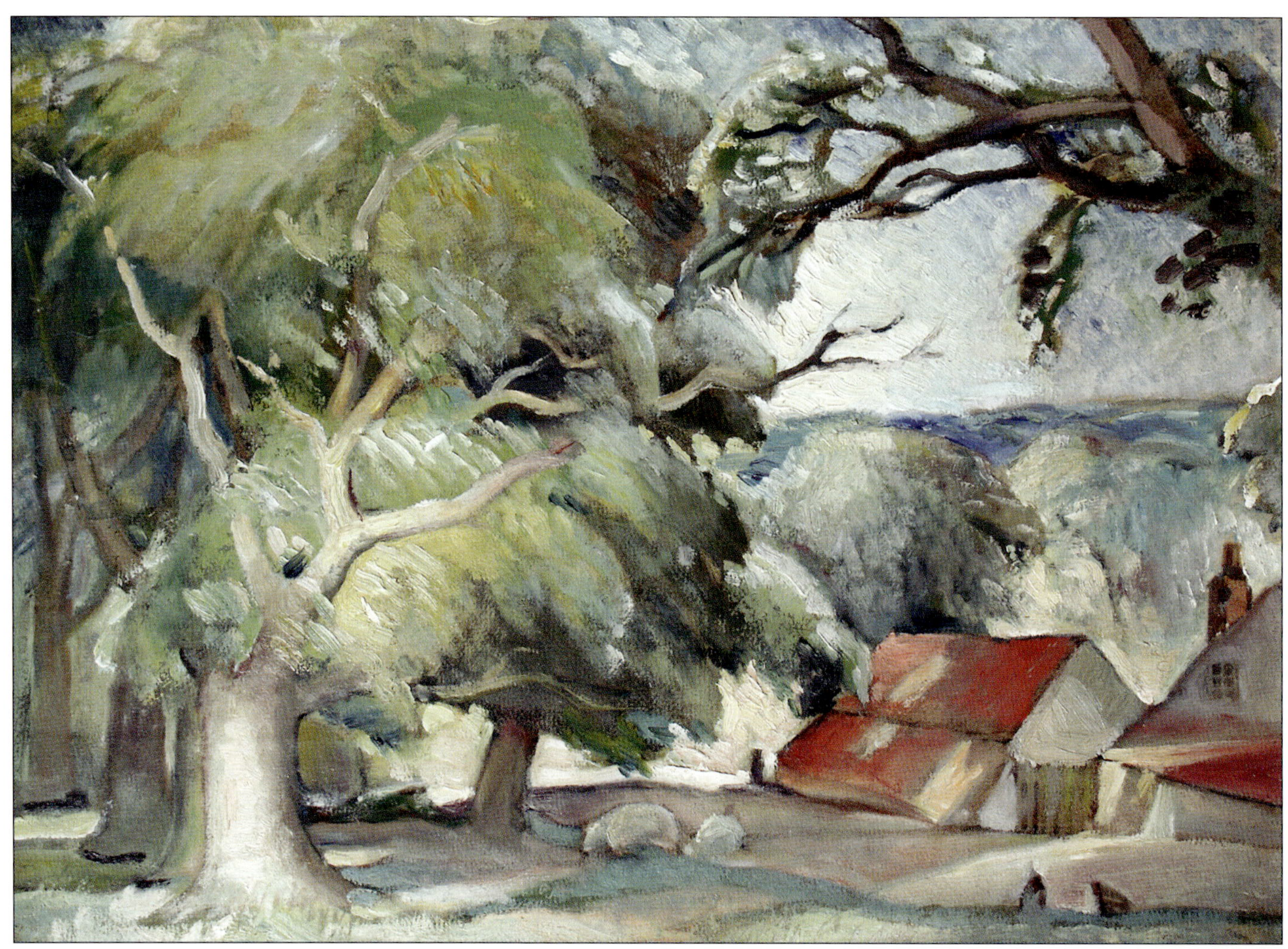

Summer Shade.
A Farm near Cley
oil on canvas
12.5x16.5 inches

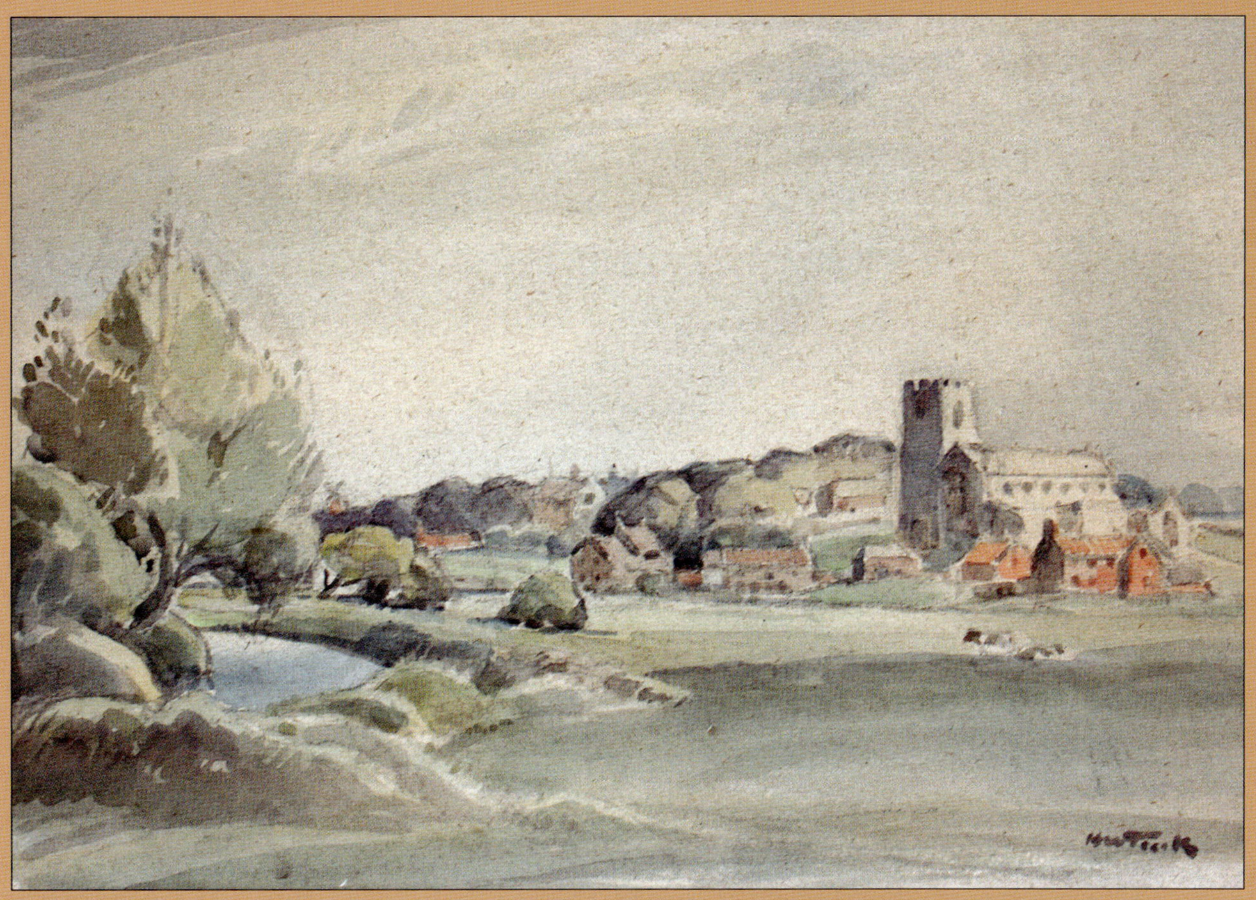

The Bend in the River.
watercolour
15x10 inches

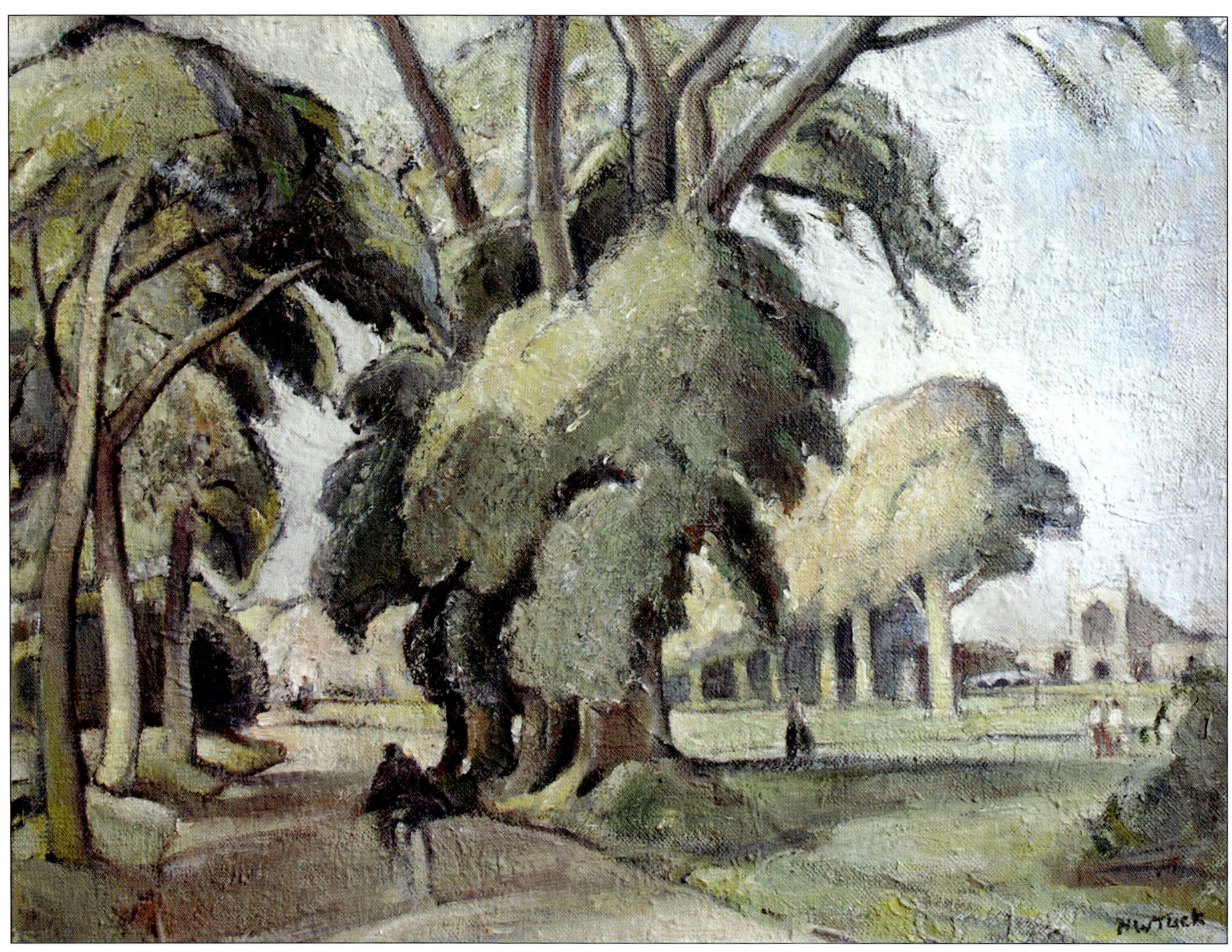

The Cyclist
(possibly Cambridge)
oil on canvas
18x16 inches

Opposite:
The Edge of the Wood
watercolour
14x11 inches

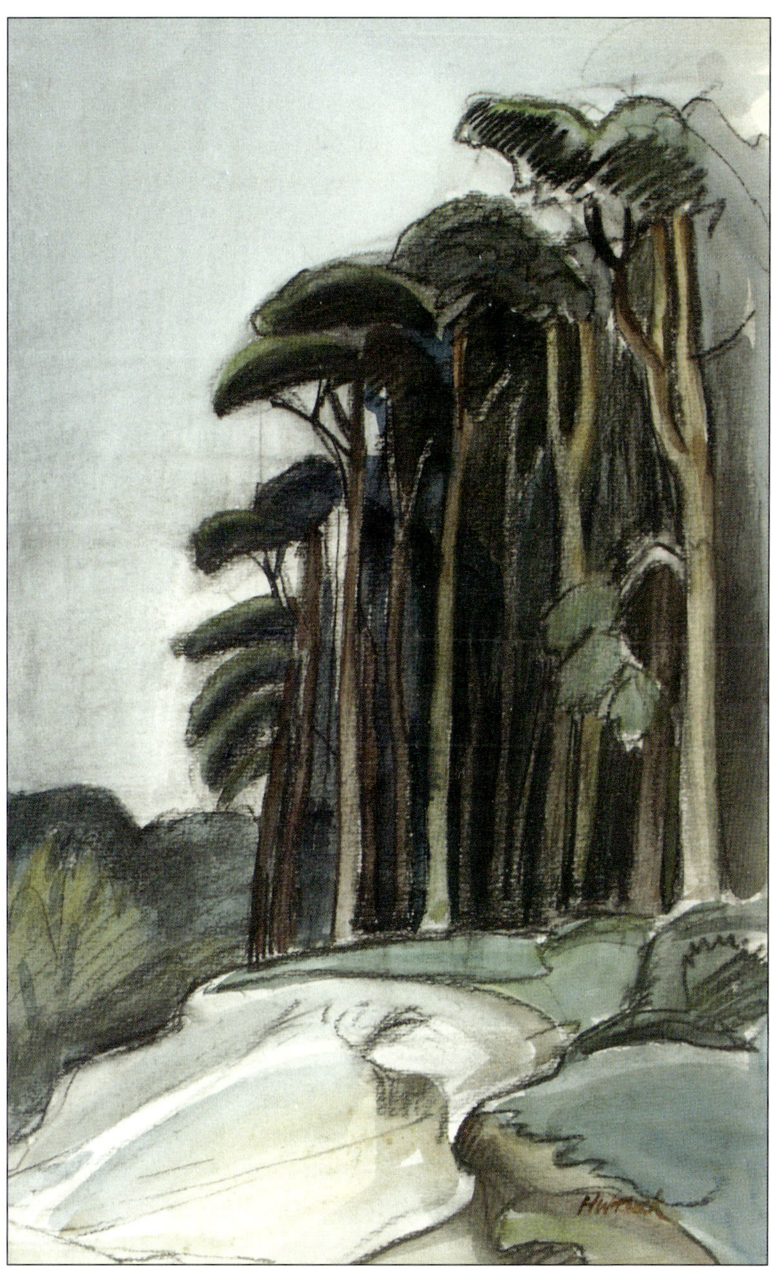

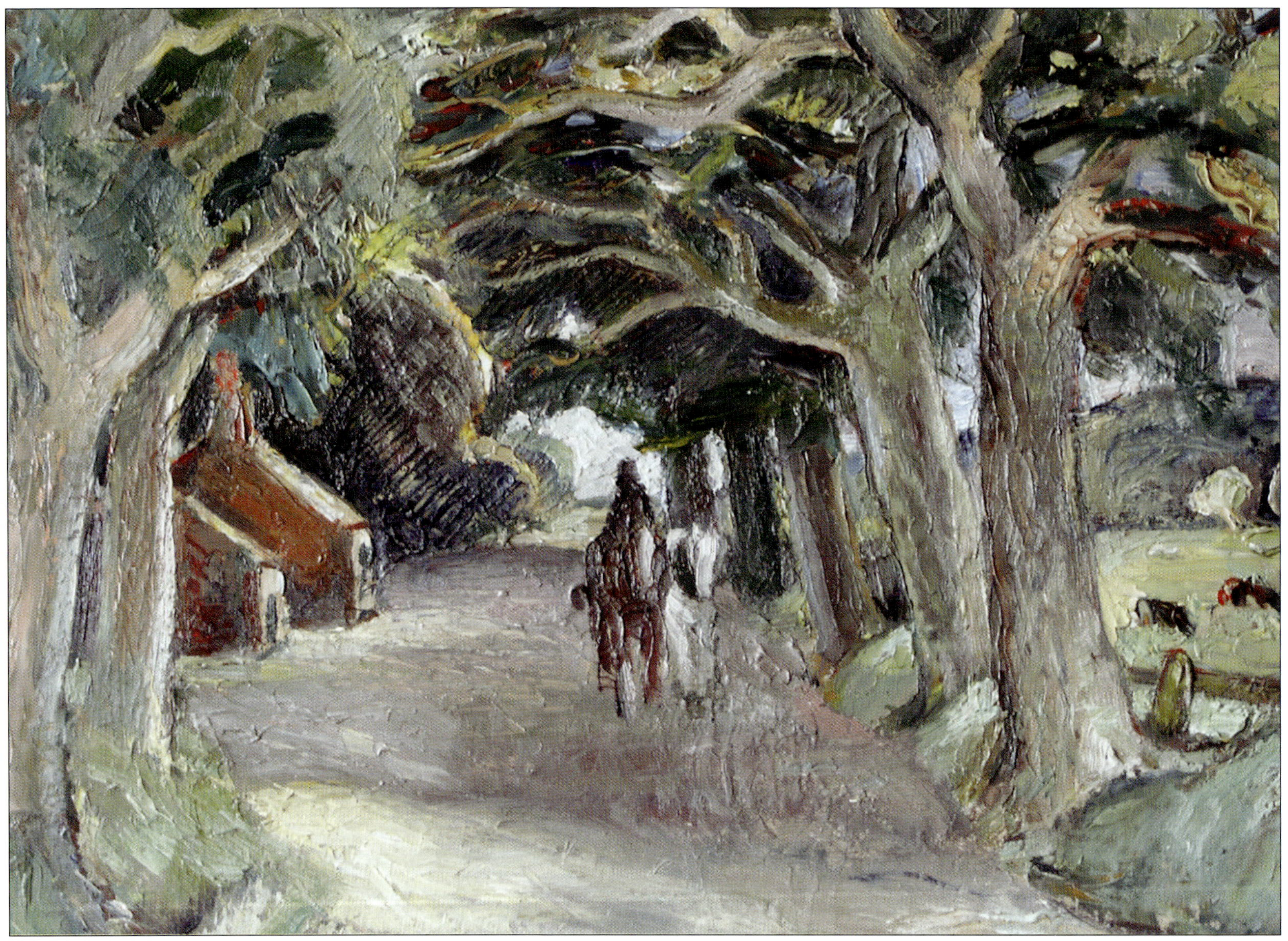

The Horse Team
oil on canvas
18x16 inches

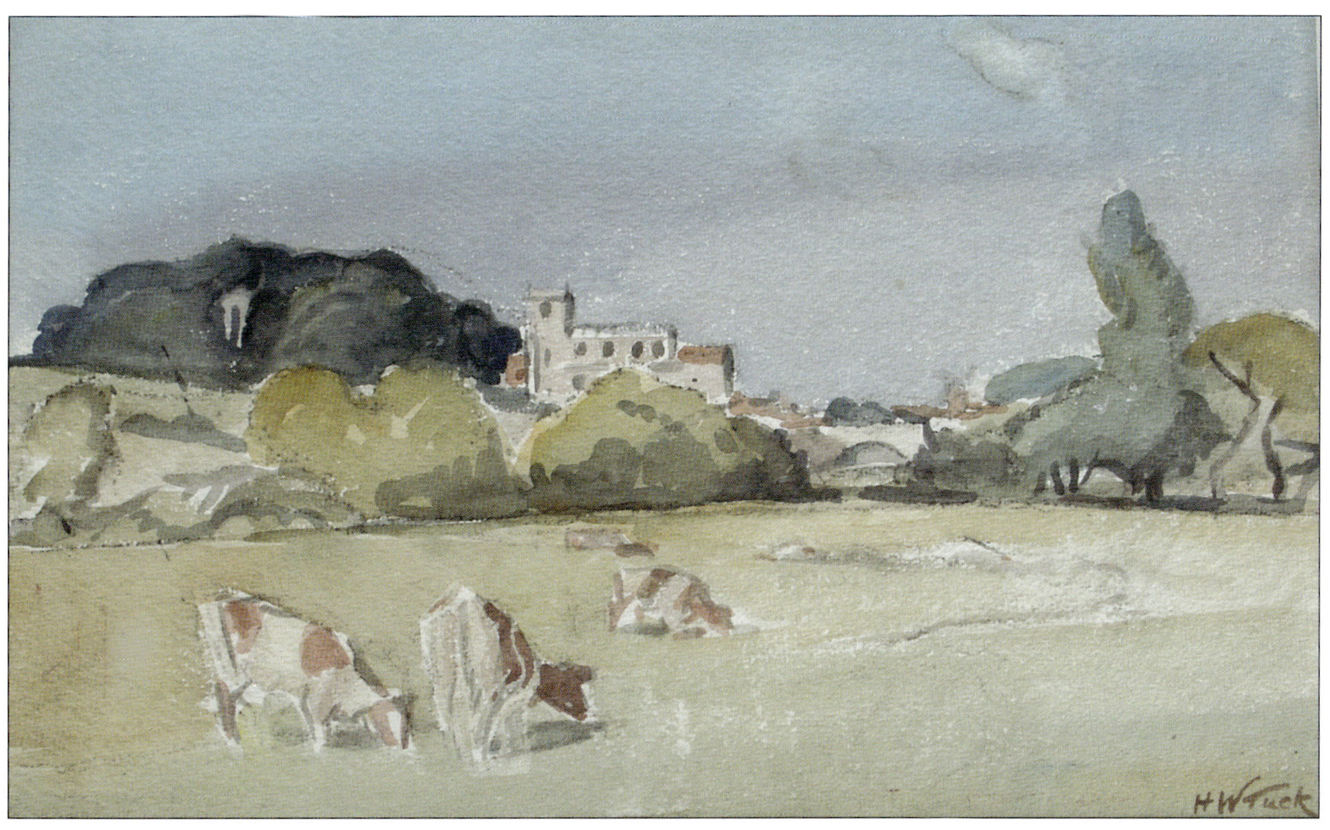

Peaceful Pastures
watercolour
14x12 inches

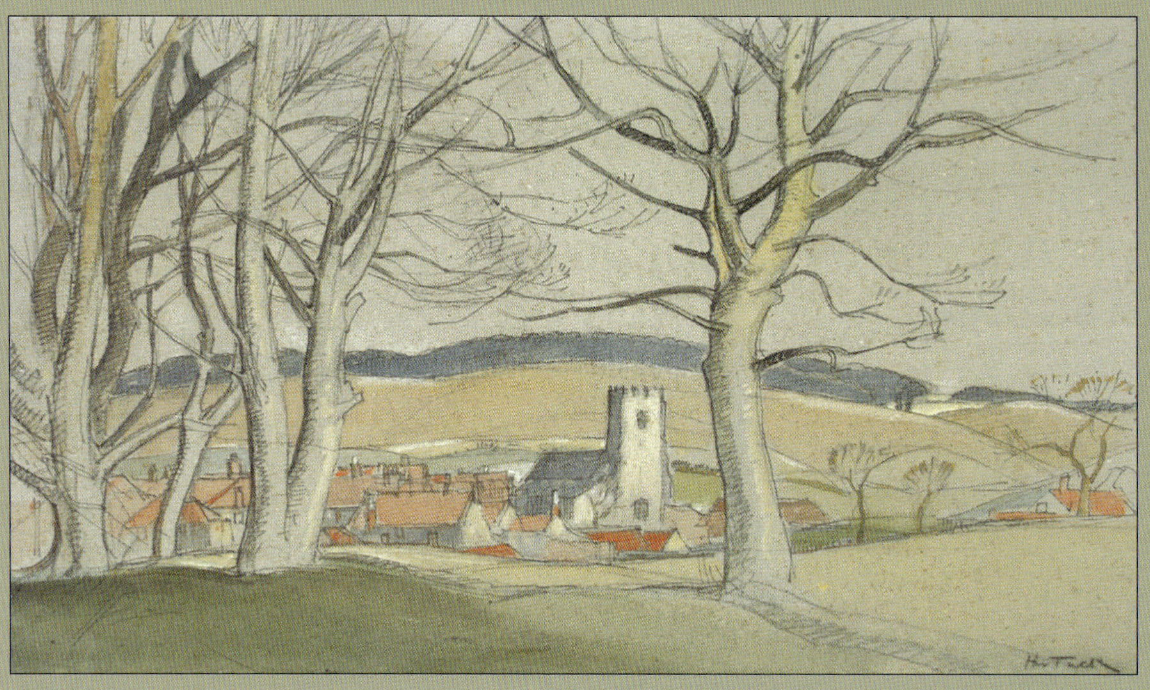

The Church, Upper Sheringham
watercolour
15x9 inches

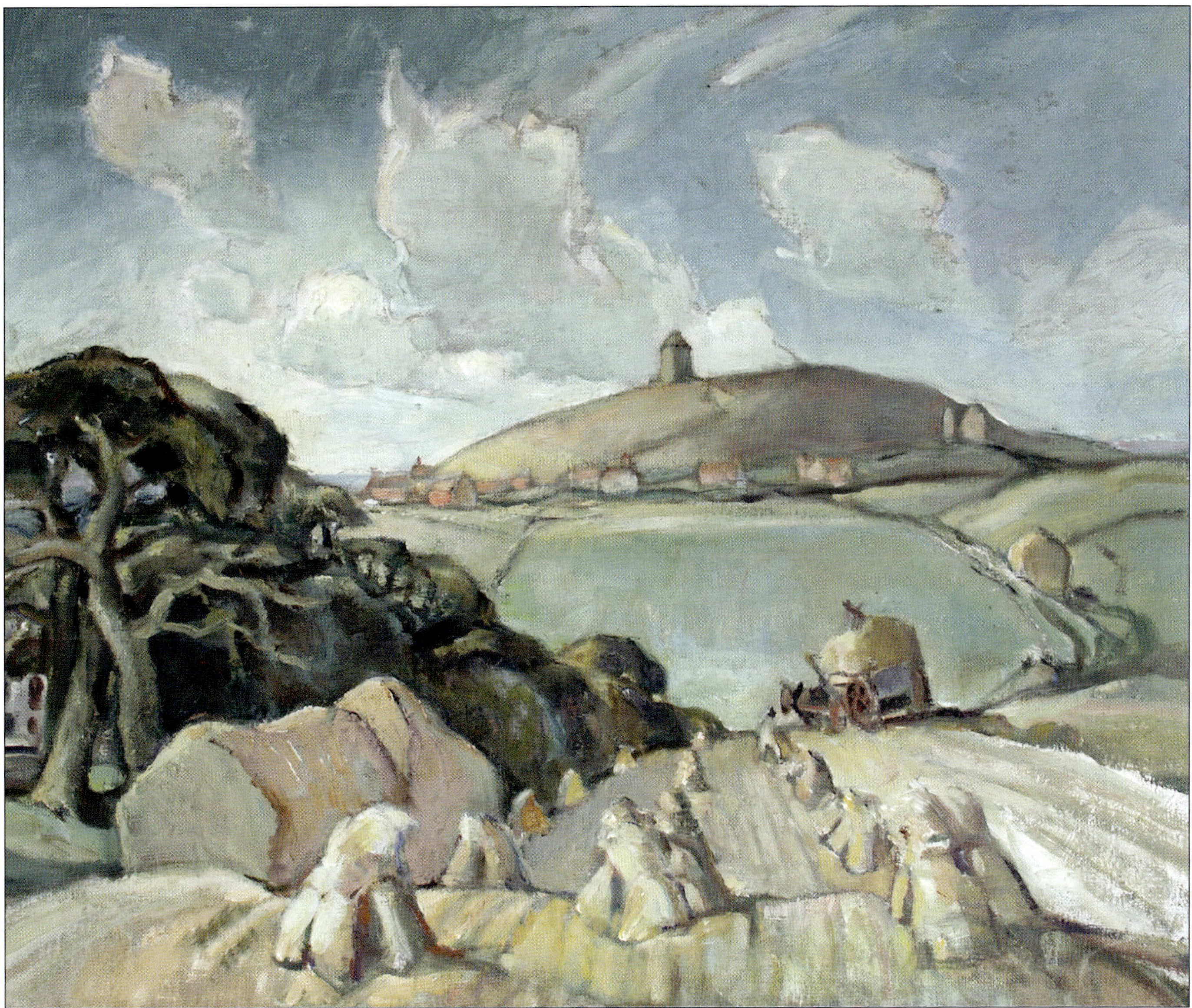

Harvest Fields: North Norfolk coast.
oil on canvas
22x18 inches

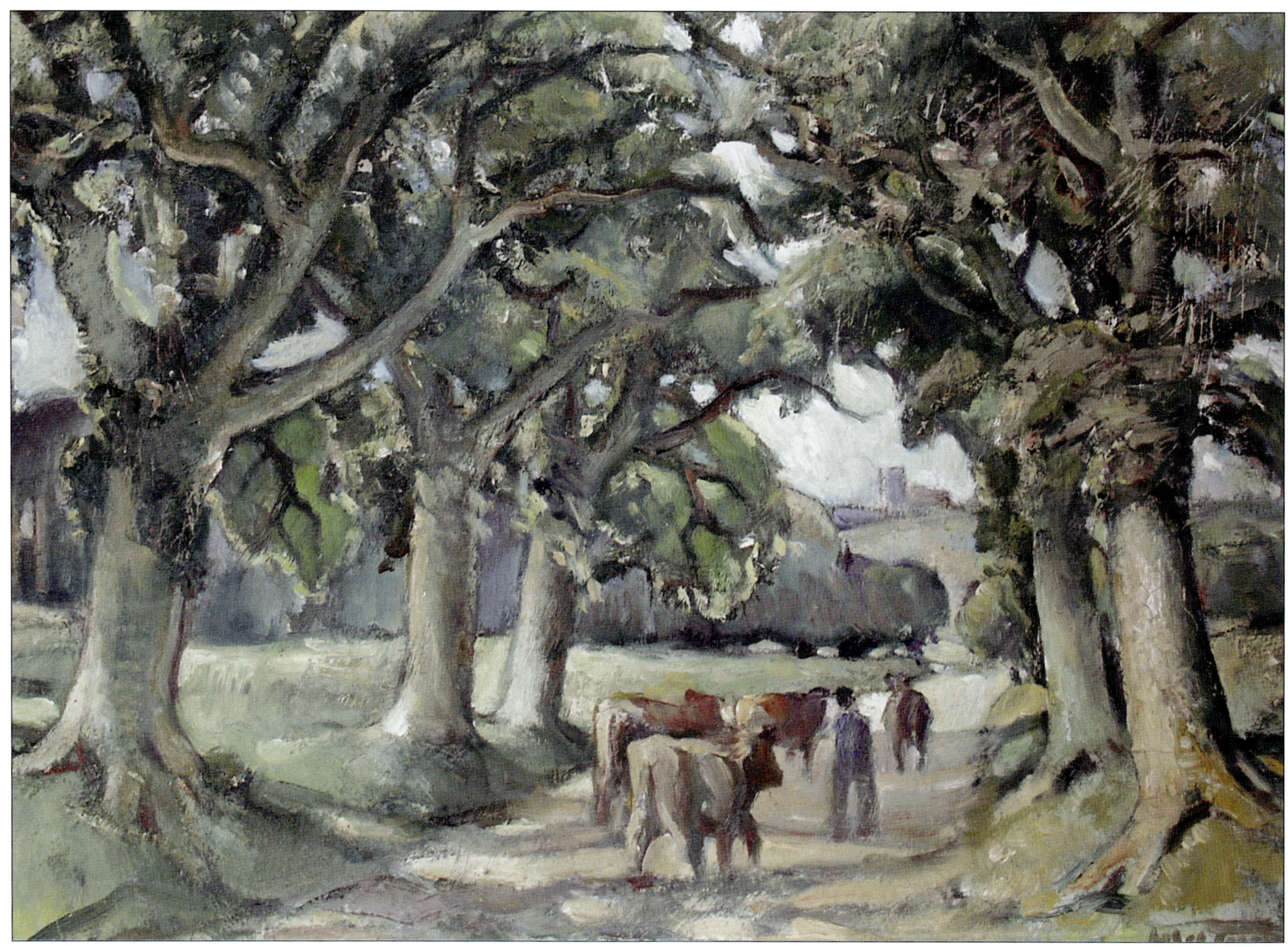

After Milking
oil on canvas
22x18 inches

Farther Afield

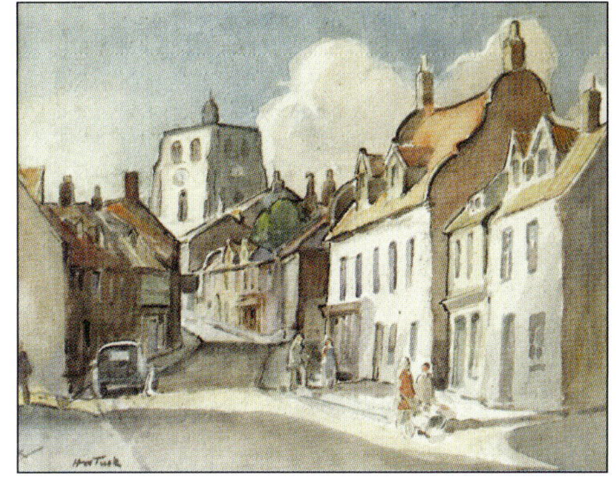

Beecles Church, Suffolk, from Blyburgate
watercolour
13x10 inches

Horace Tuck's love of his native county is amply evidenced through his paintings and from the accounts of family and friends. His frequent journeys around the county, either in his role as a peripatetic teacher, in his quest for attractive subjects to paint, and on holidays, undoubtedly provided him with a knowledge of many of the hidden nooks and corners of Norfolk and adjacent counties. But he was by no means confined to the enjoyment of the local scene.

Paintings made on his wider travels reveal that Tuck was well-acquainted with most of the British Isles, with works from the Lake District in the North, to many paintings made in Devon and Cornwall in the far South West.

Liz Keevill, Tuck's great niece, has a notebook that belonged to Tuck containing lists of 'holiday' names and addresses, noting hotels and boarding houses in towns and villages in far-flung corners of the country including Edinburgh, Ambleside, Barnstaple, Mullion,

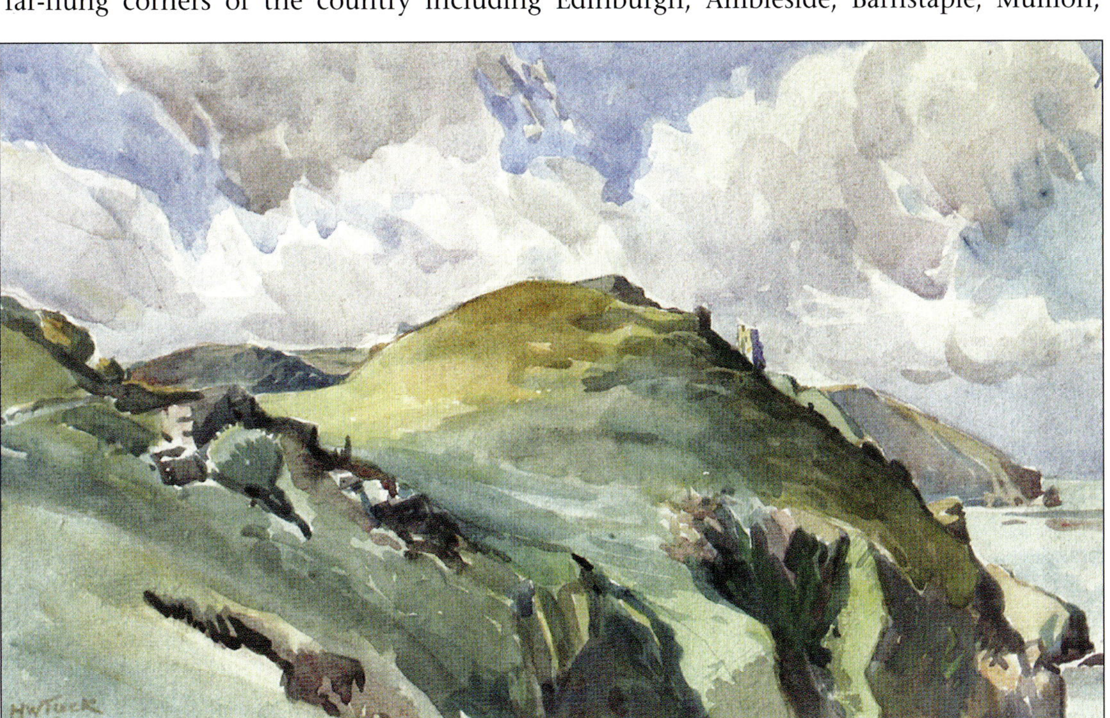

Mine Ruins on a Cornish Cliff
watercolour
14.5x10 inches

The Moorland Stream
watercolour
14x10 inches

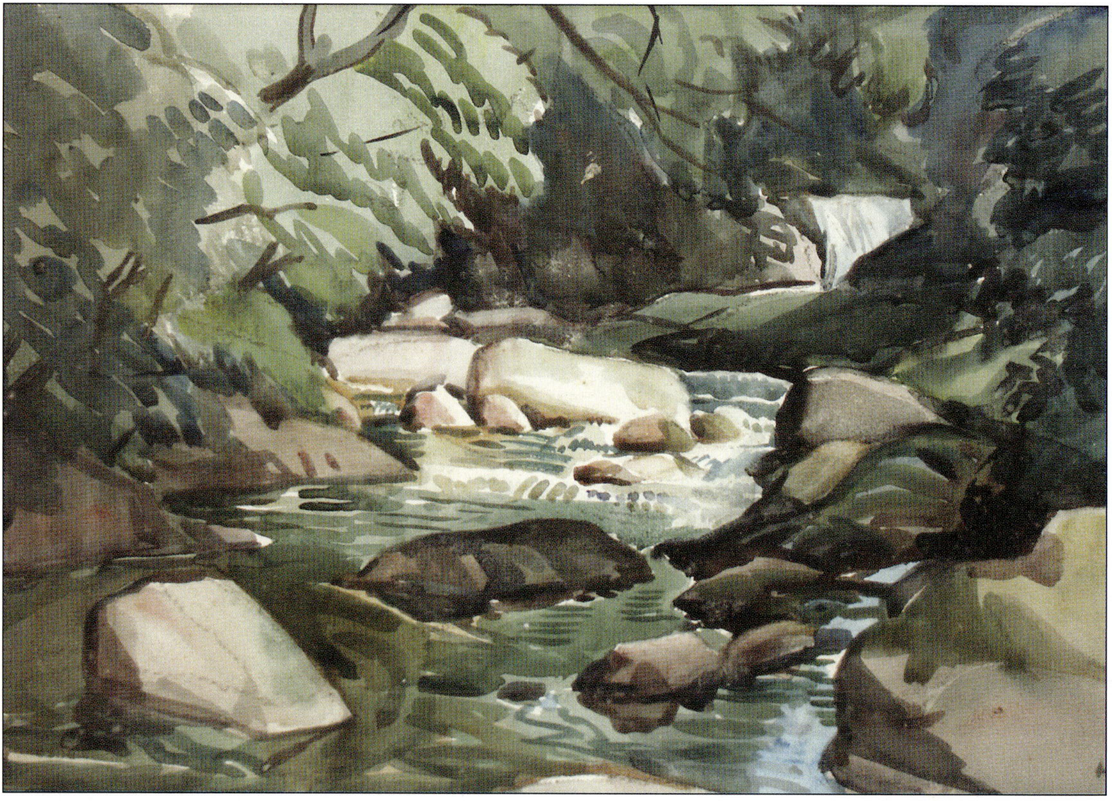

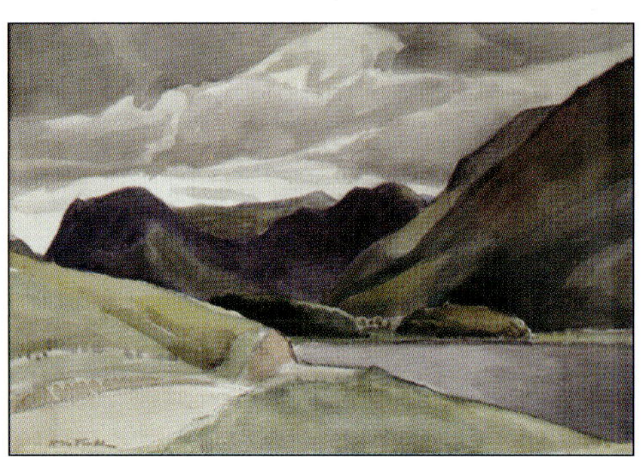

Lakeland
watercolour
13x10 inches

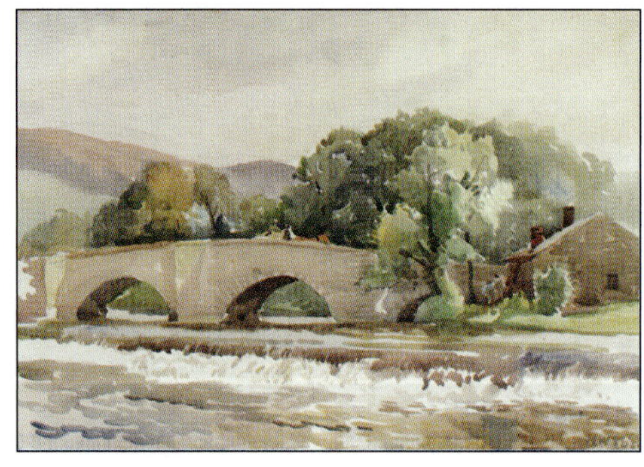

Moorland Bridge
watercolour
14x10 inches

Herefordshire, Keswick, Cumberland, Darlington, Durham and Essex. There are paintings in Cyril Nun's collection representing almost all of these holiday destinations, and similar paintings have been known occasionally to fetch up in local salerooms.

Tuck also included in his notebook useful addresses of suppliers of art materials and framers, most London-based, and names and addresses of London galleries: the Graham Gallery in New Bond Street, the Brook Street Gallery, Rushmore's in Great Russell Street, and the South London Art Gallery in Camberwell.

Travels in Europe are also frequently recorded in paint, mostly in watercolour, the medium most suited to artists on the move. The notebook contains includes addresses in Calvados (Normandy), Bruges, and Brittany, and again we have a number of examples of works completed by Tuck while holidaying abroad.

In Tuck's day train ferries provided a popular means of travel to and from the Continent from the Channel ports, Harwich being most convenient for East Anglians. Once on foreign soil, Tuck would find favourite spots in which to paint and a number of surviving works are obviously painted in and around the same location.

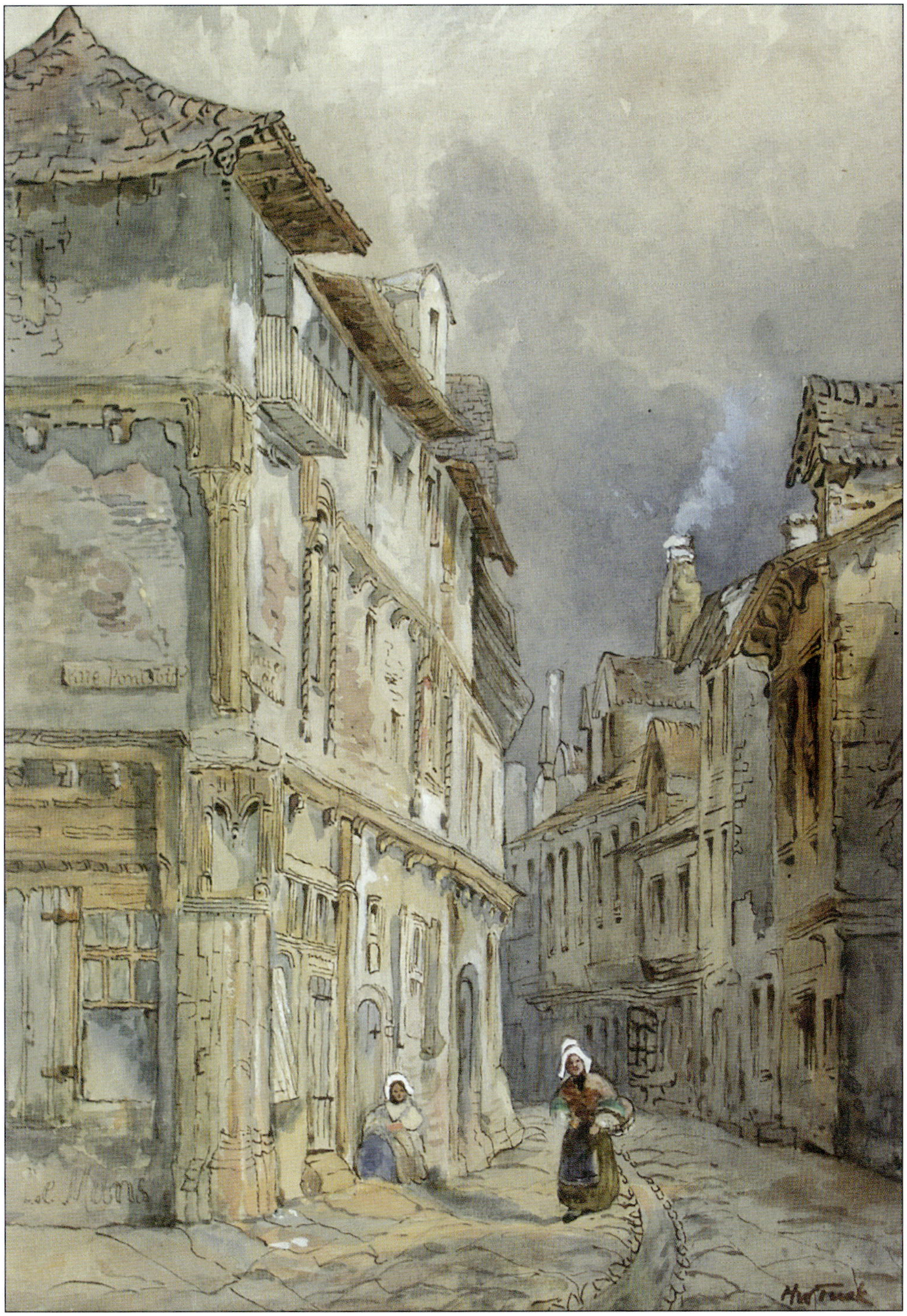

Scene in a French Town
watercolour
15x9 inches

This painting is interesting is very much in the style of topographical water-colours of the nineteenth century. Though undated it is thought to be one of Tuck's earlier pictures, painted before his style became more fluid.

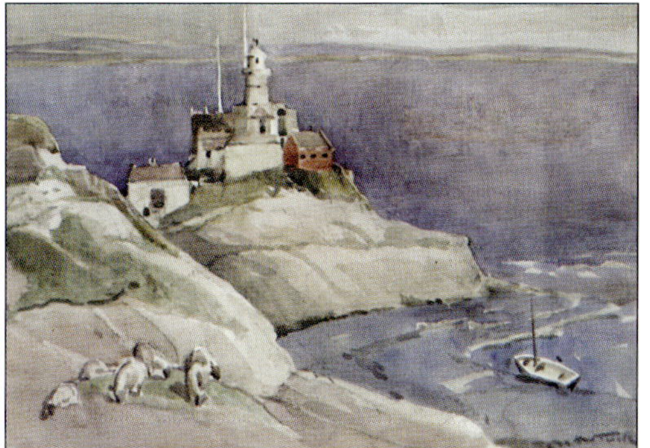

Breton Lighthouse
watercolour
14x10 inches

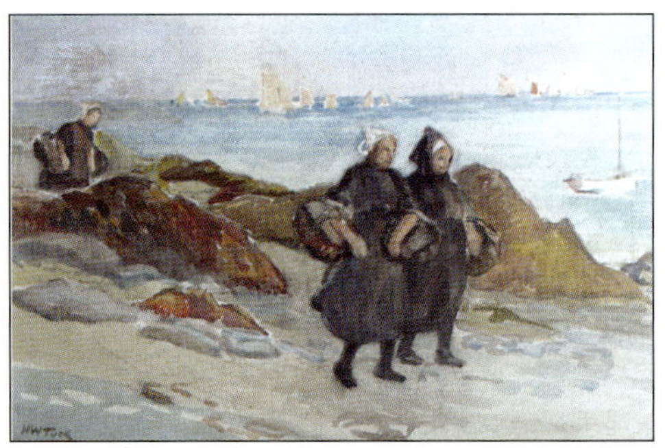

Breton Fisherwomen
watercolour
15x10.5 inches

Tuck's style for these paintings is as varied as his 'at home' works, most showing a high degree of finish and clearly were intended for sale. Sadly few of these paintings are positively identified (as is true of most of the collection) and all are undated. The location of some of those illustrated here is obvious; others are tentatively located, while some cannot be immediately identified. What is clear is that Tuck's need to paint and draw travelled with him for most of his adult life. There must be many more of his works yet to be discovered and it is hoped that this book succeeds in its aim of throwing more light on Horace Tuck and his work, both in the context of the 'Late' Norwich School, and nationally.

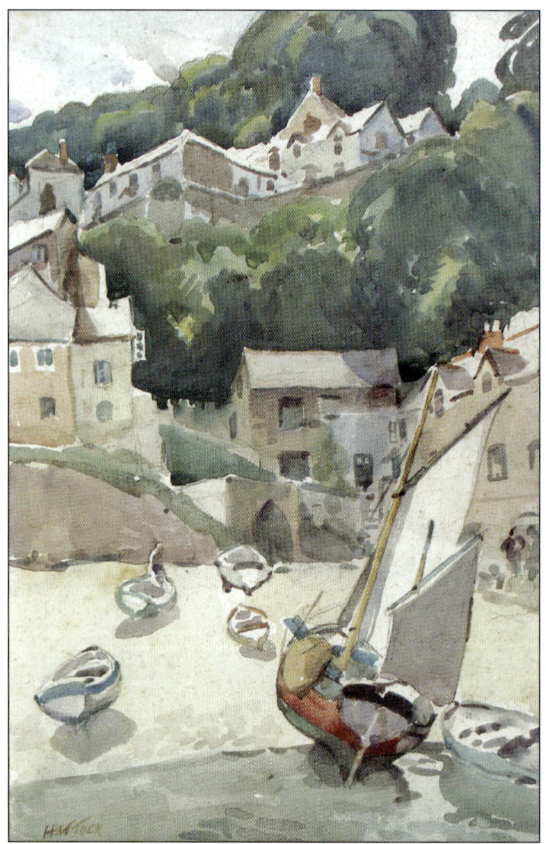

Clovelly, Devon
watercolour
9.5x14.5 inches